Silent Film and the Triumph of the American Myth

SILENT FILM

& THE TRIUMPH OF THE AMERICAN MYTH

Paula Marantz Cohen

OXFORD
UNIVERSITY PRESS

2001

OXFORD
UNIVERSITY PRESS

Oxford   New York

Athens   Auckland   Bangkok   Bogotá   Buenos Aires   Calcutta
Cape Town   Chennai   Dar es Salaam   Delhi   Florence   Hong Kong   Istanbul
Karachi   Kuala Lumpur   Madrid   Melbourne   Mexico City   Mumbai
Nairobi   Paris   São Paulo   Shanghai   Singapore   Taipei   Tokyo   Toronto   Warsaw

and associated companies in
Berlin   Ibadan

Copyright © 2001 by Oxford University Press

Published by Oxford University Press, Inc.
198 Madison Avenue, New York, New York 10016

Oxford is a registered trademark of Oxford University Press

Library of Congress Cataloging-in-Publication Data
Cohen, Paula Marantz, 1953–
Silent film and the triumph of the American myth /
Paula Marantz Cohen.
p.   cm.
Includes index.
ISBN 0-19-514093-1, ISBN 0-19-514094-X (pbk.)
1. Silent films—United States—History and criticism.
I. Title.
PN1995.75 .M37   2001
791.43'0973—dc21   00-033655

Frontispiece: Conventionally, the last shot of Edwin S. Porter's *The Great Train Robbery,*
1903 (Museum of Modern Art).

1 3 5 7 9 8 6 4 2
Printed in the United States of America
on acid-free paper

In memory of my mother

Ruth Marantz Cohen

ACKNOWLEDGMENTS

A NUMBER OF PEOPLE were indispensible to me in writing this book.

My colleague Dave Jones has been an intellectual mentor for close to twenty years. A superb critic and editor, as well as a filmmaker himself, he talked to me about initial ideas, read early drafts, and refused to let me get away with anything dishonest or imprecise. His insistence on clarity and his playful, insightful mind have made this a better book.

My sister, Rosetta Marantz Cohen, and my brother-in-law, Samuel Scheer, read the book at a crucial juncture, when I had lost patience with it, and offered encouragement and guidance. Theirs are the most discerning literary sensibilities I know, and I was aided by the sharpness of their observations, delivered in complementary vocabularies.

I owe an immeasurable debt of gratitude and love to my husband, Alan S. Penziner, whose compendious knowledge of Western culture never ceases to amaze me. He was the one who first introduced me to silent movies and convinced me to take them seriously. As a teenager, he used to make weekly visits to the New School for Social Research for screenings and discussion by the great film lover and historian William K. Everson. The silent film library that he gathered at that time, long before I knew him, uncannily anticipated the needs of this book. I can repay him in one way at least: I can now sit through a silent double feature with pleasure. I have finally become, as he says, his perfect date.

I am also grateful to Miles Orvell for reviewing parts of the manuscript with the eye of a seasoned Americanist; Mark Greenberg for his supportive role as a friend and dean; Rosemary Abbate for her insights into performance (I am convinced she would have made a great silent star); my research assistant, Brady Hammond, for his intelligence and competence; and the Drexel University students in my silent film and American literature courses whose fresh eyes and open minds helped me to think in new ways. I also want to thank my editor, Elissa Morris, and her assistant, Karen Leibowitz, at Oxford

University Press; the reviewers of the manuscript for Oxford, whose comments I found to be uniformly helpful; Frank Nesko of Movies Unlimited, the rare video store that respects film history; the librarians in the Theater Archive at the Philadelphia Public Library; and Terry Geesken and Mary Corliss at the Film Stills Archive of the Museum of Modern Art.

A final thank you goes to my beloved parents—my father, Murray S. Cohen, and my late mother, Ruth Marantz Cohen—who taught me how to think and raised me to love ideas.

Parts of chapters 3 and 4 first appeared in the literary journal *Boulevard*.

CONTENTS

Silent Film and the Triumph of the American Myth

We've gone beyond Babel, beyond words.
We've found a universal language—
a power that can make men brothers and
end war forever. Remember that.
Remember that, when you stand in front of
the camera.

                    D. W. Griffith to Lillian Gish

INTRODUCTION

THE PHOTOGRAPH, taken in England in the early 1920s, shows two couples: Lord and Lady Mountbatten (right), members of the British royal family, and Douglas Fairbanks and Mary Pickford (left), American movie stars.[1] The four figures have arranged themselves in a stunt pose for the camera. Both women are perched on the right shoulders of the men; the men have their left legs and left arms raised as if to dramatize the ease with which they hold the women aloft. The photo relays a sense of communal fun, yet a close examination shows some telling details. Mountbatten's face is taut with concentration, and he is holding Fairbanks's hand for balance. Lady Mountbatten is similarly uneasy and is grasping Pickford's shoulder.

What is clear is that Fairbanks and Pickford—Doug and Mary, as they were then known to the world—occupy the dominant position in the photograph. Doug is the fulcrum of the group, the base on which the whole precarious structure rests. Mary looks perfectly at home on his shoulder; it is a position she had occupied many times before. Whereas the British couple appear washed out in their pale outfits, the Americans seem vibrant and alive—their mix of dark and light clothes perfectly in tune with the camera's black-and-white world. The effect is heightened by Fairbanks's deep suntan and the casual stylishness of his sports jacket, in contrast to Mountbatten's stodgy double-breasted suit.

But what is most striking about the Americans are their smiles—broad and relaxed, displaying a confidence missing in their hosts. Smiling for the camera was, of course, the movie star's stock-in-trade, but there were also excellent reasons for these stars to smile at the time this photograph was taken. They had only just married, having shed their original spouses to hardly a murmur of public protest; they were both near the peak of their careers, beloved by audiences as far away as Russia and Japan; and they had recently formed with D. W. Griffith and their best friend, Charlie Chaplin, a new movie company, United Artists, destined to make them even richer than they already were. The couple was, quite simply, the envy of the world—why else would British nobility be trying so hard to imitate them?

The photograph may seem like a trifle—the record of one moment of fun in the lives of four famous people—but it is more than that. It is a tribute to the burgeoning power of a new form of representation, the moving picture, to elevate its favorites and delegate others to the background. No matter that

Preceding page: Douglas Fairbanks and Mary Pickford with Lord and Lady Mountbatten (Broadlands Archives)

Mountbatten's family could be traced back to Charlemagne and that his wife was the granddaughter of the richest man in England. Fairbanks and Pickford seem the more significant figures. They dominate the photograph because their movies gave their looks a context that they carried with them wherever they went. Doug's suntan and sports clothes and Mary's cherubic smile and game pose were all components of an American relationship to experience that had been projected on the screen and become part of a universally shared visual language. It is a language we still understand today; for whether or not we recognize Doug and Mary in the photograph, we know, based on the cues of their appearance, that they are "stars."

To see the English aristocrats made pasty seconds to the American movie stars is to see a graphic enactment of the shift in power from Europe to America that was occurring in the first three decades of the twentieth century. Douglas Fairbanks and Mary Pickford were the distilled representatives of that power. They were the purveyors of a uniquely American conception of character, shaped and disseminated through film, that would, with apparent ease and in the most genial spirit imaginable, usurp hereditary privilege in its own backyard.

How did the medium of silent film produce a Douglas Fairbanks and a Mary Pickford? How did celluloid characters like these promote the idea of the self-made American and elevate it above that of the European aristocrat? How, in short, did the movies help bring about the triumph of a new set of values and goals associated with American ascendancy in the twentieth century?

To answer these questions, one needs to answer a number of related ones. First, how did America forge a connection to the movies that would be more powerful than that of any other country? Second, how did the movies consolidate imagery associated with America in a compelling way? And third, how did this consolidation produce an image that could serve as a model for all Americans and become the prototype, the world over, for a modern kind of self? I will try to answer these questions in the following chapters, but I begin here by laying the groundwork for the relationship between film and America as it would take shape during the silent era.

Although many countries contributed to the development of film technology and production at the beginning of the twentieth century, the United States had emerged as the unrivaled center of world filmmaking by 1920. Several factors help account for this. There was the influx of ambitious immigrants to American cities in the 1880s and 1890s that lent muscle and imagination to a primitive industry. There were the unrestricted economic conditions of turn-of-the-century America that allowed for the proliferation of the first store-front movie theaters—or nickelodeons—that generated a continual demand for new films. There was the extraordinary resource of California, with its cheap real estate and fine weather, where the American film industry had the good sense to move in the mid-teens. And there was the reduction of foreign competition as World War I devastated Europe, giving American film an advantage that it would never lose. None of these factors, however, explains the profound symbiosis that has existed between America and the movies from the first decades of the twentieth century onward.[2]

The alliance between film and America was the result of more than economic opportunity and available human and natural resources, though it drew on these factors for support. It rested on film's ability to participate in the *myth of America* as it was elaborated in the course of the nineteenth century. The groundwork for the myth had been laid very early in the history of the nation in such works as St. John de Crèvecoeur's *Letters from an American Farmer* and Thomas Jefferson's *Notes on the State of Virginia*. The authors of these works were men with cultural ties to Europe who had cast their lot with America. They described their new country as a world in the process of being born—at once limited in having no conventionally agreed-upon past to draw on for guidance and advantaged in being free to create a future unhindered by the past. By the 1820s, their ideas had crystallized into a philosophical self-conception—a national myth. "Unlike the Roman myth," explains the cultural historian R. W. B. Lewis, "which envisaged life within a long, dense corridor of meaningful history—the American myth saw life and history as just beginning. It described the world as starting up again under fresh initiative, in a divinely granted second chance for the human race, after the first chance had been so disastrously fumbled in the darkening Old World."[3]

Alexis de Tocqueville, who visited the United States in the 1830s, connected the American myth to the kind of art he predicted the country would produce. "Among a democratic people," he wrote, "poetry will not be fed with legends or the memorials of old traditions. . . . The destinies of mankind, man himself taken aloof from his country and his age and standing in the presence of Nature and of God, with his passions, his doubts, his rare prosperities and inconceivable wretchedness, will become the chief, if not the sole, theme of poetry among these nations."[4] Tocqueville's notion of a country stripped to its essential components and of an art built directly from them would be echoed by the first great American poet, Walt Whitman, when he called for a new kind of cultural expression proper to the form of American life.

Film appeared at the opportune moment and with the properties necessary to meet that call. Like America, the medium was seen at its origins as primitive and naive. In any discussion of early film, the first examples given are of unmediated slices of life: people kissing, trains arriving, boxers throwing punches. The ordinary subject matter and seemingly random documentary techniques of early film made it an object of contempt to a cultured audience, who saw it as the entertainment of the riffraff, destined to remain on the programs of vaudeville houses and burlesque halls. Up through the 1950s, the question of whether film was an art at all continued to be a valid subject for debate, and much of the impetus behind early formalist and esthetic filmmaking was presented in terms of the medium's need to lift itself from its crude beginnings and overcome its raw material ("a film is not *shot,* but *built,*" declared V. I. Pudovkin, who, with Sergei Eisenstein, is seen as the father of film formalism[5]).

But what the formalists tried to overcome, others embraced as a unique strength. In being "the only art that exhibits its raw material," film possessed, according to the great proponent of realist cinema, Siegfried Kracauer, the unique ability to "excavate" and "redeem" reality. Another German theorist of the 1920s, Walter Benjamin, argued that it was precisely film's distance from traditional, "high" art that gave it the potential to reach the people and transform their relationship to established power relations.[6] Benjamin stressed the mechanical aspects of film that could revolutionize perception much in the way the steam engine and the cotton gin had revolutionized production. Both Kracauer and Benjamin saw in cinematic realism the opportunity to clear away the artifice of established culture that obscured a true and empowering vision of reality. This was precisely what American poets and politicians, from Crèvecoeur and Jefferson through Whitman and Theodore Roosevelt, had conceived to be the nation's mission for civilization as a whole.

The connection between film and America was not lost on early critics. "Our soil has no Roman coin or buried altar or Buddhist tope," wrote the poet Vachel Lindsay in 1915; film, he said, could stand in place of these things as a "new hieroglyphics" proper to America's democratic character. "It is natural that when a new art appears in the world it should choose a new people which has had hitherto no really personal art," pronounced the French critic Élie Faure in 1920, "especially when this new art is bound up, through the medium of human gesture, with the power, definiteness, and firmness of action." French film, Faure maintained, "is only a bastard form of a degenerate theater," whereas "the Americans are primitive and at the same time barbarous, which accounts for the strength and vitality which they infuse into their cinema."[7]

Film, such statements suggest, was like America itself: strong in its limitations, innovative in its artlessness.

Behind this tendency to link America and film was the idea of authenticity—of a privileged relationship to reality—that both the country and the medium were seen to share. In the mid-nineteenth century, photography had already emerged as an American medium by establishing itself as a direct conduit to the real, offering, as one commentator of the period put it, "the concrete representation of consummated facts."[8] The daguerreotype image is "*infinitely* more accurate in its representation than any painting by human hands" and achieves "identity of aspect with the thing represented," proclaimed Edgar Allan Poe in 1840. In the 1860s, the eminent jurist Oliver Wendell Holmes, whose enthusiasm for photography led him to invent a new version of the viewing device known as the stereoscope, lauded the photographic image as a kind of "cast," or second skin, for reality. He called for the creation of a National Library of Images, which could save the public money spent on traveling to see the real thing. "Matter in large masses must always be fixed and dear; form is cheap and transportable," Holmes maintained—a statement that has the photograph stand to reality much as paper currency stands to gold. Samuel Morse, inventor of the telegraph and extensively involved with developing photographic technology in America, went even further in erasing the distinction between reality and image, conceiving of photographs as he did aural recordings—not as "copies of nature but portions of nature herself."[9]

Contributing to the American enthusiasm for photography—and subsequently for film—was the new position that the observer was encouraged to occupy with respect to the image. Photography was revolutionary in that it replaced the hand with the eye as the instrument of representation. In doing so, it seemed to transfer the locus of power from the creator to the observer.[10] This shift conformed to the democratic principles on which America had been defined as a nation: it took away the presumption on the part of the photographer to a privileged role since the photograph appeared to record simply what was there; at the same time it made everyone a critic since observers could invoke their own sense of reality to compare with the photographic image (art photography, which would take issue with this kind of thinking, did not emerge until the end of the century). In the case of portrait photography, the democratic impulse was taken further because it became possible to conceive of the portrait as the work not of the photographer but of the subject being photographed: "The artist stands aside and lets you paint yourself," Ralph Waldo Emerson declared. "If you have an ill head, not he but yourself are responsible."[11] It seems appropriate that the two figures most associated with American democracy in the nineteenth century, Abraham Lincoln and Walt Whitman, were both enamored of photography and had themselves photographed extensively during their lifetimes.

With the advent of moving pictures, this democratic transfer of power from artist to spectator was radically intensified. Movement was no mere addendum or seasoning to photographic realism; it was a catalytic agent, transforming the very nature of realistic portrayal. Movement on film introduced duration to the recorded event, and since we experience duration in real time, this seemed to bring the "pastness" of the thing imaged into the present. Film's rendering of movement also made possible a multiplication of realistic effects, as elements captured in photographs were now combined and their effects amplified—a vivid example of what Herman Melville had described as the American thirst for "more reality than reality itself can show." Film could also register involuntary movement and movement captured unaware: sneezing, crying, the behavior of children and animals—providing access to experience unavailable to any other form of representation. Finally and most important, movement on film precipitated the development of film narrative, which made possible an unprecedented involvement of the viewer with *character*—an involvement that could hardly be achieved in photography and painting and that was more intimate than anything possible in theater. As a result, the film spectator came to identify with the events on the screen and to feel like a vital participant in what was being portrayed.[12]

Thus, the property of movement, central to film, added another layer or dimension to photographic realism. It produced the sense that reality was being not only recorded but also enacted, and it solidified and deepened the spectator's role as the focus and determinant of meaning.

In the context of film's intensively realistic, spectator-based esthetic, we can isolate three elements that became the raw material of film and which also happened to be defining characteristics of the American myth. In isolating these elements, it is helpful to refer back to Tocqueville when he described America in counterpoint to Europe as a country stripped of history and its associations. What, then, remains? "*Man* . . . in the presence of *Nature* . . . with his *passions* . . ." (my emphasis). What remains, to translate this statement into images, are the *body,* the *landscape,* and the *face,* moving dynamically in combination. These elements are at the center of any discussion of film as an American language. They are the building blocks of the American myth, and their interaction accounts for the emergence of American film as the dominant form of representation in the twentieth century.

The elements of body, landscape, and face constitute, on some level, what Emerson referred to as the "nouns" of nature—those concrete facts of experience that make up our fundamental sense of reality.[13] Psychoanalytic film theory has suggested that the cinematic representation of these elements causes the spectator to regress to earlier psychic states: film's representation of the body evokes a sense of physical invulnerability and wholeness; its representation of space, a sense of superhuman power and control; and its representation of the face, a sense of emotional intimacy with a monumental parental figure. In each case, the cinematic image is said to correspond to a fantasy that has its origin in the most primal stage of our development as sentient beings. Such claims, which may sound outlandish to those unfamiliar with psychoanalytic vocabulary, find additional support in common sense. Even the simplest and most untutored film spectator lives in a world of bodies, landscapes, and faces and therefore brings highly charged, personal associations to bear on their images.[14]

That said, it must be added that the way in which we see these elements is not simply, and not even primarily, a matter of our private experience. Film's appropriation of bodies, landscapes, and faces was not the unmediated rendering of reality that might be supposed. Each element had already acquired definite meanings in American life through association with other forms of representation. The body had been showcased in burlesque and vaudeville; the landscape, in landscape painting and moving panoramas; the face, in photographic portraits and the histrionic forms of theatrical acting favored in "lowbrow" theaters. Each, in short, had derived a set of meanings by being given wide circulation through mostly popular, American forms of cultural expression. Film took these already coded elements and combined them, representing a world that retained much of the vitality, coarseness, and democratic appeal of the expressive forms in which they had been showcased individually. And this continued to be true even after film had incorporated many highly artificial techniques and had moved to plush movie palaces designed to attract more moneyed and sophisticated patrons. A good deal of effort has gone into trying to explain how American film evolved from a lower-class to a middle-class diversion but less into how it managed to retain its lower-class audience. The answer lies in part in the way film's ability to seem real grew out of elements associated with lower-class, specifically American forms of entertainment; the elements then continued to be marked as authentic through opposition to a more elitist, "artful" culture associated with Europe. This conceptual link to the authenticity associated with popular culture also helps explain why American film has retained its opposition to European formalism, despite continual innovations in the realm of special effects and editing. The body, landscape, and face, when presented in an American context, have continued to figure as ostensibly "real" elements, even as they are highly manipulated and radically altered.

An understanding of film's raw material may also bring a new perspective to the issue of film language. Theorists have long tried to find equivalences between linguistic expression and cinematic expression. Early in film history, the great Russian filmmakers Pudovkin and Eisenstein equated the shot with the word, each seeing the creation of meaning as a slightly different result of what happens when individual shots are combined. Decades later, Christian Metz tried to elaborate and qualify this early formalist approach by applying Saussurian linguistics to film operations. But if we consider that film's raw materials—the elements of body, landscape, and face—were the result of a particular representational history and carried distinct meanings that were transferred to film, these elements assume a more formative role in the creation of cinematic meaning than has been acknowledged. We can dramatize the point by noting the cause-and-effect relationship between each of the three elements of the raw material and each of the three most important film operations: the cut, the long shot, and the close-up. The cut was developed to enhance physical properties and bodily movement; the long shot, to render expansive and panoramic views of landscape; and the close-up, to register facial appearance and expressiveness. In other words, it was to serve the elements of body, landscape, and face that the operations arose—not the other way around.

Furthermore, all three of these cinematic operations were necessary if the three elements of the raw material were to be dynamically combined. To see that a body exists in a specific landscape and has a specific face requires the kind of editing and camerawork associated with the cut, the long shot, and the close-up. By extension, more varied and complex combinations of the basic elements call for the development of additional operations: to show bodies and faces of two or more and to place them in a landscape requires the two-shot, the reaction shot, the wide shot, and so forth. Admittedly, these operations, by making possible the integration of elements never before dynamically combined, brought into being an altogether new vision of reality than had existed in previous forms of representation. But the fact remains that the elements carried with them meanings that launched film in one particular direction and not in another. I should add that the three primary film genres of comedy, western, and melodrama can be understood in the same way as the film operations. Although the genres are generally believed to have been adapted to film because of a drive to imitate literary models, it seems just as likely that they were appropriated because they served the raw material of film so well. Comedy was suited to showcasing the body; the western, to showcasing landscape; melodrama, to showcasing the face.

In conceiving of film's raw material in terms of only three elements, I am, of course, collapsing other elements into my scheme or leaving them aside for later treatment. "Things," for example, might well constitute an element of raw material. Erwin Panofsky argued that "movies organize material things and persons," and Vachel Lindsay in his early book on silent films included chapters devoted to furniture and to architecture.[15] But it is a property of film to allow for a great fluidity between states—especially in silent film, where speech is not present as an anchor to meaning. Pudovkin argued that in film the distinction between individual and object is obliterated, and Lindsay himself illustrates this thought in his discussion of the early film *Moving Day,* in which the furniture proceeds to walk out of the house with its occupants. This movie is a very crude example of what would be more subtly achieved later, for example, in Douglas Fairbanks's films, where whips, swords, and ropes become extensions of the protagonist's body, and in Buster Keaton's films, in which a wide range of things, from hats to ocean liners and trains, become quasi-animate companions. The beginnings of this fluid connection between people and things can be traced to vaudeville, which relied heavily on the creative use of props, but film took it further because of the capacity of camera movement and editing to perform transformations on a scale and with a verisimilitude impossible in any other medium.

More important elements overlooked in my three-element lexicon are written language, music, and simultaneous sound. Early films used intertitles, written cards inserted at intervals to explain the moving images, and one might be tempted to include these titles (often witty and artfully designed with illustrations and elaborate borders) as a fourth element of raw material. I do not include them because they seem to me to be transitional forms. They either point back to a literary tradition from which American film, by virtue of its status as a nonliterary, "real" space, was positioned to oppose or forward to simultaneous sound. In this sense, they resemble music. Musical accompaniment has been an ongoing part of film since its beginnings—though its function has changed radically in the shift from silent to sound films. During the silent period, it served, like intertitles, as an aid in following the narrative; after the advent of talking pictures, it acquired an atmospheric function like color and wide-screen projection, assisting the appeal of the dynamic image but not necessarily integrating with it.

As for speech, it is a crucial component of film language, but it is a belated one. Indeed, the absence of simultaneous sound in early film seems to me one of its most fundamental characteristics—what allowed it to emerge as a distinctive new medium and gave it access to a worldwide audience. The appeal of silence to early filmmakers and viewers cannot be overstated. James Quirk, the first editor of the fan magazine *Photoplay,* waxed on about in it in 1921 as the medium's "rarest and subtlest beauty." He connected it to the fundamental processes of nature: "All growth is silent. The deepest love is most eloquent in that transcendent silence of the communion of souls."[16] The Hungarian critic Béla Balázs singled out silence as the means by which film would retrieve a physical language that was more primal than words and which had been lost after the invention of the printing press. Both Griffith and Chaplin were adamant in connecting film's power to its silence. Griffith maintained its importance in making film a "universal language" capable of promoting world peace. Chaplin focused on its compatibility with the art of images and clung to it longer than anyone else (he made his last silent film, *Modern Times,* in 1936). However, what seems most important about the absence of simultaneous sound in early films is that it soldered the alliance between film and America, establishing their mutual connection to a reality outside the artifice of words.

Words as an obstacle to reality had been a motif in American literature throughout the nineteenth century. James Fenimore Cooper built his famous series of novels, the *Leatherstocking Tales,* around a frontier scout, ill at ease with the language of civilization, who placed his trust in the visual signs of the wilderness and earned himself the nickname "Hawkeye" from the Iroquois. The American transcendentalist philosophers Emerson and Henry David Thoreau similarly elevated the properties of vision over words: to "see" was to cut through the clutter of bookishness and received opinion that impeded a fresh perspective on life. Whitman, prolix though he was and engaged with the voluptuousness of language, also faulted words as limited and potentially misleading. More than any other writer, he invoked the elements of body, landscape, and face as ultimate points of reference: "If I shall worship one thing more than another it shall be the spread of my own body"; "The masters know the earth's words and use them more than audible words"; "Writing and talk do not prove me/I carry the plenum of proof and everything else in my face."[17]

Given the limitations and derivative associations that words carried for American writers and thinkers and the fact that popular entertainment was largely musical and physical and involved few words, film's early development without simultaneous sound confirmed its connection to a reality bred out of American experience. When speech finally entered films, it had given the other elements a head start.

Body, landscape, face—film took these "nouns of nature" that had been represented previously in scattered and relatively static forms and melded them into narratives about a new kind of self. This self had already made an anticipatory, if incomplete, appearance in American literature. The existential byproduct of the American myth, as R. W. B. Lewis argued over four decades ago, was the "American Adam": "a figure of heroic innocence and vast potentialities, poised at the start of a new history."[18] This figure was a kind of ideal form in the literature, an ambitious representation but not a fully realized one in view of having to inhabit a medium that was, by definition, derivative. Lewis and others have pointed out that American novels, plays, and poems, despite native themes and authors, remained wedded to styles of storytelling more European than American. At the same time, indigenous forms of entertainment like vaudeville and burlesque were inadequate to the representation of a new kind of self. They contained no unified narratives and hence no means of depicting a sustained idea of character with which their audiences could identify. In short, there was no place, before the advent of narrative film, for the realistic embodiment of the American myth—for the portrayal of an American who was contending successfully with a dynamically changing world.

Silent film did what earlier representational forms could not do. It gave realistic expression to the American myth and provided dynamic visual narratives that could serve as models for how to *be*. Film did away with the idea of the self as deeply conditioned, inherited, or divinely imposed. It initiated a new trust in the value of surface meaning and in the possibility of constructing a self as the product of surfaces.

The star system as it evolved during the silent era was the outgrowth of the films whose moving images flooded the consciousness of their audiences. The movie star expressed, in the most distilled possible way, a conception of the self as a mutable surface. Now, individuals with no education or social standing could be transformed on screen into figures of glamour and authority. Unlike theater, there were no words to qualify the image. Also unlike theater, "acting" seemed to disappear as a mediating form: stars were manufactured *through* their films; they did not exist outside them.

The great stars of the silent era were both self-made and audience-made in a combination that reconciled two opposing strands of the American myth: individualism and democracy. On the one hand, they extended concepts of physical self-reliance and resourcefulness associated with the American frontiersman and applied them to the material of personality. On the other hand, their ability to shape themselves to the needs of their audiences reflected a new kind of public, consensual process in the creation of the self that was in keeping with the democratic principles of the nation. This conjunction of individualism and democratic conformity was in turn adopted by the audiences themselves through the exercise of their consumer power. Consumerism extended the notion of visual display, central to silent film, into the marketplace by allowing the public to imitate a star through the purchase of a sofa, a dress, a lipstick, or a hair tonic. Fan magazines, which had gained large circulations by 1919, featured articles and advertisements with titles like "The Fifth of a Series on How to Use the Motion Picture to Suggest Furnishings for Your Home" and "Ladies Look to Your Legs" (with advice from a former Sennett bathing beauty).[19] Such articles may seem silly, and it is now commonplace to condemn the materialism they evoke as a symptom of exploitative capitalism. But the reality is more complicated. The consumer culture that movies fostered certainly had trivial and oppressive aspects, but it also had creative and liberating ones. A movie-inspired consumer culture supplied opportunities for self-expression by providing a pool of varied but finite elements—a material alphabet (the plastic extension of Vachel Lindsay's "film hieroglyphics")—through which people who had no other means of asserting their will or expressing themselves in tangible ways could construct their lives as Americans.

The arrival of speech mostly carried forward what silent film had begun: "A few months ago Londoners laughed at the sound of American slang," observed the French filmmaker René Clair soon after the advent of talking pictures, "but today nobody seems surprised and tomorrow London speech may be affected by it." History has borne Clair out, not just for Londoners but also for Parisians—surely the most resistant of populations—and for the inhabitants of more remote locales as well. Nor was this simply a matter of American films penetrating foreign markets. Foreign filmmakers also came to America and incorporated themselves into the national psyche ("Uncle Sam's Adopted Children," as *Photoplay* dubbed them in 1926). Vachel Lindsay had anticipated the potential of film to Americanize the world: "There is not a civilized or half-civilized land but may read [film's] Whitmanesque message in time, if once it is put on the films with power," he prophesied in 1915.[20]

By beginning its life without simultaneous sound, film became a uniquely effective vehicle for the representation of the American myth. It kept the myth alive even when the country could no longer claim to be the *tabula rasa* it once was, and it supported the myth even in the face of its own transformation, first, with the coming of sound and, later, with the advent of television and video. In its dynamic integration of body, landscape, and face, film and its spinoffs have sustained the American myth and sold it to the world.

This is, I know, a controversial statement. The American myth is no longer seen in the positive way it once was, and the "selling" of the myth is no longer equated with the unequivocal triumph of democratic ideals. Indeed, the whole "myth-symbol school," as it has been called, has come under attack over the past several decades as attention has shifted "from myth to rhetorics"—from a monolithic, univocal account of what it means to be American to a more fluid, multivocal chorus of accounts.[21] The newer perspective has involved discovering what has been repressed and marginalized in the narrative of American history and culture, and it has looked severely on past scholarship that imagined it could reduce America to one set of goals and interests. It is with this work in mind that I want to explain my continued belief in an American myth—at once broadening my terms to encompass recent approaches and narrowing them to make clear where my own concern lies.

In critiquing the viability of the American myth, scholars have taken issue with an earlier approach to American studies that based its conclusions on a circumscribed set of literary texts.[22] These scholars have pointed to the inadequacy of literature as a shaping force in culture, arguing that culture is the product of a multiplicity of influences that stretch beyond and, indeed, eclipse the literary. This seems to me right, but what they have overlooked is the fact that film—particularly silent film—was a new form, radically different from literature in the nature and extent of its influence. As a mass medium—and the first genuine mass medium to take a narrative form—silent film made it possible for a heroic, optimistic ideal about America to extend beyond its more elitist, theoretical origins as articulated on paper by the nation's Founding Fathers. It gave those high-flown words about freedom and opportunity a dynamic form and made them available to a diverse audience. Moreover, although the formulas of the studio system may have supported certain stereotyped notions of what it meant to be an American, the films themselves—in being richly composite, moving images open to the gaze of a variegated public—complicated these stereotypes. Film historian Richard Dyer has described Hollywood films as "leaky" vessels, not the closed systems that one might imagine, which is to say that by their very nature these movies made possible an elasticity in the conception of self that each viewer took away from the experience of watching them.[23]

At the same time, the representation of reality that silent film offered, although being in one sense open to variable interpretation, also harmonized and smoothed over differences, bringing a diverse America to a belief in the possibility of remaking oneself according to certain prescribed guidelines. The groups that were largely excluded in this regard were African Americans, Asians, and Native Americans. Silent film could not harmonize the visual coordinates associated with these groups as well as it could the largely nonvisual characteristics associated with Polish, Irish, Italian, and Jewish immigrants. Moreover, since silent film achieved many of its effects through visual contrast, it often seemed to assimilate ethnic minorities at the expense of racial ones— Jewish characters, for example, rendered less exotic, "whiter," in the context of black characters.[24] There was also the added problem of cultural conditioning. The country's history of injustice toward Indians and blacks had given rise to defenses and rationalizations that were more deeply embedded in the culture than the attitudes toward newer immigrant groups. The films reflexively adopted these in their narratives and, in doing so, became a new and powerful means of disseminating and reinforcing established prejudices.

Yet without denying such unfortunate attributes of the medium and while admitting that, overall, it did not transcend the culture that produced it, I argue that even at their worst, silent films exposed injustice by telling their stories in dramatic visual form. Consider *The Birth of a Nation:* by representing its most egregiously racist sentiments in many of its most visually striking scenes (one thinks of the repugnant rendering of the black state legislature during Reconstruction), the film had the capacity to mobilize black protest in a way never before expressed against a cultural representation; it sparked a national debate about the portrayal of the African American that continues to this day. Perhaps a more noteworthy protest, because it occurred within the medium itself, was the 1919 film *Within Our Gates,* an indictment of racial prejudice made in rebuttal to *The Birth of a Nation* by the black filmmaker Oscar Micheaux. What is particularly noteworthy about this film and serves to support my belief in the ability of the American myth to sustain itself in new contexts is how completely it adapts an ideal of America to its own perspective. Although it begins with a gruesome lynching, it ends with the hero voicing his patriotism and counseling the heroine: "We were never immigrants. Be proud of this country always!"[25] The statement uses the immigrant as the foil for an American identity, just as the immigrant used the African American for the same purpose. It illustrates my contention that as long as films continued to espouse the possibilities for self-assertion and self-creation, it was possible for people (even those pointedly excluded from the imagery of mainstream films) to appropriate the values of the American myth for their own use.

In a broader sense, film has operated as a self-corrective medium if only as a result of its persistent drive to do something new. The silent director and producer Thomas Ince, for example, was so devoted to offbeat approaches in his films that he sometimes inverted established norms and took the Indians' point of view on westward expansion.[26] Ince's films were admittedly the exceptions of the period, but they anticipated the westerns of the 1960s and 1970s, whose inverted conventions were connected to more widespread social awareness. Griffith of all people voiced the salient point at the heart of all reform movement when he proclaimed that "the task I'm trying to achieve is above all to make you see."[27] "Seeing," of course, can be partial and it can be flawed, but it can also pick up, unpredictably, on the seemingly negligible detail or it can note where a detail that ought to be present is missing. By representing America to itself, silent film offered its audiences the opportunity to "see" the limits and omissions of its representations and, in time, to demand revision.

The esthetic and entertainment value of silent film may not be readily apparent to the uninitiated. Most people think only of faded images and jerky movements when they think of the silent era, and it requires a certain amount of patience and attentiveness—not to mention a well-scored print of good quality projected at the right speed—to experience the seductive power of silent film. Yet if the effort is made, it is repaid many times over. There is a beauty and grace to silent films that have never been equaled in talking pictures, which explains why so many eminent critics, from Vachel Lindsay to Rudolph Arnheim and Aldous Huxley, saw the advent of talkies as a diminishment. We are fortunate that many silent films are now finding their way onto videotape in remastered versions with original scores. Since it is a property of film to make us lose ourselves, these films are invitations to time travel: the dated dress and decor, and even the lack of speech, eventually cease to be obstacles, their strangeness dissolved away by the power of visual narrative. Film historians have warned that the vast majority of silent films, like the vast majority of films today, were mediocre or worse, but one advantage of returning to the era rather than living in it is that some of the sifting has been done for us. What we have available tend to be the better examples of the medium.[28]

Along with the esthetic value of silent film is the historical value. Just as it is impossible to fully appreciate Italian Renaissance art without knowing its roots in Italian medieval art, so to understand Hollywood movies of the 1930s and 1940s we must know their roots in silent movies of the teens and 1920s, when the studio system and what is called classic Hollywood cinema first took shape. American silent film is the geological substrate, the cultural unconscious, if you will, of the Hollywood movie, which still conditions our sense of what a movie is like. It deserves study for what it can teach about American film as a dominant cultural form.

Finally, the value of the silent film extends beyond its esthetic appeal and its importance in film history. Its greatest value is as the source of a way of seeing that powerfully informs our present lives. Watching these films with attention to the historical trends and contexts that shaped them helps illuminate how America articulated a sense of itself at the beginning of the twentieth century that it would go on to strengthen and elaborate as the century progressed. Silent film consolidated and rendered believable the American myth that had circulated in truncated, scattered, and inchoate form in the nineteenth century. It gave birth to a new kind of consciousness, centered on the dynamic image, that would have far-reaching effects on our future as a nation and on the shape of the world. Although it is certainly possible to parse the films of the silent era and uncover exclusionary, oppressive, and conflicting messages, it is also possible to look at that era as a unified moment in our history when the country found a voice by keeping silent.

One final note: this book does not involve the kind of archival research that is presently being done by many film historians. I am not a film historian but a cultural critic for whom the silent era offers a wealth of material for understanding American experience, past and present. My intention is to demonstrate that American silent film was a unique site, where ideas associated with America found a congenial home, where they were consolidated and given an unprecedented power to persuade a vast public of their truth and desirability. To demonstrate this thesis, I deal not only with the silent era but also with the nineteenth-century culture that preceded it, selecting figures and motifs from both periods that I think carry a maximum of meaning and returning to them again and again as useful points of reference. In taking this approach, a number of important filmmakers and screen presences have been shortchanged. Chaplin, for example, is treated perfunctorily in these pages (his English roots and his Dickensian sensibility make him less connected to the American myth as I define it). Wonderful stars such as John Barrymore, Ronald Colman, Janet Gaynor, Charles Farrell, Louise Brooks, Vilma Banky, Betty Bronson, and Colleen Moore, not to mention fine directors like Raoul Walsh, John Ford, King Vidor, Rex Ingram, and Joseph von Sternberg, are referred to only in passing or not at all. These casualties are largely dictated by the needs of my argument. My hope is that readers may be inspired to judge their appeal and importance for themselves. Leading a modern audience back to the silent era is, after all, the ultimate goal of this study.

1

LITERARY ANTECEDENTS OF AMERICAN SILENT FILM

A T ONE POINT in Mary Pickford's 1917 film, *The Little American,* Mary's character, a young American woman who has recently arrived in France to visit a relative, finds herself caught in the throes of World War I and faced with a band of vicious "Huns" who have broken into the chateau where she is staying. Her eyes wide with fright, her hands plucking nervously at the lace of her collar, Little Mary reaches into the front of her dress and pulls out a ragged square of cloth—a tiny American flag—that she waves in front of the enemy. It is the kind of small but noble gesture common in American silent films that makes even the most jaded spectator gulp with emotion. In this case, the little flag does not stop the marauders; they proceed to rape the servants and pillage the chateau. But Mary's symbolic gesture is a powerful statement of affiliation and character. It makes clear that she will find a way to defeat the enemy—that no risk is too great. Soon, she is communicating with the French army through a hidden wireless; escaping from a firing squad; and converting her lover, an officer in the German army, to the cause of freedom and justice. She does all this through pluck and resourcefulness, her fragility belying a steely determination and courage.

This film, an enormous success at its release, dramatized in female form what Mary's future husband, Douglas Fairbanks, was dramatizing on screen in male form: that the American was capable of triumphing in even the most extreme situations of oppression or danger. Neither Doug nor Mary uttered a word in the course of their ordeals; their medium did not allow for speech. But their silence was not, as it might have been a century earlier, the mark of inarticulateness and cultural deprivation. Quite the contrary; it was eloquent. It enhanced rather than diminished their power.

"No religion, no manners, and above all, no language, essentially her own," pronounced a European commentator about America in 1825. "No dim traces of the past—no venerable monuments—no romantic associations," wrote the British essayist William Hazlitt of the same period.[1] America, such statements implied, was a backward Europe, deprived of the material for cultural greatness. In the face of such views, it is not surprising that many American writers decided to cross the Atlantic to remedy their cultural deficiencies. Both Washington Irving and Mark Twain lived for extended periods in Europe, and both Edith Wharton and Henry James spent the larger portion of their working life

Preceding page: Mary Pickford in *The Little American,* 1917 (Kobal Collection)

abroad. The influence of a European literary tradition was strong even for those who were devoted to the idea of a uniquely American literature. James Fenimore Cooper, whose work would extol the American wilderness, was inspired in his subject matter and style by the British novelist Walter Scott; and Ralph Waldo Emerson, the most important advocate of a national literature, found his first intellectual mentor in the British moral philosopher Thomas Carlyle.

Yet even as American writers suffered from a sense of inferiority with respect to Europe, they also saw themselves as having advantages that Europe lacked. Their models were the Founding Fathers, who had seen in America's newness the source of its promise: "We have it in our power to begin the world again," declared Thomas Paine. "The Creator has made the earth for the living, not the dead," pronounced Thomas Jefferson.[2] Both statements reflect the conviction that the nation's laws had to be shaped out of present American experience rather than past European custom. The same spirit, applied to a national esthetic, meant that the American writer had to invent a new literature: "Of the great poems received from abroad," asked Walt Whitman, "is there one that is consistent with these United States. . . . Is there one whose underlying basis is not a denial and insult to democracy?"[3] Whitman's question is a challenge to himself and to American writers in general to stop imitating past literary models and find, in their absence, more authentic materials for representing experience. "We want a national literature," wrote Henry Wadsworth Longfellow, "commensurate with our mountains and our rivers. . . . We want a national drama in which scope shall be given to our gigantic ideas and to the unparalleled activity of our people. . . . In a word, we want a national literature altogether shaggy and unshorn, that shall shake the earth, like a herd of buffaloes thundering over the prairies."[4]

Ralph Waldo Emerson represents the initiating philosophical figure in meeting this epic challenge of a national literature. Born in Boston in 1803, he had begun his career conventionally enough, attending Harvard and then proceeding into the ministry, where he was ordained as pastor in the church of the great Puritan forefathers, Increase and Cotton Mather. The Mathers represented an austerely revisionist religious doctrine that encapsulated some of the purer ideals associated with the myth of a new beginning in America. Yet those ideas were also bound up with Calvinist notions of sin, and they opposed the faith in natural law that had lent optimism and vitality to the new republic. Emerson's Boston church had revised that early Puritanism into a more open and accepting Unitarianism, but Emerson came to see this as an unsatisfying compromise—a way of holding on to the structures of past belief while jettisoning much of its more unpleasant and oppressive content. In pursuit of material for a meaningful theology, he initially looked abroad, as so many talented Americans had done. He quit the ministry and traveled to England, where he met the Romantic poets Samuel Coleridge and William Wordsworth and the great essayist Thomas Carlyle.

The philosophy espoused by these writers—their rejection of established religion and their embrace of a more personal conception of life grounded in nature and the imagination—would become the core of Emerson's own philosophy. But he would also give these ideas a nationalist turn by attaching them to the concrete reality of his country's landscape, resources, and people. America, Emerson came to believe, was the literal expression of the ideals of freedom and natural law that the Romantic poets and their successors had championed in more abstract terms. For Wordsworth and Coleridge, nature was a mediating form, a vehicle for the exercise of the imagination; but for Emerson, it was the American continent itself that was "a poem"—"its ample geography dazzles the imagination." As the promoter of a new, indigenous form of expression, he counseled writers to turn away from Europe and study America—"the climate, the soil, the length of the day, the wants of the people, the habit and form of the government"—in short, to make the present facts of American life as important a source of inspiration as the learned teachings of the past.[5]

If Emerson was the philosopher of a national literature, James Fenimore Cooper can be called its first practitioner. Cooper, like Emerson, followed a path that began conventionally, then swerved in a more original direction. He was born in 1789 in New Jersey to a wealthy family and briefly attended Yale, where he failed to apply himself and was asked to leave. Before embarking on a career as a writer, he lived in the style of an English country squire, apparently indifferent to issues of national identity and culture. He turned to novel writing on a whim, having boasted that he could improve upon a novel by Jane Austen and thereby producing a mediocre imitation of a British novel of manners. With that book, Cooper found his vocation; he would soon find his subject, abandoning the model of Austen for that of the historical novelist Walter Scott (eventually earning himself the nickname "the American Scott"). But if Cooper came to echo Scott in his style, as Emerson echoed Carlyle, he also found, as Emerson did, a native theme that would distinguish him from his literary mentor. That theme was American history. Hazlitt and other European commentators had called this an oxymoron—America had no history, they said—but Cooper worked with rather than against their claim. American history, as he conceived it, was its absence of history in the European sense. If the country boasted "no venerable monuments," it had the advantage of space unoccupied by monuments. It had wilderness and prairie, open to the actions and imagination of the first white settlers, who were engaging at first hand with nature and with the "natural man," that distillation of acuity, courage, cunning, and violence that was Cooper's characterization of the Native American.

Cooper's most celebrated novels are a group of five books called the *Leatherstocking Tales,* which deal with America's emergence into "civilization" out of the frontier experience of its recent past. The books are noteworthy not only in their theme but also in the way their theme is dramatized by the order of their composition. The first, *The Pioneers,* composed in 1823, deals with the settlement of the Hudson River Valley, occurring at the time that the novel was composed; the last, *The Deerslayer,* written in 1841, is set in the 1740s, when the area was still in a state of wilderness. The progression backward is important because it reflects the author's embrace of the American myth—the conviction that the very newness of the country, once believed to be a detriment, was a mark of nobility and value. In transforming the frontier scout Natty Bumppo from a peripheral, aging character into a young hero, Cooper was in effect embracing his American cultural inheritance and trying to do it justice in his fiction. D. H. Lawrence, one of many Cooper admirers to theorize on the chronology of the *Tales,* would see the progression backward as an expression of cultural independence—of the birth of America from its European parent: "She starts old, old, wrinkled and writhing in an old skin. And there is a general sloughing off of the old skin, towards a new youth. It is the myth of America."[6]

The "shedding of the skin" that Lawrence associated with the American myth was, of course, the shedding of the trappings of European civilization and, in particular, the shedding of an inherited language. Cooper's Natty Bumppo is most himself when he exists outside of his language and simply reads nature directly: "Better and wiser would it be," he declares in *The Deerslayer,* "if [man] could understand the signs of nature and take a lesson from the fowls of the air and the beasts of the fields."[7] Bumppo, known by the Indians first as Deerslayer and then as Hawkeye, is the prototype from which all the heroes and heroines of American literature can be said to spring. Though few are so literally immersed in nature as he is, most are similar in choosing to ignore the conventions of society and to operate as much as they possibly can outside the constraints of language. Thus, Hawthorne's Hester Prynne is a social pariah who achieves moral stature through her unwillingness to explain herself; Twain's Huck Finn ends by throwing down his pen and heading for the territories where civilization—and language—will not impede his freedom; and Melville's Bartleby and Billy Budd both become martyrs as the result of their silence.

Henry James's American heroes and heroines are particularly interesting examples of this pattern. Although James expatriated himself on the basis of America's lack of a European-style history and culture, he went on to write books that elevated the American innocent at the expense of the wily and socially adept European. Christopher Newman, the title character of *The American,* heroically loses the woman he loves rather than engage in the social machinations necessary to win her; Isabel Archer, in *The Portrait of a Lady,* is marked as the novel's heroine by an idealism that allows her to be duped into a mercenary marriage; and Adam Verver, the American millionaire art collector in *The Golden Bowl,* emerges, through his unwillingness to speak about what he knows or doesn't know, as the book's most profoundly humane character.

These characters are not comprehensible in the traditional terms by which we know characters in literature. Lacking the desire or ability to articulate what they think or feel, they do not inspire us to imagine their inner lives. It would be wrong to say that they are repressed in the classic Freudian sense; the idea of a personal psychology hardly seems to make sense when thinking about a Hester Prynne or a Bartleby. Even James's characters, for all their talk, seem less deep than intricately and elaborately superficial. The effect of these characters is not literary in the conventional sense but something closer to pictorial or, to anticipate the direction of my argument, cinematic. One remembers Huck and Jim on the raft, gazing up at the stars; Billy Budd being drawn up to heaven, an aureole of light surrounding his head; and Hester Prynne posed before the town elders, the scarlet letter emblazoned on her breast. In each case, the literature seems to be aspiring to what the literary critic Richard Poirier called "a world elsewhere"—though not, as he would have it, to a more abstract, metaphysical world but to a more concrete or, at least, a more image-based one.[8]

What these novels might be said to express through their scenic representation of character is a yearning for a nonliterary literature—for a mode of expression that could escape the constrictions of literary or verbal language and approach experience directly. "I'm glad [the lake] has no name," announces Bumppo at one point in *The Deerslayer,* "or, at least, no pale-face name, for their christenings always foretell waste and destruction."[9] "Naming," Bumppo's words imply, *causes* waste and destruction. Elsewhere in American literature, what Bumppo associates with environmental devastation is expressed as a larger cultural devastation: a distortion of meaning, a loss of correspondence between words and things: "I had better never see a book, than to be warped by its attraction clean out of my own orbit, and made a satellite instead of a system," writes Emerson. "I did not read books the first summer," announces Thoreau in describing his sojourn at Walden Pond, "I hoed beans." "A morning-glory at my window satisfies me more than the metaphysics of books," proclaims Whitman.[10] The call, in statements like these, is to bypass words for things, literature for life. Accordingly, "vision" becomes the fundamental metaphor for understanding. Emerson, in his most famous phrase, dubs himself "a transparent eyeball"—a dramatic rendering of the effort to absorb and mirror the world in its material existence without the mediation of language.

Such statements are, of course, paradoxical since they ignore what they themselves are made of. Being dependent on words, they reflect a larger, intractable world of convention and artifice. In the novels, this is expressed in the protagonists' ultimate failure to win their object or to accommodate themselves to their society. Cooper wrote his *Leatherstocking Tales* backward to highlight the affinity of his hero with the American frontier spirit, but if we read the novels in their chronological order we see that that hero is destined to be marginalized—not only by age but also by the encroaching forms of a civilization where he can never be at home. If we return to Emerson, we see that frustration expressed in a different way. Emerson's dependence on past literary models remained embedded in his style, not only in its obvious echo of Carlyle but also in the very references through which he hoped to evoke the casting off of such influence. When, for example, he calls for a "genius in American life" who can celebrate the vitality of American culture in all of its "barbarism and materialism," he immediately compares such a genius to Homer, who, he claims, represented the vitality of Greek culture as a "carnival of the gods."[11] It is an analogy that betrays his enmeshment in the Western classical tradition that he was trying to escape. "Emerson had his message, but he was a good while looking for his form," noted Henry James, voicing the paradox and making clear its connection to a given medium of expression.[12] As a result of his dependence on past forms, Emerson seems less the apostle of a new American literature than its anticipatory prophet: "Our day of dependence, our long apprenticeship to the learning of other lands, draws to a close," he announced toward the beginning of "The American Scholar," concluding with a series of calls that echo the Twenty-third Psalm: "We will walk on our own feet; we will work with our own hands; we will speak our own minds. The study of letters shall be no longer a name for pity, for doubt, and for sensual indulgence. . . . A nation of men will for the first time exist, because each believes himself inspired by the Divine Soul which also inspires all men."[13] These words place the new beginning in a future mystically transfigured. But how is the transfiguration to happen? Although Emerson abandoned his pulpit to preach a literary gospel, his writing seems a reformulation of the apocalyptic sermon, with the future poet in the place of the messiah, to be fervently but passively awaited.

Some of the same tendencies are discernible in Emerson's disciple and friend, Henry David Thoreau. More austere and intense than his mentor, Thoreau had many of the attributes of the monk or classical stoic: he was solitary and ruminative, indifferent to fame and the world's praise, and essentially unemployed except in a vague quest for meaning. Whereas Emerson had translated the clerical ministry into a secular one, Thoreau was more radically cut off from traditional forms of vocation and required an altogether different form in which to relay his thinking. His effort to leave history and literary models behind is most successfully embodied in *Walden,* his record of the two years he spent alone by a New England pond. The book expresses its author's intensive quest for the authentic experience in nature—his attempt to return, so to speak, to Deerslayer's golden youth through the contrivance of a consciously staged event. If the country cannot go back to its "purer" frontier history, Thoreau might as well be saying, the individual can at least simulate that return by leading life with the same simplicity and involvement with nature.

Yet although *Walden* has the form and tone of a latter-day scripture, its ambition is so great that logical omissions and inconsistencies spring into relief against it. We read, for example, that Thoreau has been placed in jail for not paying his taxes but not how he happens to be released; that he has purchased the walls of his house from a poor family but not what becomes of that family after he has dislodged them; and that he abandons his noble experiment after two years but not what he plans to do afterward to exercise the lessons of his retreat. These gaps are glaring because they call into question the assumption on which the work rests: that this is the definitive hymn to the righteous life. But Thoreau diagnoses the problem himself and situates it in language: "I am convinced that I cannot exaggerate enough even to lay the foundation of a true expression. . . . The volatile truth of our words should continually betray the inadequacy of the residual statement. Their truth is instantly translated; its literal monument alone remains."[14] As with Emerson, though in a different way, some ground has been cleared from which to see into the future, but that vision remains obstructed by the "literal monument" of words.

The philosophy that both Emerson and Thoreau espoused was one of transcendence—an effort to use words to bypass words, to master what Thoreau would term "the language [in] which all things and events speak without metaphor."[15] But the result, inevitably, fell short of the aspiration. One feels, reading these two writers, the combination of passion and stiltedness that is the mark of their power, but also of their difficulty, and that explains their limited appeal to a wide audience.

Of all the American writers of the nineteenth century, Walt Whitman comes closest to transcending the literary nature of his medium. Whitman's background was more solidly democratic than either Emerson's or Thoreau's. The son of a carpenter, he was mostly self-taught and mixed easily with people from all walks of life. His poetry is likewise a poetry of movement and inclusion, a restless striving to experience and encompass life in all its variety and dynamism:

> Urge and urge and urge,
> Always the procreant urge of the world.
> Out of the dimness opposite equals advance, always substance
>   and increase,
> always sex,
> Always a knit of identity, always distinction, always a breed of life.[16]

The great Americanist critic R. W. B. Lewis once noted that reading Whitman feels like reading "the first poem ever written."[17] Certainly, Whitman's use of language and prosody were a revelation in their time; his influence on modern poetry was enormous; and his effect, even today, seems stunningly original. But his poems, for all their novelty and verve, are also difficult and verbose—very much a weighty enterprise. He prepared to write *Leaves of Grass* by engaging in an extended reading program, steeping himself in the classical works of Western culture; when he began writing his own poetry, he self-consciously diverged from the tradition he had taken such pains to learn. This may explain his limited appeal to many readers. For to appreciate Whitman it helps to know from what he is departing, making his poetry more difficult to grasp than the more conventional, elitist poetry that he repudiates. Vachel Lindsay, who would hail film as a Whitmanesque art, would nonetheless fault Whitman for "not persuade[ing] the democracy to read his democratic poems."[18]

One senses Whitman's own frustration with the limitations inherent in language in "Song of Myself," the most famous poem in *Leaves of Grass*. The poem is filled with Emersonian juxtapositions about the restrictiveness of "speech" and the expansiveness and largess of "vision." But Whitman also goes further than Emerson, making tangible and sensory invocations, particularly to his own body, the ultimate point of reference: "If I worship one thing more than another, it shall be the spread of my own body or any part of it."[19] The statement is made poignant by its implied desire for the words to become flesh. Indeed, Whitman's effort as a poet is always to move beyond what he has spoken—to move, as it were, off the page and into the world:

Not words of routine this song of mine,
But abruptly to question, leap beyond yet nearer bring;
This printed and bound book—but the printer and the printing-office boy?
The well-taken photograph—but your wife or friend close and solid
    in your arms?[20]

This passage runs through different representational media, designating each of them as inadequate and partial. Direct physical contact, the poet seems to say, is the only truly satisfying goal.

There is a correlation to be drawn between Whitman's effort in such passages to transcend the limitations of words in the casting of images and the ongoing revision, supplementation, and reordering of *Leaves of Grass* that preoccupied him for the last thirty years of his life. That compulsion to revise—to create a continuum of experience on the page—reflects a desire to *live* in the poems, to turn them into a surrogate body that his readers could literally take in their hands. His insistence in certain contexts that words *are* things supports this view. Only in Whitman's great prose work *Democratic Vistas* does he finally seem to give up the effort for direct connection and embrace the futurism of Emerson, bequeathing the struggle, as he puts it, to "some two or three really original American poets (perhaps artists or lecturers) [to] arise, mounting the horizon like planets,"[21] to achieve the task that he has been unable to complete. The uncertainty about the form that the future seer will take seems significant.

One could argue, finally, that the most successful expression that Whitman forged in his time was the myth of himself: the image of the archetypal American, encompassing different extremes and phases of being—from the bawdy roustabout and free spirit of youth to the kindly guru of old age. Helping in the formation of his many personas was Whitman's great enthusiasm for being photographed and the fact that photographs exist from various stages of his life. Among the many well-known images, the earliest, from the frontispiece of the first edition of *Leaves of Grass,* is perhaps the most memorable. It shows him with his black hat pushed back and his shirt sleeves rolled up, standing jauntily—one hand in his pocket, one on his waist. The photograph is unusual not only in its casual presentation (formal attire was generally prescribed for portraits) but also in seeming to catch its subject in the moment (an effect difficult to obtain given the long exposure time required for photography of the period). Whitman seems to be inviting the observer to see him in the midst of life: "You shall stand at my side and look in the mirror with me," he commands in "Song of Myself," and he extends the image of himself being watched in the invocation to "Poets to Come" in the "Inscriptions" portion of *Leaves of Grass:* "I

Walt Whitman, engraving from daguerreotype, from frontispiece to the
first edition of *Leaves of Grass,* 1855 (Culver Pictures)

am a man who, sauntering along without fully stopping, turns a casual look
upon you and then averts his face,/ Leaving it to you to prove and define it,/Ex-
pecting the main things from you."[22] These lines foretell the kind of casual intimacy and remoteness that would characterize the film actor's relationship to
an audience—an audience that would make its own meaning out of the odd intimacy it forged with the moving figure projected on the screen.

Whitman would represent himself throughout his life as actively engaged
with different kinds of people from different walks of life: he visited Civil War
veterans in their hospital beds; he rode the New York ferry with the immigrant
masses; he crossed the plains with the cowboys and western settlers: "I am
large, I include multitudes," he boasted of his protean ability to inhabit multiple and changing roles.[23] In this boast, he anticipated a new form of self-presentation; for it is precisely the ability to mirror the dynamic life of a large and
diverse public that would be the defining characteristic of the movie star.

Thomas Edison's first film: *Fred Ott's Sneeze,* 1893 (Museum of Modern Art)

In 1893, a year after Walt Whitman's death, Thomas Alva Edison opened the first motion picture studio, the Black Maria, behind his industrial laboratory in West Orange, New Jersey. There, with the technical help of his employee, William Dickson, and the cooperation of his handyman, Fred Ott, he produced his first film, a few seconds of footage known to posterity as *Fred Ott's Sneeze.*[24]

It is interesting to compare Edison, the embodiment of American ingenuity and know-how, to Whitman, the first truly original American poet. Both the "Wizard of Menlo Park" and the "Old Gray Bard" were sons of carpenters, both were largely self-taught and voracious readers, and both were aggressive self-promoters. Yet the differences are equally striking and can begin to be explained—at least for the purpose of this study—as the result of their different historical positionings. Whitman, born in 1819, was a New Yorker, and although he would travel throughout the country later in his life and make the vastness and variety of the continent one of his central themes, his experience of America began as an eastern one.

Edison, more than a quarter of a century younger than Whitman, was born in Ohio and spent the first seven years of his life at the edge of the western reserve, an area being rapidly transformed by the technological and commercial forces of midcentury. In the course of the years that the Edisons lived in Ohio, canal transportation vied with developing railroad transportation, and the railroad finally won as it proliferated in a spurt of growth in the next decade. In 1854, the Edison family moved to Michigan, where the railroad was also in the process of transforming the landscape and changing the nature and rate of industrial production. Confronted with the roar of the train and the tapping of the newly invented telegraph, Edison was inspired to put his imprint on the things that were driving that forward motion. If Whitman, at the threshold of a technological future, needed to describe nature in original ways that would influence the theoretical shape of that future, Edison, in the full flush of technological change, needed to control nature in original ways—to remake the world through things rather than words. And yet, to reaffirm the kinship of these two influential figures, the "things" that Edison sought to control were almost all concerned with communication, what had preoccupied Whitman in the form of an endlessly original gush of words.

Edison invented or had a hand in improving the telegraph, the electric pen (precursor to the ditto machine), the telephone, the phonograph, and of course the motion picture camera. This string of devices would transform the nature and quality of communication in the twentieth century, carrying forward what the railroad had begun and giving concrete realization to the sounds and sights so central to Whitman's poetry.

Although Whitman had acknowledged the material and technological resources of America as crucial to the nation's identity, his view of art was ultimately removed from these things. A great chasm had opened in nineteenth-
century America between material values and spiritual ones—a separation that
had always existed as a motif in Christian thinking but which now took on
heightened meaning in the face of a burgeoning industrial culture. The writers
of the period had sought to bridge the divide through invocations to nature
and, in the case of Whitman, to the body. But the vast commercial empire—materialism as money and machinery—was generally viewed as threatening, a cor-
rupting influence that was stealing the soul of America and withering its
promise: "Men think it essential for humanity that the *Nation* have commerce,
and export ice, and talk through a telegraph and ride thirty miles an hour . . .
but whether we should live like baboons or men is a little uncertain," wrote
Thoreau.[25] This high-handed placement of "men" on one side and commercial "baboons" on the other was simply another way of marking the division
that had begun to solidify in American society between high and low culture.
Serious writing lay on one side of the divide and public amusement (circus,
vaudeville, burlesque, and soon penny arcades and nickelodeons) on the
other. Both Emerson and Whitman had invoked a future poet as the fulfillment
of their vision, but it is unlikely that they would have recognized their new messiah in the image of Edison's handyman with a cold.

Edison himself was not immune to the kind of thinking expressed by Thoreau. His devices were obvious contributions to the popular and commercial:
the burst of sound, the bright light, the moving image. But although he was eager to make money from the applications of his inventions, he had a deep and
abiding contempt for popular culture. This is clear from his approach to the development and marketing of film technology. During the 1890s, he assumed
that the peep show machine was the full extent of motion picture exhibition,
and it took two men, working an ocean away (the French brothers, Auguste
and Louis Lumière), to consolidate his kinetograph and kinetoscope into a single device for the recording and projection of images to an audience. Even
later, after Edison followed the Lumières' lead and perfected his camera, he
still did not imagine that the medium would ever serve as more than vapid diversion at the end of vaudeville and circus programs. And even later, after he
realized that big money was to be made from the nickelodeons, leading him to
embroil himself in a series of protracted law suits to protect patents for his cameras and maintain a monopoly on film distribution, he remained dismissive of
the movies as a significant form of cultural expression.

Film became a true heir to literature only when it escaped Edison's control and came into the hands of immigrant entrepreneurs like Carl Laemmle, William Fox, Marcus Loew, and Adolph Zukor—men who understood and appreciated the expressive potential of the medium. Edison had been poor as a youth, but there was nothing in his poverty to cause him to repudiate his past, only to try to improve it. His interest in technology can be seen as a dramatic and literal expression of this drive for self-improvement. Immigrants like Laemmle and Zukor, by contrast, had come to America mostly as adolescents or young men in an escape from a past that was a source of pain and embarrassment to them. As the majority of them were Jews from poor backgrounds, they had had little connection with a privileged, cultured Europe and had experienced the Old World as the site of discrimination and abuse. Neal Gabler, in chronicling the driving passions that propelled these immigrants into filmmaking, notes that in most cases they had also inherited a "patrimony of failure" and spent their lives trying to build new identities.[26] To do so, they sought both to break with the past—a break made easier because of the need to adopt a new language and culture—and to find new material to forge an identity in the present. The film industry gave them access to both. It attracted them not only because, as a new business, it had not yet developed formal economic controls that might exclude them but also because it could create narratives in keeping with their dream of remaking themselves. Silent film was ideally suited to telling stories that would address the imagination of these immigrants: it bypassed the need for a sophisticated grasp of the English language and, on a more abstract level, reflected their position of being cut off from their own histories. Whereas verbal and literary language is linked to historical time in needing to be learned and passed on, silent film, in being primarily visual and dynamic, is not.

Of all the early entrepreneurs who helped propel film beyond the peep shows that Edison had launched, Adolph Zukor is the one most responsible for its development as a storytelling device. Orphaned at a young age and adopted by an uncle who wished to train him as a rabbi, Zukor rebelled against the kind of close reading and general bookishness required for this kind of vocation. His interest was in the Bible as story and, later, in the fast-paced narratives of dime novels. When he came to America, he essentially severed his connection to Judaism and to the scholarly tradition: "No sooner did I put my foot on American soil than I was a newborn person," he is quoted as saying, unwittingly expressing himself in the rhetoric of the American myth. Although he began working in America as a furrier, his first glimpse of an Edison peep show convinced him to abandon that career and make movies his occupation. He invested in one and then a chain of penny arcades, and after screen projection

Sarah Bernhardt in *Queen Elizabeth,* 1912 (Kobal Collection)

had given rise to the nickelodeons, he bought a storefront theater and began showing movies to an audience. Soon he had developed partnerships with the jack-of-all-trades businessman Marcus Loew, the vaudeville impresario William A. Brady; and the owners of the theatrical chain, the Shubert brothers.

Zukor wanted to exhibit films in higher quality theaters, but his major concern was to exhibit longer films: "These short films, one-reelers or less, didn't give me the feeling that this was something that was going to be permanent," he explained.[27] His first move to establish permanence was to buy the French Pathé production of *Queen Elizabeth,* a cinematic record of Sarah Bernhardt's theatrical performance and, in 1912, to stage its gala opening at New York's Lyceum Theater. He then proceeded to produce similar films himself, appropriating stage stars and plays for his Famous Players in Famous Plays series. Though box office results were not impressive, the films set the industry in the direction of more serious and more sustained narratives; they specifically helped to encourage the more artful efforts at longer narrative films that were emerging from D. W. Griffith during the same period.

Zukor's understanding of the narrative value of motion pictures is at the center of his difference from Edison. Edison saw film as one in a series of devices to transform nature; Zukor saw it as a business that would make possible the transformation of himself—that would help him in his quest to assimilate into American life: "It's not like making shoes or automobiles," he explained, "where you have a model and you follow through for the year. Every picture is an enterprise by itself. There are certain ingredients you have to study, and certain times that you have to say, 'I don't think I'll take that story, I don't think I'll make it, I don't think it's what the public will take.'"[28] The implication of this statement—that to reject a film is to edit a vision of oneself and of the public—is an eloquent testimony to the kind of psychological investment that producing a film held for men like Zukor.

As Zukor's early attempts at narrative film reflect, the relationship between film narrative and literary or theatrical narrative was not clearly defined at the outset. In the short-lived Famous Players series, the films depended on a knowledge of the plays on which they were based and on generous intertitles to help audiences follow the story. Zukor's efforts at longer films were, in this sense, like most narrative films before 1912, still dependent on traditional forms of language to relay meaning. The earliest narrative films had done this by having narrators talk alongside the screens, much as pianists would later play alongside them. As films grew longer and began to depend on short fiction, novels, and plays for their sources, live narrators were replaced by intertitles, which transferred large chunks of the original literary material to the screen. Since directors had not yet learned to give shape to stories through montage, camera angles, and continuity editing, the intertitles would summarize the action in advance, relegating the moving images—medium shots taken from a fixed camera position—to the status of dynamic illustrations.

Although Zukor's Famous Players films were generally not successful, there was a notable exception: those featuring "the girl with the curls," soon to be known the world over as Mary Pickford. Pickford's films inspired an early and enthusiastic following because her image somehow asserted itself despite the limitations of the films' primitive camerawork. Viewers focused their attention on what little they saw of Pickford and imagined what they didn't see. As if demanding a close-up before the operation was commonly in use, audiences began referring to her as "the girl with the curls" very early in her career. Zukor's longer films were in part responsible for this, for by indulging the public's desire for more prolonged exposure to Mary, they sparked a desire for more of her in other respects as well: for details of her dress, her physical gestures, her face—in short, for a closer proximity to her image. And the more that the camera provided these details, the more expressive the details became and the less necessary the lengthy intertitles to explain feelings and motives that could now be conveyed through visual means.

The development of a more purely visual film language was thus the result of a combination of factors: longer films, the drive to provide closer proximity to favored performers, and the discovery of alternative forms of expression that entailed less reliance on explanatory titles. Though much of this was an organic process and cause and effect are difficult to assess, a good deal of credit for the shift from films structured according to literary or theatrical models to those reflecting a genuinely image-based language must be given to D. W Griffith (with whom Pickford, significantly, began her career). If Adolph Zukor helped pioneer the longer film, Griffith helped give it form. Though not, strictly speaking, a technical innovator, he was a great synthesizer and creative visionary, and he must be credited with the first major strides in cinematic storytelling.

Born in 1875 in Kentucky, David Wark Griffith was, as he told it, the son of proud but impoverished Southern gentry whose plantation had been burned to the ground by Union soldiers during the first year of the Civil War.[29] Griffith, Sr., colorfully if somewhat frighteningly nicknamed "Roaring Jake," had been a Confederate colonel and had regaled his son with tales of his heroism and that of his ancestors, going back to before the Revolution. These stories of the American past were an abiding source of pride to Griffith and a shaping force for his imagination. They were also the kinds of stories likely to appeal to the immigrant entrepreneurs who were seeking an American experience as a pattern for their own lives and as subject matter for their industry's films.

Although Griffith would be a great contributor to film's visual expressiveness, his first inclinations were literary rather than cinematic. He began his career as an aspiring writer and would later say that he would have preferred to have written one page of *Leaves of Grass* than all the movies that had won him acclaim. If he admired Whitman among American writers, his tastes in British literature were more conventionally Victorian. He favored Tennyson and Browning in poetry and Dickens in prose, from whom he claimed to have learned his techniques of montage.[30] These preferences seem significant: Griffith's liking for what was already an old-fashioned literary style, alongside his apparent disinterest, if not distaste, for contemporary literature, can explain both his failure as a writer and his initial success as a filmmaker. The high-flown sentimentalism that he so much admired in Victorian literature translated effectively to the screen by allowing for melodramatic incidents and expressive, if stereotypical, characters. More modern literature, which would soon begin to adapt cinematic imagery and structural techniques, was too elusive and experimental to serve a newly emerging visual medium. It could also be argued that Griffith's old-fashioned literary sensibility was more akin to nineteenth-century American writers, like Whitman, who had anticipated film in their call for a new, uniquely American form of expression.

By the same token, Griffith's attachment to a sentimentalized view of life can also explain why his popularity waned by the mid-1920s and why he eventually was unable to get financial backing for new projects. We can understood this better by a glance at the intertitles of his films.[31] Although Griffith grasped very early the need to subordinate words to images in the overall balance of his storytelling, the Victorian style that he continued to use in his intertitles would increasingly jar with the more casual, ironic spirit of the age. More significantly, perhaps, the moralizing tone of his titles reflected the kind of authorial intervention that had been effective in nineteenth-century novels but was at odds with film's visual orientation. In Griffith's 1919 *Broken Blossoms,* the approach is particularly marked, perhaps because the film is so visually arresting. The story is of a poor, abused young girl who finds temporary refuge with a Chinese shopkeeper but is eventually discovered and murdered by her drunken father. Despite wrenchingly dramatic images of vulnerability and alienation, Griffith could not resist using the intertitles as a moral bludgeon. In one scene, for example, after showing the brutal father (identified by the oddly comic name Battling Burrows) striking his helpless daughter, the titles read, "We may believe there are no Battling Burrows, striking the helpless with brutal whip—but do we not ourselves use the whip of unkind words and deeds? So, perhaps, Battling may even carry a message of warning." Both Dickens and George Eliot had used authorial intervention in this way, with the aim of explaining the psychological motives of their characters and expounding on the value of moral action. But a visual medium seems designed to reveal character by showing action and to teach lessons by showing the results of action. In this context, Griffith's sanctimonious verbiage seems not only unnecessary but also obtrusive and annoying.

By the late teens, intertitles like Griffith's had been superseded by a more phlegmatic or ironic style. Anita Loos's witty titles for Douglas Fairbanks's comedies were as far from Griffith's sentimental moralizing as one could get (although Griffith had actually employed Loos, early in her career, to write some of the intertitles for *Intolerance*). The general trend favored succinctness over wordiness: less was more. Vachel Lindsay, whose rabid enthusiasm for silent film tended to make him veer toward extremism, went so far as to suggest that music, as well as intertitles, be eliminated and that films evolve into pure expressions of dynamic visual imagery. His idea was that audiences should talk about the images passing on the screen as one might talk about a painting in an art museum.

Lindsay's views were impractical—it is very hard to watch silent films without music (though certain French exhibitors in the 1950s and 1960s screened

them in this way in an attempt at purity). Nor were intertitles ever entirely eliminated despite the acclaim heaped on German filmmaker F. W. Murnau's 1924
The Last Laugh, which managed to tell its story with enormous effectiveness
without using any. Lavishly decorated titles actually became something of a fad
during the early twenties; Alfred Hitchcock's first job in 1921 for the British
branch of Famous Players Lasky was as a title card designer. But the purists
who opposed intertitles were right in principle. They recognized that silent film
had become a medium in which words were, if not superfluous, of minor importance; at their best, they could pass before the eyes of the audience without
registering their source in another medium. Late silent films, like the magister-
ial *Sunrise* and the tragically frenetic *The Crowd,* reflect this view. They are so
beautifully paced and sustain such a compelling continuity of action and character that the intertitles seem like mere grace notes, their literary aspect
drained away by the atmosphere of the images.

In considering the fate of the word in silent films, it is also worth noting
how literary adaptations fared during this period. The temptation to adapt the
classics, as in the temptation to insert lengthy and flowery intertitles, reflected
the continued lure of a literary culture that would never entirely disappear
(though film's success in purging literature as a serious rival has been so great
that literary adaptations today seem less about evoking literary works than
about substituting for them). Adolph Zukor's Famous Players series was an
early example of adaptation, in this case from the stage to the screen; the results, though not impressive, were historically important in building the respectability of the industry and providing a rationale for the longer film.

Beginning at around the same period and continuing for the duration of
the silent era, a steady stream of adaptations of American literary classics also
occurred. Among the better known are *Uncle Tom's Cabin* (1910), *Huckleberry
Finn* (1920), *The Last of the Mohicans* (1920), and *The Scarlet Letter* (1926).
These films are noteworthy because they are based on literary works that seem
to anticipate cinema in their frequent use of visual metaphors and scenic moments. Some of these films were not the first screen adaptations of their classic
sources; all were not the last. The very fact that these literary works were subject to multiple screen adaptations suggests that they stood as a challenge to
filmmakers, and that after each attempt there remained the sense that the objective—a successful translation of a great book to film—had not been achieved.

But the problem had an additional dimension. These films not only failed
to reflect the quality of their literary sources, an admittedly difficult task, but
also fell short of other films of the period whose sources were not as good. Con-

sider, for example, two films, *The Scarlet Letter* (1926) and *The Wind* (1928), both produced by Irving Thalberg, directed by Victor Seastrom, and starring Lillian Gish. One is based on Nathaniel Hawthorne's classic novel, the other on Dorothy Scarborough's contemporary potboiler. *The Wind* is gripping cinema; *The Scarlet Letter* is mostly turgid and uninteresting. Although Hawthorne's novel was full of a certain kind of scenic effect that distinguished it from the European novel of the same period, the force of this effect derived from a literary conception of society that could not be translated to the screen. In the Scarborough novel, however, the character's suffering is bound up with something visual and dynamic—the wind as a violent and relentless physical force—and its extreme tangibility (the very quality that makes the novel melodrama rather than great literature) is what suits it for adaptation. Hitchcock, who liked to assert his loyalty to the visual language he mastered during the silent era, often stated that he preferred to base his movies on lesser, melodramatic works like Scarborough's than on classic works like Hawthorne's. His rationale was that great literature was too fully the product of its own medium to be successfully adapted.[32]

Erich von Stroheim's 1924 *Greed* is another example of the inherent problems attached to the adaptation of literature to film. Stroheim became obsessed with faithfully transferring the powerful Frank Norris novel *McTeague* to the screen, and he essentially filmed the book page by page. The result was a monstrosity of 42 reels that he reluctantly cut to 24, and which was then taken from his hands and cut to a generally incoherent 10. The film is what is commonly called a brilliant failure. It has a fetishistic power that might be compared to Whitman's *Leaves of Grass*—where Whitman's poem strains at times to be a visual work, Stroheim's strains to be a literary one.

Silent film redressed the balance that had plagued nineteenth-century American writers in their relationship to Europe. It turned the deficits of the new American nation into advantages and realized in cultural terms the idea of "beginning the world again," which had been central to the American myth. D. W. Griffith would draw on this vocabulary of youthful promise in comparing film to theater: "The stage," he explained, "is a development of centuries based on certain fixed conditions and within prescribed limits. . . . The moving picture, a growth of only a few years, is boundless in its scope and endless in its possibilities."[33] Vachel Lindsay would take this idea of a new beginning further, predicting that film would reenact and improve on the original evolution of the species:

[T]his invention, the kinetoscope, which affects or will affect as many people as the guns of Europe, is not yet understood in its powers, particularly those of bringing back the primitive in a big rich way. The primitive is always a new and higher beginning to the man who understands it. . . . In this adolescence of Democracy the history of man is to be retraced, the same round on a higher spiral of life. . . . We can build the American soul broad-based from the foundations. We can begin with dreams the veriest stone-club warrior can understand, and as far as an appeal to the eye can do it, lead him in fancy through every phase of life to the apocalyptic splendors.[34]

In this passage, Lindsay enthusiastically links the newness of the medium to its mission; its primitivism is connected to its destined power.

What Lindsay termed "the bringing back [of] the primitive in a big rich way" involved the transformation of the word into the moving image—a transformation that involved a death struggle. Word and image represent two opposing ways of figuring reality. The power of the word lies in its ability to penetrate surfaces—to turn people inside out and make available an internal life normally hidden from view. This had been the basis of the psychological novel, the narrative form that had flourished in the nineteenth century. The ascendancy of silent film meant that images would have to do the work of words; as Erwin Panofsky put it, both actions and inner states of mind would have to be spatialized.[35] But actions and inner states are not equally susceptible to spatialization. With moving images as the basic form for narrative expression, less could be said about feeling and thought and more could be said about action. Or to put this differently, less could be said about the past and more about the present; less about being, and more about becoming. "Becoming" had been one of Emerson's favorite words, and he had elaborated on it in his explosive little book *Nature* in a fashion that might be said to have forecast the rhythm and vitality of film: "Life only avails, not the having lived . . . it resides in the moment of transition from a past to a new state, in the shooting of the gulf, in the darting to an aim. This one fact the world hates, that the soul *becomes;* for that forever degrades the past."[36] This philosophy of action—inherently visual and dynamic, antihistorical and anti-intellectual (despite the intellectual source espousing it here)—was the American relationship to experience and would be expressed with unique intensity and power through the medium of silent film.

HOUDINI, KEATON, AND THE RISE OF THE BODY

N EAR THE beginning of the 1928 silent film *Submarine,* there is a thrilling
action sequence involving its two main characters, played by Jack Holt
and Ralph Graves. Holt is a navy diver who locates underwater wrecks that
would pose a threat to ships, and Graves is the radio operator who communi-
cates with him during his dives. Having just completed a successful dive, Holt,
wearing only his swimming trunks, is standing at the stern of the boat. As an order is given to blow up the wreck he has just located, the camera tilts down to
show that his leg is caught in the coil of rope attached to the explosive. The
rope uncoils and a few seconds later he is pulled overboard, and we see his
body being carried underwater. The camera now returns to the deck, where
Graves registers what has happened. He grabs a knife, pulls off his shirt, and
dives into the water. An underwater shot shows him swimming toward Holt,
struggling with the rope, and finally cutting his friend free. An aerial shot now
shows the charge exploding, then shifts to the crew, watching from the deck, as
they turn away sadly—they assume that Holt and Graves have perished in the
explosion. But a second later, the two men surface near the side of the boat. As
they climb aboard, they move jauntily. "I was getting loose when you butted
in," reads the intertitles for Holt's character, supporting the playfulness of the
men's body language but also underscoring that without Grave's courage and
athletic prowess Holt would now be dead.

The scene accomplishes a number of things. It displays a wonderful acro-
batic feat, not just by the actors (or their screen doubles) but also by the camera
in its ability to produce both aerial and underwater shots. It also offers a sus-
penseful rescue narrative, an ingenious elaboration on the last-minute rescue,
introduced to film by D. W. Griffith twenty years earlier. Finally, it dramatizes a
relationship—it asserts the powerful friendship that exists between these two
men by testing that friendship in the most direct possible way (later in the film,
a woman will test the friendship less directly but more severely). The scene is
spectacle, story, and character profile. It links the protagonists to abstract values and personal emotions at the same time that it glories in exhibiting their
bodies and their capacity for action. Both Holt and Graves, it should be noted,
were superb physical specimens whom Frank Capra, directing his first feature
drama, made a point of showcasing as "real men"—without their shirts and
without makeup.[1]

The combination of muscularity, camaraderie, and suspense encoded in
this scene reflects the multiple meanings attached to the male body in Ameri-

Preceding page: Jack Holt in *Submarine,* 1928 (Museum of Modern Art)

can film during the silent period. To understand how these meanings came to the medium, one must understand how the body was perceived in nineteenth-century American culture and, specifically, what role it played in performance prior to the rise of film.

In 1893, the year that Edison produced *Fred Ott's Sneeze,* the World's Columbian Exposition, America's first world's fair, was held in Chicago. According to the historian Henry Steele Commager, the Exposition marked a moment of transition in American history. It announced the passing of "an America predominantly agricultural; concerned with domestic problems," to a "modern America, predominantly urban and industrial, inextricably involved with world economy and politics."[2] The two Americas, past and future, were mirrored in the shape of the Exposition itself. Part of the site was occupied by the so-called White City, a constellation of imposing buildings that housed exhibits devoted to a technological and cultural future. These buildings included the Zoopraxographical Hall, which featured photographic studies by Eadweard Muybridge on locomotion, and the Electricity Hall, which featured Edison's inventions, including a demonstration of his kinetoscope. The other part of the exposition, and by far the more popular, was neither architectural nor technological; it was

The World's Columbian Exposition, Chicago, 1893: The midway, looking west toward the ferris wheel (Culver Pictures)

the Midway Plaisance—a strip of open space that was billed as the greatest live entertainment center in the world. Among the featured acts on the midway (and at its extension, the Coliseum, nearby) were Florenz Ziegfield's vaudeville review; Buffalo Bill's Wild West Show and Congress of Rough Riders; David Belasco's latest theatrical production, *The Girl I Left Behind* (in which Apache warriors swooped down on the audience from the wings); and a beauty pageant billed as the World's Congress of Beauties ("40 Ladies from 40 Nations").

There was also a wide array of supplementary acts, the product of the vaudeville circuit, which had grown into a vast source of mass entertainment over the previous decade. One of these was a magic act by a young magician named Harry Houdini. At the time, Houdini did not stand out from the many live performers on the Midway Plaisance; he did not draw crowds on the order of, say, Little Egypt, performing her *danse de ventre* next door. But his career was only beginning. In a few years, he would emerge as the most popular live entertainer in the world, having learned and borrowed from performers like Little Egypt. Houdini would come to represent a uniquely American conception of the body, consolidating a physical idea that had existed in scattered form in the public imagination over the course of the nineteenth century. Significantly, his successor would not be another live performer like himself but a new medium destined to transform the very nature of performance as it had been known up to that time. The movies, which in 1893 were a mere technological curiosity tucked away on the other side of the Columbian Exposition, would come to dominate mass entertainment by 1920, appropriating the body for its own purposes and eventually usurping even Houdini, the consummate live performer of his age.

He was born Ehrich Weiss in 1874, the son of a Hungarian rabbi who came to America to improve his fortune but only succeeded in sinking his family deeper into poverty. Rabbi Weiss was a man of the book and a failure; his son, a man of the body, would be a success. Uneducated and socially unconnected but a gifted natural athlete, Ehrich Weiss epitomized the concept of the American, cut free from the traditional rites, customs, and class affiliations of Europe. He apprenticed for his vocation not by studying the Talmud but by swimming, running, and boxing—excelling, one could say, in the art of strenuous play. "Were it not for my athletic boyhood," he would later explain, "I would never have been Houdini."[3]

Legend has it that the first trick to inspire the young Houdini was paligenesia—the cutting up of the body into pieces and its magical reincorporation at the end. It is a trick that puts the body in the foreground but pushes beyond what is possible through physical exertion. Paligenesia was also the favorite

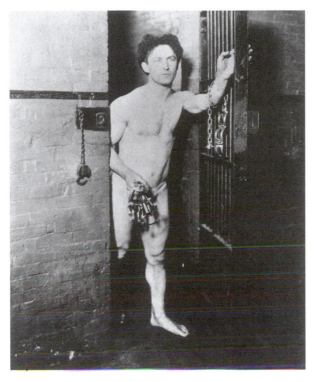

Harry Houdini after one of his prison cell escapes (Photofest)

trick of the French magician and film pioneer George Méliès, who had
adapted the idea to a primitive notion of montage. Houdini's innovation, however, was firmly rooted in live performance. He took paligenesia as the structure for an act that sought to blur the line between the possible and the impossible, to leave in doubt whether a feat had been done through natural means or
through trickery—a confusion that could be effective only when the performer
confronted his audience in the flesh. When the vaudeville impresario Martin
Beck first saw Houdini perform with his wife, Bess, in a dime museum act in
1901, he immediately recognized the originality and appeal of this approach.
He advised the couple to throw out their more conventional tricks, using cards
and animals, and concentrate on the physically grounded feats: the trunk-sub-
stitution trick, known popularly as the Metamorphosis, in which Houdini and
Bess appeared to change places inside a locked trunk in a matter of seconds,
and the handcuff escape, which would become Houdini's signature feat and
would be elaborated in the course of his career into escapes from packing
cases, milk cans, Russian "rolling jails," and even a gigantic, dead sea turtle.

Beginning from that point in 1901, Houdini had in hand the key to success: the uniqueness and power of his performance would turn on the fact of his body. The effect was helped by a certain oddity in his physical appearance. The eminent literary critic Edmund Wilson, an avid Houdini fan, described him as "a short stocky man with small feet and a very large head."[4] It was a body that gained its sense of reality—of "thereness"—through its very lack of ideal form. Magicians had traditionally hidden themselves under capes and turbans in an effort to deemphasize their bodies and enhance the mystery of with their craft. Houdini took the opposite tack and began performing in bathing trunks, a loin cloth, or (in private demonstrations) nothing at all. He presented himself as a "natural spectacle," claiming that his tricks were not tricks in the conventional sense but acts of physical dexterity, examples of what the body was capable of in its most trained and developed state: "There is so much that is marvelous and wonderful that can be accomplished by perfectly natural means," he boasted, "that I have no need to find recourse in humbugging the public."[5] The claim, of course, was disingenuous—he humbugged the public to achieve many, if not most, of his feats. But the spirit of the remark was true insofar as he relied on amazing physical prowess to accomplish the humbugging. (If, for example, he needed to escape a difficult pair of handcuffs, he might swallow the key in advance and regurgitate it later—a physical feat as impressive, in its way, as the feat it was designed to assist.) Since he performed many of his early escapes behind a screen or cabinet, it ultimately seemed less important to the public how he moved from point A—where he was trussed, manacled, hung upside down, or stuffed inside a trunk or sack—to point B, where he bounded on the stage, hands in the air, dripping in sweat. What mattered was his appearance at the end, free and intact, physically present to shake hands and pose for photographs.

Houdini's spectacular, physically grounded feats were the culmination of America's century-long preoccupation with live entertainment that was centered on the body. As shown by the Columbian Exposition, vaudeville, burlesque, circus, and the uniquely American derivative of the circus, the Wild West Show, had had a thriving existence over the course of the nineteenth century. Even so-called legitimate theater, as performed in America, depended on physically prepossessing stars far more than acting talent or expertise, and the "matinee idol," swooned over by "matinee girls," was a uniquely American phenomenon.[6] Europe, of course, was not immune to the charms of physical display; it had its music halls and cabarets, which featured their share of seductive flesh. But these forms of entertainment were less direct (one might say, more artful) in their appreciation of the body; there was nothing in European physical spectacle to compare with the brash sexuality of American burlesque.

Nineteenth-century America's fascination with the body can be explained in a number of ways. First, it can be seen as a response to Puritan values and prejudices. This may seem paradoxical, but if we consider the inciting tendencies of repression (tendencies that Michel Foucault and his followers have amply addressed), we can see that one of the legacies of Puritanism in America was a more intense fascination with the body than might otherwise have been the case.[7] By the same token, Puritan reticence about sexuality served as an impetus to the development of alternative, "innocent" forms of bodily performance. In the 1880s, impresario Tony Pastor decided to turn vaudeville into wholesome family entertainment by eliminating cruder varieties of display, an initiative that did not so much cover up the physical as divert it into multiple, less explicitly sexual channels.[8] Houdini had briefly managed a "girlie show" early in his career, but it was by abandoning this line of work and developing his own act that he made his fortune (and in later years he would present himself as very much of a prude). The lesson was the same as in Pastor's family vaudeville: bodies that capitalized on feats of wonder rather than sex and that placed physicality in a broader context would attract a larger, more desirable audience.

Entertainment that was centered on the body can also be linked to the experience of the American frontier and, a bit later, to the conditions of the American cities. The westward movement created a vast arena and appetite for physical spectacle, allowing for forms of public expression that had been judged improper by more decorous and culturally conventional Easterners. By the same token, as immigrants flooded the cities at the turn of the century, an entertainment that focused on the body found an enthusiastic audience. The physical orientation of vaudeville and burlesque had a special appeal to a diverse ethnic population, many of whom had no knowledge of English and no familiarity with traditional, literary forms of expression.

In addition, the American focus on the body can be seen, on a symbolic level, as an expression of cultural independence. It served as an alternative to the European focus on the word, substituting an individualized physical ideal for a more august cultural history. Paul Bunyan, Johnny Appleseed, and Daniel Boone, heroes that embodied American spirit and know-how, were all represented as large, muscular, dynamic men—towering figures, who rivaled in strength, size, and solidity the tall trees through which they strode. Much of the mythic stature that came to be associated with Abraham Lincoln was a function of his imposing height and physical presence. As Nathaniel Hawthorne observed, Lincoln was "the veritable specimen, physically, of what the world seems determined to regard as our characteristic qualities."[9] Building on similar assumptions, Henry James portrayed his protagonist in *The American,* a figure representative of the national type, as "in the first place, physically, a fine man," and Francis Parkman described his heroic frontier guide in *The Oregon Trail* as "six feet high, and very powerfully and gracefully moulded . . . proof of what unaided nature will sometimes do."[10] The physical characteristics in these cases were meant to connect with a sense of the nation's health and vitality. One is again put in mind of Lincoln, whose "Americanism," as the scholar J. G. Randall noted, is "revealed with an effect that is almost startling if one looks at the full standing form . . . and then tries to imagine that figure in court costume, with knee-breeches, close fitting stockings, and buckles. There was little of Europe here."[11] Randall strips Lincoln down to differentiate him as a "real" body from his artificial European counterpart. The effect is not unlike the one Houdini produced when he stripped down for his acts and presented himself as the quintessence of the strong, able, and natural man.

The physically impressive and robust American also served other symbolic purposes. Not only was he a foil to the presumably effete and physically attenuated European, but he was also a counterweight to the mechanical and commercial aspects of American society itself. Whitman, in seeking to cut away what was false and conformist in American life, made his ultimate call to the body as the source of an organic, as opposed to a mechanical, understanding of experience. In similar fashion, at the end of the nineteenth century, physical regimens associated with Fletcherism and the physical culture movement were promoted as the antidote to a routinized, mechanized workplace and to the rat race of a consumer society.

But if the drive for physical health and display ran counter to commercial and industrial tendencies in the culture, it also reflected a kinship with those tendencies. The physical regimens meant to ease the stress of a mechanized workplace were, at the same time, very much derived from that workplace. The prescriptions for eating, drinking, sleeping, and sexual activity depended on ideas about energy flow and efficiency that were basic to the principles of division of labor and mass production. By the same token, even that apotheosis of organicism, Walt Whitman, although extolling the body in the flesh, was also a great advocate of the photographic camera, a mechanism capable of turning the body into an infinitely reproducible and manipulable image. It was during the 1880s that the experimental photographer Muybridge, laying the groundwork for motion picture technology, compiled his series of animals and

Eadweard Muybridge's locomotion photographs, c. 1887 (Photofest)

humans in different phases of motion. His studies presented the body as a mechanism that could be analyzed like other mechanisms. Muybridge was helped in his work at the University of Pennsylvania by the painter Thomas Eakins, who used photographic images to assist his rendering of the human body in his paintings.[12]

This, then, was a paradox of the nineteenth-century American body. It stood as the site of pure, unmechanized nature on the one hand, and as the representative and adjunct of the machine on the other hand. Many facets of nineteenth-century American life can provide insight into this idea of the body as it evolved before the advent of film. For my purposes, however, Houdini seems to be an exemplary figure in exploring these meanings. He approached his own body and promoted it to the world in terms of the two seemingly opposing attitudes described above: elevating it in its human potential and displaying it as a mechanism, manipulable like other mechanisms. In raising the physical issues that he did in the way that he did, Houdini can be seen as an advance man for the movies, whose formal and esthetic properties would take his efforts much further in both directions.

At the heart of this drive to explore the body in the full range of its abilities and attributes was Houdini's increasing involvement with the idea of "exposure."[13] On a literal level, this manifested itself in his habit of stripping down in the act of performing and in his increasing tendency to perform his escapes in full view of his audience. On a more abstract level, his preoccupation with exposure took the form of revealing what he took to be fraud in his profession. The idea of abolishing fraud among magicians would seem to be an exercise in absurdity, but at this historical juncture it can be connected to a general cultural preoccupation with the distinction between the real and the imaged, which was beginning to be eroded with the introduction of photography. As already noted, both Oliver Wendell Holmes and Samuel Morse, figures of authority in nineteenth-century American culture, were inclined to ignore the distinction; Houdini was determined to enforce it. Early in his career, his drive to expose fraud was mostly a random, personal response to his enemies in the profession. It involved leaping onto the stage during other magicians' acts to demonstrate how their tricks should be done or writing clumsily furious letters to newspapers, accusing his rivals of improper methods. In the last decade of his life, however, the drive to expose became more generalized and was addressed to the more weighty antagonist of the spiritualist movement. Spiritualism, with its belief in supernatural events and occult powers, had, as its central premise a denial of the reality and integrity of the body.

Public interest in spiritualism had emerged early in the nineteenth century, had declined in vogue as the century progressed, and had then gained a new and ardent following after World War I, when so many grieving families were looking for solace. The movement can also be seen as another reaction against developing industrialism and an attempt to find meaning beyond the values of an increasingly competitive, materialistic society. Houdini had actually begun his career by making spiritualist claims, and many of his escape techniques had been inspired by early spiritualist acts. But by the time he achieved celebrity, spiritualism had become a direct threat to his style of performance.

All of Houdini's late exhibition tours were organized to discredit the spiritualists. The acts featured meticulous replications of feats that his spiritualist rivals claimed to produce through supernatural means. He showed how "mediums" used their legs and feet like hands and hid tools or materials in their mouths or elsewhere on their bodies. He explained how "spirit photography" depended on simple techniques of double exposure, and he demonstrated how mirrors, magic lanterns, and hidden cameras could project ghostly faces on walls or windows. He brought audience members to the stage and blindfolded them (since mediums liked to perform in the dark) and then proceeded to show how, lacking sight, they could be easily led to false assumptions about what was going on around them. Visiting many of the celebrated spiritualists who had launched the movement, he got them to explain how their feats were done. (The Davenport brothers, for example, who had caused a sensation earlier in the nineteenth century by "dematerializing" in and out of intricately tied ropes, entrusted him with their secret rope tie.)

If Houdini's first performances had been about dazzling the public with the outside of the body, these last performances were about exposing its inside. The ability to swallow picks and keys or hide them in the orifices of his body, in his hair, or in the thick skin on the sole of his foot was a function of the body's density. The ability to trick the eye through duplicitous movements or the play of mirrors or lights was a function of the subjectivity and malleability of human visual perception. Revealing such tricks of the trade was exposure in the most profound sense: it lay open to view the body's properties and defined the parameters within which it functioned. In retrospect, the revelations seem to be last-ditch attempts to salvage the live body for performance by demonstrating its density and dimensionality. They point forward, as well as back. For if the body was something that spiritualism tried to discredit, it was also something that film—for all its ability to show motion and to produce an illusion of depth— would be unable to render except as a two-dimensional, surface image.

Houdini's crusade against spiritualism can also be taken as a social allegory, marking the kind of historical transition that Henry Steele Commager had referred to when he described the Columbian Exposition as a passage from a traditional America to a modern one. Houdini's crusade dramatized tensions between an Old World and a New, between America's link to a European past that was associated with words (a tradition rooted in forms of meaning historically derived or taken on faith) and a more confident, democratic present that was associated with bodies, soon to be reconstituted as images. By debunking spiritualism, Houdini was able to symbolically take on a rival that film would annihilate more completely—history itself, with all the prejudices, conventions, and cultural accretions that made it an enemy to the self-made, first-generation American. Houdini was waging a war, in this sense, on behalf of the American myth.

The Margery case, the most famous spiritualist case in which he was involved, reveals dramatically the difficult position between worlds that Houdini occupied toward the end of his career. Margery was the name used by an alleged medium named Mina Crandon, the second wife of a highly respected Boston neurologist. The magazine *Scientific American* had agreed to award a prize of $2500 to any medium whom it judged to be authentic. Margery had been put forward as a candidate for the prize; and Houdini had been asked to serve on the committee assigned to investigate her claim. His response was immediately skeptical, but he found little support for his opinion on the committee. The others were impressed by the Crandons' social and scientific credentials and unimpressed by Houdini, whom they dismissed as a lowly magician, an immigrant, and a Jew. Houdini proceeded, much as he did in his vaudeville acts, to try to expose Margery through his standard methods of demonstration, only now these did not have the predicted effect. Instead of being convinced, the committee resisted and doubted at every turn, and the investigation came to seem more like a sadistic farce than a scientific study. Houdini devised ingenious ways to trap Margery, claimed he had done so, was ridiculed or discounted by the others, became more strident and sensationalist in his attempts at proof, and was rendered more negligible and laughable in the process. In the end, after some very ugly name-calling, the committee was disbanded, unable to arrive at a consensus. It eventually took a group of Harvard psychologists, with no affiliation to the committee, to expose the Crandons for the charlatans they were.

The case reveals how fully Houdini's association with the body, empowering in some contexts, limited him in others. On the stage, his awkward English had gone unnoticed or had enhanced his act by serving as a foil to his astonishing physical feats. But in more refined and serious circles, his unpolished speech undermined his credibility or rendered him ridiculous. He might say he had performed a trick through natural means, he might even explain how he had done it, but his mode of expression was so clumsy that no "gentleman" would care to listen. Arthur Conan Doyle, the eminent British author, was a champion of spiritualism and a friend of Houdini until their differing viewpoints caused a spectacular falling out. Doyle insisted that Houdini possessed supernatural powers, and when Houdini vehemently denied this, his vehemence convinced Doyle even more that he was lying. It was a strange reversal of established custom: the magician trying but failing to convince his audience that his tricks were *not* acts of magic. The situation is even stranger in that Doyle's most famous literary creation, Sherlock Holmes, was devoted to explaining, through rational means, the most seemingly irrational crimes. But, then, Holmes was also the consummate gentleman, a model of refined education and manners, who relied primarily on abstract thought—logical deduction rather than concrete experience—to solve his cases.

Houdini's failure to convince a venerable establishment of what he knew to be true demonstrated the limits of his influence. He might draw crowds for his performances at the Palladium in London and the Hippodrome in New York, but his success in these settings was as a showman in which his body was a source of entertainment, not explanation. He had no authority in the realm of words, and despite his efforts to gain such authority—writing books and newspaper columns and establishing affiliations with universities and museums—he was discounted when he tried to render judgment on "elevated" topics like spiritualism.

But if Houdini had no authority in the Old World, in which words counted more than bodies, he could operate only so far in the New World, where live bodies were metamorphosing into images. Early in his career, he had thrown himself enthusiastically into the new medium of film. At one point, he owned both a film-processing and a film production company, and he appeared in some half dozen films, as well as a fifteen-episode serial, in the course of his life. But despite extensive promotion, his movies were never as successful as he hoped, and he eventually abandoned his film career to devote himself fully to his antispiritualist crusade. Indeed, the crusade can be read as a covert reaction to his lack of success in film and an unconscious effort to fight the encroaching power of the motion picture in the public imagination. By opposing spiritualism, he was asserting the validity of the live body over the spirit body; but ironically, it was the cinematic body that was far more of a threat and was destined to render the live body obsolete.

One can explain the relationship between the live body and the cinematic body by connecting Houdini's failure as a movie star to the idea of the "secret" on which he based his performances. Since so much of his career was involved in exposure—in showing how tricks were done—the Houdini secret (and he invariably used the term in the singular to suggest one essential mystery behind the many superficial ones) must refer to something less technical than existential, connected to what it means to perform live for a mass audience.

His last major feat dramatically demonstrates this. It was billed as a "live burial," devised to replicate—and hence discredit—the performance of an Egyptian mystic who was making a hit on the vaudeville circuit by remaining sealed inside a coffin for close to an hour. The Egyptian claimed that he was able to survive by putting himself into a spiritually induced trance. Houdini insisted that he could achieve the same thing with controlled breathing, and he staged a demonstration to prove it. After an extensive promotional buildup, he succeeded in breaking his rival's record and revealed that the coffin contained enough air to sustain life for over an hour if one carefully rationed its use. But his demonstration can hardly be said to have resolved the mystery. For how does one manage to control one's breathing, to remain calm and composed, when confined inside a sealed box for almost an hour and a half? Barring a source of oxygen in the coffin (which some skeptics insist he must have had), the secret becomes the function of his unique physical and psychological constitution. It was "Houdini himself," as his wife explained, "that was the secret."[14]

Put another way, the secret lay in the alliance between a public boast and its verification in the body. It meant never letting the verbal claim lose contact with the physical proof—of never, that is, being off guard or offstage. Houdini's life was a sustained performance. He always referred to himself in the third person, and he called his wife, even in private, "Mrs. Houdini." He did not smoke or drink—such things were not good for the reputation or the body—

Houdini, emerging from the casket in which he had been sealed and
submerged underwater for one and a half hours, 1926 (Photofest)

and he spent his life in hotel rooms, traveling from one performance site to the
next. This was public life of an extraordinarily intense and sustained kind. It reflects a profound need to maintain a public persona, to avoid returning to the
helplessness and lack of definition that was the poor immigrant boy, Ehrich
Weiss.

It seems fitting, then, that Houdini's death can be traced to a moment in
which exposure of the body failed to be supported by that generally vigilant
public self. The precipitating events occurred in Houdini's dressing room one
evening after a performance. Several visitors were present, and one, an
overzealous college student, took it in his head to challenge Houdini's strength
by suddenly administering a series of punches to his stomach. Death from a
ruptured appendix followed a week later. It may seem ironic that the death occurred not in a spectacular act of physical exposure but in a private and petty
one. But it also makes sense that Houdini would die as a result of distracted-
ness, offstage rather than on. The technical secret of surviving such punches, as
he had explained on other occasions, was the simple one of tensing the stomach muscles in anticipation of the blow. In the relative relaxation of his dressing

room, he had shown himself off guard and unprotected; he had lost hold of the "secret," and what otherwise would have been a challenge became an attack.

In another sense, of course, the body simply gave way, as for all of us it inevitably must; even Houdini would have had to weaken and die eventually. But mortality can have different meanings in different historical contexts. Houdini's death carried symbolic weight at this particular juncture: it spoke to the insufficiency of the live body as a vehicle for a sustained public identity and to the need for a new form of representation that would remedy that insufficiency.

Houdini and the vaudeville acts that he embodied were fleeting assertions of the "real" in the history of representation—privileged moments when the democratic spirit of the nation was correlated with a sense of physical experience. In vaudeville and burlesque, uniquely American forms of entertainment that flourished at the turn of the century but had begun to disappear by the 1920s, bodies displayed themselves on the stage in vivid and direct fashion, and other bodies were clamorously involved in watching them and one another. These bodies were present in the most corporeal sense—no darkened theater and flickering images interfered to evoke disembodiment.[15] Houdini's act, which featured his oddly shaped body stripped almost naked and dripping in sweat, also relied on "citizens committees" to be present on stage to verify his procedures, to search him, and to act generally as surrogates for the public in the seats below. He often asked strangers to feel his muscles and, as his last fatal encounter demonstrates, encouraged them to test his body in more extreme ways as well.

What Houdini did, above all, was force his audiences into an identification with him as a mortal being at the same time that he elevated himself above them, as stronger, more dexterous, and more courageous than they could ever be. He existed as a heroic ideal of physical talent and training, testimony to what a human specimen at its best was capable of achieving. Although his feats involved many techniques that drew on illusionism and that anticipated the rise of film, their ultimate fascination lay in the appearance of his body in the flesh as the ground for everything he did. It was the reality to which all the tricks ultimately came home.

It is this placement of the real body at the fulcrum of meaning that subverted Houdini's appearance on film. Despite vague aspirations to stardom, he never really conceived of film as anything but an addendum to live performance. He expected his films to bring more people to his shows, and he expected movie audiences to project what they knew of him on stage onto what they saw on screen. In his 1922 film, *The Man from Beyond,* a dummy is used when the protagonist is supposed to plunge over Niagara Falls. Audiences familiar with Houdini's bridge jumps and other dangerous feats tended to believe they were seeing the real thing, and ads for the film encouraged the belief. But such "sleights of mind," as one might call them, were not sustainable in the long term. Other Houdini films did not exploit externally conditioned assumptions as effectively and were box office disappointments. Seeing these films today, one can only be struck by how bad they are. The physical oddness that contemporaries like Edmund Wilson found compelling in live performance looks simply unprepossessing on the screen. Houdini could not act; he could not move with any fluency or grace; he could not even kiss the leading lady with any conviction because he saw it as a sign of infidelity to his wife (though no stranger to another kind of duplicitous kiss: his wife sometimes transferred a handcuff key from her mouth to his during a mid-performance kiss). He was a master of illusion, but he could not pretend in the spirit of fiction, only in the spirit of truth.

Houdini's undistinguished film career recalls the lackluster results of other turn-of-the century figures when they attempted to appear in movies. Helen Keller's film, *Deliverance*, promoted as rivaling *The Birth of a Nation*, was a flop; Buffalo Bill came across less convincingly as a cowboy on screen than actors who had never been out west; Sarah Bernhardt and Isadora Duncan were both grave disappointments on film. All of these figures were cinematic precursors—they possessed many of the attributes that we now associate with the movie star, yet a chasm separated them from what they anticipated. Their appeal derived from being densely material and calling into play a variety of sensory systems.[16] Helen Keller awed the public by communicating through touch; Isadora Duncan's bare feet slapped the boards of the stage as she danced; Sarah Bernhardt toured after she had lost a leg to gangrene, her public reveling in the physicality of that loss, for it asserted that she was on loan to them only for so long and would soon irrevocably disappear. Film, as Walter Benjamin has argued, declares nothing to be irrevocable or irreplaceable. We can see our favorite stars in their freshest youth long after they have been interred. But these precinematic figures were wedded to a particular moment. Despite the hopes that Houdini's fans entertained that he would return from the grave, his death marked the end not just of him but also of the type of performance that had brought him such extraordinary fame.

The shift from the live body to the cinematic body as the focus for mass entertainment occurred when the technological aids that were deployed to strengthen and support the body eventually subsumed it. Paligenesia, that trick that so fascinated the young Houdini, relied on a partial substitution of facsimiles (false body parts and trick lighting) for the real body. Film completed the process not just for the individual body but also for the larger cultural body, that is, for mass entertainment as a whole. Vaudeville houses had originally shown films as addendums to live performances, but by the late teens, vaudeville acts had begun to be brought into the movie palaces as supporting entertainment for the films (as late as the 1960s, Radio City Music Hall was using live acts to prime its audience for the show's centerpiece: a high-visibility movie).[17]

Admittedly, film has never entirely severed its connection to live performance. In the early years of the silent era, narrators provided commentary on the screen images, and, later, piano players, bands, and even orchestras performed live next to the screen. With the arrival of feature films and the birth of the star system, performers would sometimes make appearances in movie theaters as a way of adding flesh to their cinematic images.

A more enduring link to live performance has been through special effects. Like physical feats, cinematic effects can be a source of intense wonder and can produce a visceral reaction in the spectator. The French director George Méliès distinguished himself from other magicians very early in the history of film by understanding the difference between real effects and cinematic effects, in which another level of manipulation is necessary to produce the response achieved on stage from mere sleight of hand.

Special effects, in this sense, are another turn on primitive film's initial "attractions," which were themselves a turn on the shocks and thrills of vaudeville acts like Houdini's.[18] Just as the earliest attractions (trains arriving and boxers throwing punches) soon ceased to shock and amaze once audiences became accustomed to the novelty of movement, so special effects have had a tendency to wear thin over time, as demonstrated not just by the dinky look of a Méliès film as it appears to us today but also in the ever-strained fate of the James Bond films. And the same can be said for live performance. Houdini experienced a need to continually "up the ante" of his physical feats, reaching into the stratosphere of contortionism, manacles, water cells, and coffins to keep his audience engaged. In the public's escalating appetite for thrills, we thus see another kinship between cinematic special effects and live physical feats.

All of which is to say that what distinguishes the live body from the film body does not lie in the realm of special effects, however bizarre or astonishing these may be. It is not what the human body can appear to be or do that film explores in a new way; it is what that body can *mean.* Only, that is, when the body could relay a new kind of sustained meaning did film find itself in a position to vie with and eventually replace live performance in the public imagination. The turning point occurred with the introduction of narrative to film.

The escape that Houdini performed on the stage was a simple progress from disruption and bondage to freedom and wholeness: paligenesia. The escape of a character from a situation in film can hardly be defined by so simple a technical label. Narrative film inserts into the movement from one state to another the idea of a subject. The reverse shot (when the camera returns to the person whose point of view it initially started from) intercedes between the shot and the audience's gaze, and we receive the experience in a mediated way. Our interest and enthusiasm are directed less to what the character does than to what we feel propels that action and turns the character into a consciousness, a figure who has chosen to do that particular thing and not another. In the case of Houdini's movie performances, the existence of an antecedent meaning, an identity outside the space of film, interfered with the meaning of the reverse shot. When Adolph Zukor developed his Famous Players in Famous Plays series, recruiting stage stars for films based on theater productions, the result was similarly unsuccessful because these well-known personnages siphoned attention away from the narrative. Knowing that one was watching the great Sarah Bernhardt was a distraction from the illusionistic continuity required. Films would engross the spectator only when the performers were produced *inside* rather than outside of their movie roles. Thus the only performer in Zukor's series who achieved real success was Mary Pickford, whose character had been forged through her earlier film roles with the Biograph and IMP companies, not through her appearances on stage.

The radical change in the meaning of the body that came about with the rise of narrative film can be demonstrated by the career of Buster Keaton. Keaton's transition from the vaudeville stage to silent film points up the differences between the live body and the cinematic body, between the escape as feat and the escape as narrative, and between the America of 1910 and the America of 1920. By the same token, Keaton's failure to accommodate himself to talking pictures reflects the new factors that sound introduced in the representation of the body and that rendered his particular brand of physicality obsolete.

Both Houdini and Keaton grew up in the West as itinerant performers. Both were gifted athletes and technologically astute tinkerers, and both would achieve (at least for a period of time) a high degree of control over the shape of their performances, producing work of unusual originality and broad public appeal. But they were also a generation apart. Houdini and his wife had been friends with Keaton's parents on the vaudeville circuit. The two couples had traveled together, and Houdini is said to have coined the nickname "Buster" when Keaton fell down a flight of stairs at the age of six months. Given this history, it is easy to see the two figures as a metaphorical father and son: not only did Keaton make a successful transition to film, which Houdini attempted but was not able to achieve, but he also used his films to critique the process of filmmaking, much as Houdini had critiqued his own craft through his crusade against spiritualism.[19] Keaton's film career seems to take up where Houdini left off in the representation of the body.

Keaton's performing career began early, as a child in his parent's vaudeville act. His most commonly assigned role was as a "human mop," in which he was thrown around the stage by his father, who grasped a valise handle sewn into his clothes. When the father lost his grip on one occasion, the young Buster flew into the crowd, an experience that might help explain why he eventually abandoned the family act for the movies, where the possibilities for physical control were far greater. But his early role as a prop in his family's sketches may also have set the direction for his film persona—his subsequent use of his body as a mechanized prop, a cog in the wheel of narrative.

Keaton's first movie job was in 1917, working on a series of improvised shorts with the then popular comedian Roscoe "Fatty" Arbuckle. Keaton's impeccable timing, his creative invention of gags, and his instinctive ability to ad-

Buster Keaton (age five) with his parents in their vaudeville act,
The Three Keatons, 1900 (Photofest)

just his performance to the camera led to increasing autonomy and recognition, and he was soon allowed to make a series of short comedies on his own. The success of the short films led to longer ones: a run of eleven brilliant feature-length comedies made between 1923 and 1928.

Keaton's career traces an evolution in the body's role in film. In his earliest two-reelers with Arbuckle, the distinction between extemporaneous performance and finished film was small. The cast, which generally included Arbuckle and the premiere Mack Sennett comedienne, Mabel Normand, simply arrived on the set and began to improvise. It was "freewheeling chaos," Keaton's biographer, Rudi Blesh, explained: "the story, like Topsy, just grew."[20]

In the two-reel films Keaton directed and starred in during the next three years, he went beyond setups and gags to develop what he called "laughing sequences"—episodes that were strong on cause and effect. The plots of these films, though rudimentary, were also based on a narrative premise: the building of a house (*One Week*); the launching of a boat (*The Boat*); the record of an automated house gone haywire (*The Electric House*); or the performance of a stage show in which all the characters, including the audience, are played by Keaton (*The Playhouse*). Hardly plots in the developed sense that we associate with character-based stories, these films nonetheless traced an action from its beginning to its end and, in doing so, allowed for the emergence of a coherent character. It is in these films that the Keaton persona was born—the poker-faced little man, surmounting obstacles through a kind of dogged and mechanical energy. In vaudeville, as Keaton told it, he had learned not to smile through the proddings of his father, who had noted that the straight face of the child brought more laughs. In film, that poker face, now hardened into a habit ("I *couldn't* smile"), became a distinguishing mark of character ("a face that ranks with Lincoln's," James Agee would say), its meaning no longer topical but sustained and existential.[21]

In the early twenties, his reputation solidified by the shorts, Keaton began to make feature-length films. It was an important shift in form. Comedy had been the last of the genres to advance to the longer format that Adolph Zukor and D. W. Griffith had pioneered in an effort to improve the medium's prestige and broaden its appeal. This belatedness can be explained by the genre's link to its vaudeville roots and to the live body. It had seemed to producers that audiences, coming to see singular stunts, would not have patience for longer films with plots.[22] Then came the idea to subordinate the stunts to the plots rather than the other way around, much as vaudeville, once the dominant entertainment, had been subordinated to movies. This entailed turning the comedians from simple clowns into resonant characters.

Chaplin, Keaton, and Lloyd had begun to make this change in their shorter films, but whereas these had evolved a character through a sustained, though abbreviated, plot, the feature films assumed a character at the outset. They were predicated on the idea that the comedians were personalities before they were stunt men and that the stunts were extensions of their personalities. In each case, the plots turned on moving the character from a low point to a high point—from defeat to triumph. In Chaplin's case, it was defeating powerful and arrogant adversaries. For Lloyd, it was navigating the obstacles of the big city and besting the bullying sophisticate. For Keaton, it was transforming oneself from ineptitude to mastery. Both Chaplin's and Lloyd's plot lines were derived from literary sources. Chaplin's is the Dickensian plot of the little but virtuous man struggling against an oppressive system; it draws on the sentimentality of Victorian melodrama and fiction. Lloyd's plot is related to the dime novels of the turn of the century, epitomized in the Horatio Alger stories that focused on hard work as the key to success.[23]

In Keaton's case, however, the feature films do not have a literary inspiration but are directly related to physical experience. An inept, ungainly youth, often shown to be effete or bookish, is transformed into a model of heroic energy and athleticism. With their focus on physical transformation, these plots are different from the standard success story of rags to riches; in fact, Keaton's character often begins as well-off, even rich. Instead, they trace a movement from formality to freedom, from European to American values—a story that recalls the life journey of Harry Houdini, who moved from a confining rabbinical household to an exuberant vaudeville stage. Keaton's plots also charted a further line of development from Houdini to Keaton himself, that is, from the vaudeville stage to the movies and from the real to the cinematic body.

Keaton is a uniquely self-reflexive figure in silent film because he associates his character's acquisition of physical mastery with the capabilities of his medium; he makes it clear that the hero's success is the result of what film can do for him. Early in most Keaton films, his character's ineptitude is represented through the pratfalls of the vaudeville stage: to be ordinary is to be associated with live performance. But later, when he executes his more spectacular feats, the properties of film are emphasized. In *College,* his final sprint home to save the girl uses the speeded-up film process; in *Our Hospitality,* his magnificent rescue of the girl from the waterfall uses quite transparent film editing that substitutes a dummy for the girl's body; and in *Steamboat Bill Jr.,* his heroism during the hurricane depends on obvious setups and editing, so that people and things can be blown to precisely the places they need to be. The most explicit example of this movement from realistic stunts to cinematically concocted ones occurs in Keaton's 1924 film, *Sherlock Jr.*[24] The film is divided into a "real" first half—in which the hero is framed by his rival for theft of his fiancée's father's watch and ends up back at the movie theater, where he works as a projectionist—and an "illusionary" second half—in which he dreams himself into a movie on the screen and becomes the celebrated, infallible detective, Sherlock Jr., who solves a crime that involves a girl and a villain who resemble his fiancée and rival. Once inside the movie, the Keaton character becomes a magician and escape artist, capable of extricating himself from any trap that is laid for him. And what particularly characterizes the transformed Buster is the ease with which he operates in a body that had been awkward and cumbersome for the "real" Buster.

In *Sherlock Jr.,* Keaton not only dramatizes the difference between real and cinematic experience but also exposes the mechanism of the cinematic process itself. His character doesn't just fall asleep and then appear inside a film; rather, he falls asleep and then has his "dream" self jump into the screen and have to undergo violent shifts in scenery as the movie being projected cuts from one scene to the next. Only after having laid bare how film works—how it uses representational fragments to simulate continuity and produce the illusion of impossible feats—does the character finally assume his heroic role inside the film.

The film also lays bare the mechanism behind the making and unmaking of cinematic character. It shows how character is produced through the body's insertion into a narrative and how it is destroyed when the body's place in the narrative shifts. We see this during the transitional episode, when Buster tries to enter the movie and finds himself at the mercy of a film editor run amok. Although Buster has the appearance of a coherent character with comprehensible motives when he jumps into the film, the editing changes, which prevent him from getting his bearings, turn him into an automaton or animated prop, until continuity returns and he becomes the detective, Sherlock Jr., inside the film. The transitional footage demonstrates that without a consistent context, the idea of character simply cannot be sustained. The same principle operates more subtly once he assumes the role of Sherlock Jr., as two sequences, taken together, demonstrate. In one, we see him playing billiards with the villain, who has hidden a bomb in one of the billiard balls. As Sherlock plays, he continually misses the explosive ball. The scene is exquisitely drawn out, depending for its suspense on hair's-breath misses of the most fantastic kind. Here is the infallible Sherlock Jr. in a position of superhuman control over the objects around him; he cannot miss because the film has cast him as the master of this particular universe. But in a complementary scene toward the end of the film, the locus of control is reversed. Sherlock is shown riding on the handlebars of an unpiloted motorcycle, rushing headlong through traffic but missing a colli-

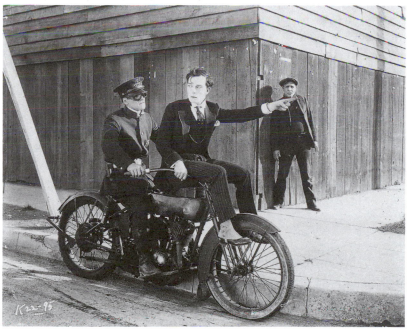

"Real" vs. "dream": Keaton in the two parts of *Sherlock Jr.,* 1924
(Everett Collection and Kobal Collection)

sion much in the way the billiard ball had managed to miss a collision with the explosive ball. The character has taken the place of the billiard ball and, instead of controlling the objects in his world, he is now one of the objects being controlled.

What characterizes the body in film is precisely this ability to move back and forth from subject to object. Critics have noted that Keaton's films, unlike Chaplin's, are outdoor films that make strategic use of the far shot to reveal the mechanism of experience on the largest possible scale.[25] But it is also true that Keaton's films often start indoors, move outdoors, and then return indoors at intervals as a means of emphasizing the interplay between an all-encompassing design and the singular force of human agency. Even the most spectacular panoramic stunts in a Keaton film are ultimately grounded in the Keaton body, as well as its extension, the Keaton face, which manages to coalesce both subject and object in its resonant stillness and implacability.

The shifting position of the human body from subject to object in *Sherlock Jr.* has other implications as well. Ultimately it becomes a commentary on the way cinematic representation fits into reality and alters it. At the end of the film, the "real" character awakens from his dream beside the movie projector to find his fiancée standing beside him. She has come to announce that she has proven his innocence in the theft of her father's watch. As they stand together near the projector, with the film passing behind them on the screen, Buster watches the footage over her shoulder for cues on how to express his feelings. As the screen hero puts his arm around the heroine's shoulders, he puts his arm around his fiancée's; as the screen hero kisses the heroine, he does the same. Finally, the last frame of the film cuts into the future to show the screen couple with their children on their knees. Buster scratches his head: he cannot imitate this. The sequence encapsulates the role that movies, by this time, had come to play in people's experience. For while film can do things that life cannot directly imitate, it is nonetheless enmeshed in the lives of its audience as a source of meaning and a guide for action and values. It overlaps with the rhythm and form of reality, and it usurps control even as it provides lessons in a more expansive and controlling consciousness. What one critic has termed "the essential filminess of [Keaton's] screen image" can be taken to denote the essential filminess of experience itself—the sense that reality is interpenetrated with its representation on screen, that life is an extension of the movies.[26]

Both Chaplin and Lloyd, though very different in the particulars of their comedy, were similar to Keaton in the self-conscious presentation of their bodies in the context of their films. Through their distinctive costumes, makeup, and movement, they introduced an exaggerated idea of character that underlined their own constructedness. All three of these silent comedians were, in this sense, satirical glosses on the serious male stars of the period (a variation was the baby-faced Harry Langdon, who parodied Lillian Gish). The bodies of such stars as Douglas Fairbanks, John Barrymore, Ramon Novarro, and Rudolph Valentino are entirely infallible, an effect amplified and extended through costumes and props. Thus, in the Fairbanks swashbuckler *Don Q, Son of Zorro,* the hero, preparing to go out, is shown to magnificent physical advantage as his servant helps him on with his jacket, his cape, and his gloves and is handed a variety of whips to try out, all the while smoking a cigarette with dashing and graceful dexterity. A similar dressing scene occurs in Valentino's *Blood and Sand. Sherlock Jr.* has a scene that echoes them, in which Sherlock is assisted in dressing by his valet. But here the effect is decidedly tongue in cheek; the character is dreaming himself into the swashbuckling role of invulnerable hero.

In general, the comedians either italicize the bodies of screen heroes, as Keaton does in this scene, or invert them through an array of pratfalls and physical tics. Utterly removed from the realm of the superhero, the comedians show that life is more a matter of tripping over an obstacle than leaping over it and that their successes owe more to film's deus ex machina than to their own talent and ingenuity. At the same time, the films also manage to applaud the triumph of their characters, despite the artificial aids involved. They make us embrace a concept of reality in which such characters, the "losers" of real life, may triumph. Thus, they connect with their audience in important ways, for whereas the bodies of the screen heroes evoke a fantasy of will and expertise, the comedians are the physical embodiments of a more randomly benign destiny that we may all, sometimes, have the good luck to encounter. In Keaton's case, this includes the idea that technology is an unpredictable variable in modern life, destructive at times but also at times useful and even lifesaving.

One physical presence that deserves his own footnote is Lon Chaney. Neither a man of action nor a man who was satirizing action, Chaney devised a repertoire of physical grotesques that found no counterpart elsewhere in silent film and no correlative later. Called the "Man of a Thousand Faces" (much publicity centered on his makeup case, with false noses and hairpieces, that he carried with him everywhere), his gift was actually more physical than facial. On some level, Chaney was a contortionist in the tradition of Houdini, but like Keaton, he was also Houdini's cinematic heir, putting his extraordinary physical capabilities to work in a narrative form. The sinister grace of his beckoning hands as he seduces the girl to his lair in *Phantom of the Opera,* the toadlike

Lon Chaney in *The Phantom of the Opera,* 1925 (Museum of Modern Art)

jumps with which he springs across space in *The Hunchback of Notre Dame,* and the balletic moves through which he straightens his twisted body as he pretends to be cured of deformity in *The Miracle Man* are examples of an esthetic that seems bred from the unique conditions of silent film. In no other medium would the body hold such uncontested sway, and no other actor would use the medium to make bodily mutilation and deformity interesting and even beautiful. Although Chaney's films do not comply with present norms of political correctness, it is still possible to be moved by them and to understand their enormous popularity with audiences.[27]

Until now, I have been discussing the role of the male body in American silent film. I would like to end this chapter by dealing briefly with how women's bodies figured—or rather, failed to figure—in the medium.

In the 1970s, with the advent of feminist film theory, it was put forward that the female body occupied a central structuring role in classical film narrative, although a dehumanizing one. The woman's body, critics argued, was a sexual magnet or fetish, which by focusing unwanted desires and fears, gave the spectator (generically understood to be male) an illusory sense of power and freedom. The theory has since been qualified for Hollywood films in general, and it seems to me to be decidedly wrong with respect to silent films.[28]

Silent film did not capitalize on the physical objectification of women so prevalent in the history of representation, for a number of reasons. One is simply a function of prevailing social norms. Men were allowed to strip down for action sequences; women were expected to remain trussed up in layers of clothing. Indeed, the layered look, even during the freer, jazzier period of the mid- to late 1920s, appears to have been a basic part of the female esthetic. In those instances when women's bodies were highlighted, it was to make very specific moral points. One thinks of Joan Crawford's wild Charleston in *Our Dancing Daughters* or Nita Naldi's bovine physicality in DeMille's *Ten Commandments,* both designed to show that these women had crossed the line of moral acceptability—one to be reclaimed to a good life after a series of trials, the other to die at the hands of her corrupt lover and, by her own admission, to be headed straight for hell.

Another reason for women's relative absence as bodies in silent films is that comedy, the premiere physical genre of the period, with its reliance on pratfalls and stunts, was dominated by men. Some women, like Mabel Normand, Marie Dressler, Beatrice Lillie, and Marion Davies, performed stunts of a sort, but usually this involved a parody of their femininity; for example, Lillie tries to act the part of a seductress in the 1928 film *Exit Smiling* and, failing, escalates her behavior to the point of caricature—collapsing onto sofas and chairs and throwing herself onto her unwilling partner. Again, audiences simply were not prepared to accept too much of this sort of thing—it jarred with common conventions of modesty and propriety. *Exit Smiling* was not a box office hit and essentially drove Lillie out of movies. Davies, likewise a gifted physical comedian, was consistently underrated; her *Show People,* a charming satire not only of the female star but also of early Hollywood more generally, did not receive the acclaim it deserved.[29]

However, the relative absence of women's bodies in silent films probably had less to do with genre restrictions and issues of propriety than with the alternative use to which women were put—as the site of an intense and varied facial expressiveness. Even the famous screen vamps were not physical objects of the type we now associate with *Playboy* centerfolds. A range of size and shape was associated with the vamp, whose sexuality seemed more a function of dark eyes, heavy brows, and pouting lips than of a voluptuous body. As I shall discuss later, women in silent films were most strongly identified with their faces, whose expressiveness carried some of the meaning once relayed by psychological literature. The result was a sexual division of labor—male bodies and female faces, the one relaying character through action, the other through emotion.

With the advent of simultaneous sound, the triumph of the body that silent film had made possible was necessarily compromised. It was not just that the timbre of voice and style of speech had to match the beauty and grace of the body presented on screen; the content of the words also had to reflect the quality of the image—a matching that would prove, in most cases, impossible to achieve: "It isn't that Mr. Gilbert's voice is insufficient; it's that his use of it robs him of magnetism, individuality, and strangest of all, skill," wrote one critic, seeking to explain why John Gilbert, only a few years earlier Hollywood's greatest male star, failed so miserably in talking pictures.[30] It seems inevitable that Keaton's voice, which wasn't terrible, should sound like vulgar croaking when we finally hear it in his first sound film, *Free and Easy*. The narratives that had been possible in his feature films of the 1920s could not be sustained with sound, where the voice anchored the body more completely in a given context, making extreme transformations less convincing. Keaton, as well as Chaplin and Lloyd, had been able to deconstruct their physical images without negating the physical triumph of their characters. This was a delicate balance of meanings that the intrusion of the voice would disturb.

Sound would never totally usurp the dynamic image of the body in film, but it would impinge on it enough to require the emergence of a new kind of physical type. James Cagney, a major Warner Brothers star of the 1930s, was the emblem of a cruder and scrappier physicality that could never have succeeded in silent films; he had neither the physical grace nor the sublime ineptitude to support their transformative themes. Cagney brings us back to the awkward energy of a Houdini, elevating that awkwardness through the brash insistence of a voice to match the body's crudeness. In Houdini, that crudeness had the raw power of fleshiness, but in Cagney it became part of a narrative of aggression, acquisitiveness, and feistiness—a narrative suited to the economic and cultural challenges of 1930s America.

3

HART, FAIRBANKS, AND THE VITALIZATION OF LANDSCAPE

THE CAMERA pans across the towering cliffs of a canyon, then moves in to locate a man on a horse at the top of one of the cliffs. Moving closer, it shows the man in full shot, his body erect in the saddle, his face lean and weathered as he stares out into the distance, pensive, before resuming his ride.

So begins the 1914 *The Bargain,* William S. Hart's first feature-length film, but it might just as well be the opening of any number of Hart westerns or, for that matter, any number of westerns from 1914 until the present. It is a scene central to our cultural imagination, and its power lies in its latent dynamism—not man posed in landscape but man poised to move in landscape; for in a moment, the figure will ride down the cliff and across the plain.

"It is possible that the cinema was the only language capable . . . of giving [the West] the true aesthetic dimension," wrote the venerable film theorist André Bazin in his book on the western: "Without the cinema, the conquest of the West would have made of the 'Western stories' but one minor literature."[1] Bazin's claim is that the West owes a great deal to film—that without it the western landscape would not occupy such a prominent place in our national mythology. But the statement could also be reversed. Without the West as its point of departure, the development of cinema might well have been different. The West served film as the primal space for the movement of character, and it is from this space that cinematic space evolved as a dynamic component of what it means to be an American.

The importance of landscape in the development of a uniquely American identity had its origins in European art and esthetics. Landscape began to emerge as a genre in European painting in the seventeenth century when artists like Claude Poussin and Claude Lorrain began to see natural settings not just as backgrounds for historical paintings and portraits but also as worthy of attention in their own right. This new appreciation of landscape was given further impetus in the eighteenth century by philosophers like John Locke and David Hume, who grounded their notion of reality in the experience of the individual in nature. These ideas were elevated into positive rules for living in Jean Jacques Rousseau's state of nature and Friedrich von Schelling's *naturphilosophie,* which connected unspoiled natural landscape with innate moral principles, and in Edmund Burke's concept of the sublime, which made untamed nature the basis for new definitions of beauty. In the early nineteenth century, the Romantic poets incorporated these ideas into their creative prac-

Preceding page: William S. Hart, traversing the landscape (Museum of Modern Art)

tice. Coleridge based his work on the representation of extreme or uncanny manifestations of nature, and Wordsworth took as his subject nature's moral influence and nurturing power.[2]

The wilderness and open plain of the American West, being compatible with the idealized conception of nature espoused by European artists and thinkers, quickly assumed the role of a competitive resource, a means by which the nation could assert its identity apart from Europe. Initially, this took a spiritual form. The American landscape helped to justify what Sacvan Bercovitch has called the Puritan "errand" in its dissenting mission against the Anglican Church.[3] But by the nineteenth century, the symbolic role of American landscape had been elaborated in secular terms. Thus Emerson, in trying to define the "incomparable materials" that might free America from a slavish relationship to Europe and to the past, pointed specifically to "the western clearing, Oregon and Texas." And Whitman, extolling the West in an essay on the Mississippi River, focused his admiration on the unrealized potential of the surrounding landscape: "my eyes feasted on primitive and rich meadows, some of them partially inhabited, but far, immensely far more untouched, unbroken."[4] As such statements suggest, American landscape could be represented as vaster and purer than the more conventionally settled landscape of Europe. It could denote the nation's creative potential and moral superiority: a Garden of Eden to Europe's Fallen World.

The spectacle of natural landscape as the hallmark of America's authenticity and power was given vivid depiction in the work of the early nineteenth-century painter Thomas Cole. Cole was the first practitioner of the Hudson River school and is generally credited with initiating the tradition of American landscape painting. Born in England in 1801, Cole came to America when he was eighteen. While the rest of his family went on to Ohio, he remained in Philadelphia, thus freeing himself at a stroke from the strictures of a custom-bound European society and of an authoritative and demanding father (though he would later occupy a garret in his father's New York house and struggle with him over his choice of an artistic career). Cole's migration was at least symbolically a migration into open space, the reverse of that later undertaken by Henry James in his quest for greater "social density" abroad. It anticipated the migration of the Zukors and Laemmles, fathers of the American film industry, who almost a hundred years later would leave Europe behind and seek elbow room and new materials in America.[5]

Cole embraced the American landscape as a realistic means of expressing personal aspirations that meshed with national ideals. "All nature here is new to art," he pronounced in surveying the then frontier of the Hudson River Val-

ley. "No Tivolis, Ternis, Mont Blancs, Plinlimmons, hackneyed and worn by
the daily pencils of hundreds, but primeval forest, virgin lakes, and
waterfalls."[6] His most memorable works are a series of views of that valley—the
same region in which James Fenimore Cooper, writing at around the same
time, set his *Leatherstocking Tales* (Cole's 1827 *Scene from* The Last of the Mohicans is his tribute to Cooper[7]).

Yet for all Cole's interest in American landscape, his esthetic loyalties remained divided. Ten years after arriving in America, he returned to England
to study and proceeded to adapt many of the techniques of the grand style of
European history painting to his work. Like Cooper and Emerson, who had relied on European writing to nurture an indigenous style, Cole's application of
European technique to American subject matter seems at once a loss and a
gain. It kept him tethered to certain painterly conventions that were at odds
with his most original impulses, but it also allowed him to emerge as the first
important American landscape painter—the first to give American landscape
the status of historical monument: "Every American is bound to love his country by admiring Cole," declared a contemporary collector.[8]

One of Cole's most striking paintings, *Daniel Boone at his Cabin at Great
Osage Lake* (1826), is a good example of his method. Painted before his trip to
Europe, it displays the devotion to his new country characteristic of so much of
his work, as well as the compositional tendencies and interest in heroic subjects
that would be amplified by the influence of European art. The painting features a spectacular natural landscape inhabited by the figure of the frontiersman, his rifle on his lap and seated in front of his cabin. Boone's posture is regal
and suggests a heroic integration with the landscape around him, what Cole
termed, in describing the Hudson River landscape more generally, as "*natural
majesty*"—the majesty, one could say, of the first man at home in Paradise. Yet
in viewing the painting it helps to know that Boone was not some figure from
the remote past of American history or legend; he had died only six years earlier, and the solitary self-sufficiency Cole attributes to him characterized the life
of many still living in the West. The painting thus conflates a sense of origin
with a sense of contemporaneity, and it associates the mythological qualities of
the wilderness spectacle with the realistic facts of American life. Simply to live
as an American, Cole suggests in this painting, is to feed the culture, ennobling
it and providing material for representation.

In almost all of Cole's work a human figure or some artifact of civilization
(a path, an ax, the roof of a cabin) appears within a natural landscape, suggesting that in America nature at its most sublime is inhabited: individual and landscape are compatible and fitted to each other. At the same time, what also char-

Thomas Cole, *Daniel Boone at His Cabin at Great Osage Lake,* c. 1826
(Mead Art Museum, Amherst College)

acterizes Cole's paintings is a tension among various states of nature as these connect to the human subject. His canvases divide themselves into planes, or perspectives, in which wildness, pastoral tranquility, and sublime elevation are variously juxtaposed—an expression of the dynamism associated with nature as it presents itself to human use and inspiration. In *Daniel Boone,* the very different pictorial segments of the canvas express the challenge that nature presented to the frontier settler and that his life in nature allowed him to bridge. The scene, in this sense, is "composed": it relays an idea that is abstract, formal, and at odds with the kind of tangible realism that impressed early American collectors who, as one put it, "preferred real American scenes to compositions."[9]

Cole's 1836 *View from Mount Holyoke, Northampton, Massachusetts, after a Thunderstorm"* (commonly known as *The Oxbow*) is an especially interesting work from a compositional standpoint. Cole places an image of himself, the painter with his canvas and umbrella, off to the side of the view, which is divided down the middle: the tranquil pastoral landscape of the right side of the canvas, in which the painter is set, contrasting with the more violent and extreme nature of the left side, where he is seeking his inspiration. One could say that the idea of reciprocity between the "wild" and the "civilized"—of uninhabited landscape versus inhabited landscape—becomes in this painting an allegory for the representation of nature as Cole used it in his work: his art domesticates the wild but relies on it for inspiration.

Cole's highly composed renderings of American landscape have been faulted for depending too heavily on European painterly conventions and for lacking confidence in the unmediated power of nature. But such criticism misses the larger point of the work, for what is evident in these paintings is their effort, through composition, to move beyond the limitations inherent in painting itself. Cole's canvases attempt to depict the vital integration of the individual in nature but, in being static artifacts, can only show that integration as a composed juxtaposition of disparate images. The painterly arrangement of the wild and the domesticated can therefore be seen to resemble Emerson's use of visual imagery in his writing. In both cases, there is an attempt to transcend the medium of expression, with the paradoxical effect of reinforcing the medium's characteristics. In Emerson's case, the visual metaphors make the writing seem more literary; in Cole's, the dynamic juxtaposition of images makes the painting more painterly.

Late in his career, Cole addressed this paradox through another means—two monumental series of canvases, each telling an epic story. The first series, entitled *The Voyage of Life,* consists of four paintings, charting the stages of life from childhood to old age; the second, *The Course of Empire,* consists of five paintings that trace the rise and fall of empire, beginning in primal nature and returning to it. The two series are Cole's attempt to move from a spatial to a narrative rendering of the relationship between the individual and nature, but both reveal the limitations of such an approach. First, they present an allegorical representation of the human figures in the natural landscape; that is, they abandon the real for the abstract. Second, they depict a fatalistic vision of the future. What in Cole's "views" was fixed into a dynamic partitioning of the wild and the cultivated becomes, in the series paintings, a tragic march into decline and loss—a march, as it were, from America to Europe. The same movement has already been noted in the literature of the period. It is the progress of the *Leatherstocking Tales,* which, when read chronologically, begins with the young hero, centered in a wild landscape, and culminates with him as an older figure, marginalized in a domesticated one.

Cole's paintings, for all their inability to solve the problem of living in nature, reflect an acute desire to come to terms with natural landscape that con-

Thomas Cole in *The Course of Empire: Desolation* (fifth of the series), 1836
(© Collection of the New York Historical Society)

tinued to be expressed in subsequent American landscape painting in the nineteenth century. Albert Bierstadt, also a European expatriate, pushed Cole's dynamic idealism further, creating monumental canvases that contain an assortment of narrative elements arranged in a kind of "painterly montage." In his
discussion of Bierstadt, the critic Lee Mitchell notes the "cinematic effect" of
the paintings, which seem, he says, "to beg for characters and plots" and
prompt viewers to wonder when they are going to move. Mitchell also notes
that Bierstadt's work, spectacularly popular in the 1860s and 1870s, had gone
out of favor by the turn of the century. It seems probable that the rise of film
rendered it obsolete.[10]

Bierstadt has often been grouped with the luminist painters (successors to
the Hudson River school), so called because of the surreal light that suffuses
their landscapes. If we consider Cole's early effort to render American landscape in dynamic terms, we can see the luminists as carrying forward this effort
but shifting the focus from compositional to atmospheric dynamism. Luminist
painting, the art historian Barbara Novak has explained, is a kind of pictorial
realization of what Emerson was trying to articulate when he called himself a
"transparent eyeball," gazing on the wonders of nature, and what Thoreau
meant when he described his response to nature as electric, "as if I touched the
wires of a battery."[11] Indeed, the luminists can be placed at a kind of midpoint
between the inspired expression of nineteenth-century American poetry and
fiction and the dynamic, visual expression of twentieth-century American film.

The positioning gains added weight when we consider that the eerie quality of the lighting in luminist painting makes the canvas appear to be a stopped moment, a freeze frame in a cinematic epic.

The effort to represent landscape as a vital reality—as more than a mere scenic view or backdrop to other subjects—was discernible in other areas of nineteenth-century American life as well: in the theater, where efforts were made to produce extravagantly natural-looking sets and to bring horses, elephants, and Indians onto the stage; in the popularity of stroboscopic disks that projected a series of images of scenery onto screens and walls; and in the popularity of the stereoscope, a device that, by positioning photographs at different angles for each eye, gave the impression of a three-dimensional landscape.[12]

Perhaps the most striking example of the craving for a more dynamic relationship with nature was the popularity of moving panoramas, or cycloramas, which began to tour American cities and towns in the 1870s. These were painted or photographed canvases, usually eight to twelve feet high and rolled across two large cylinders positioned on either side of the stage, to produce the impression of a monumental landscape that was moving before the viewers' eyes. The prototype for this kind of perspective on nature was available through railroad travel, still a relatively novel experience in the 1870s, and it has been suggested that the railroad was the true origin of the panoramic visual sense that would be elaborated with the development of film.[13] One of the most popular late variations on the cyclorama, the Hale's Tours, made the connection explicit. This featured photographic footage of landscapes in a viewing space decorated like a railroad car, with seats on springs and blowing fans to further the effect. A Hale's Tours theater was one of Adolph Zukor's first commercial ventures, and both Carl Laemmle and Sam Warner were employed by Hale companies early in their careers.

Still panoramas of battle scenes and historical events had been exhibited as early as the 1790s in Europe, as well as in America, but the cycloramas and Hale's Tours of a century later tended to be specifically American entertainments and to be devoted to specifically American sites and vistas like Niagara Falls, Mammoth Cave in Kentucky, and the overland route to California.[14] It seems that Americans were uniquely intent on placing themselves in a more direct relationship to their own natural landscape than was possible through painting, photography, or still panorama. Yet the moving panoramas remained limited in their ability to integrate the spectator into the spectacle; they continued to enforce a position of detachment. In other words, prior to narrative film, there existed no rendering of the human figure in nature that had a dynamic component, that could serve as a guide to the realities of *living* as an American.

To understand how film would resolve the problem of the American relationship to landscape, it helps to return to the World's Columbian Exposition of 1893, discussed in the previous chapter. While Houdini's tricks and Edison's kinetoscope were entertaining visitors in different corners of the Exposition, in another corner a young historian named Frederick Jackson Turner was addressing a more sedate audience at a meeting of the American Historical Society convened for the occasion. His paper, "The Significance of the Frontier in American History," would have an enormous impact on the way Americans would think about the relationship between landscape and character.

Turner went beyond a simple extolling of America's landscape as a supreme natural resource; his interest was in landscape as part of experience, as it moved with and against its inhabitants. He argued that the country had been formed out of a particular kind of *dynamic* landscape—the shifting demarcation, or "frontier," between settled and unsettled land that had been continually pushed back as American settlement proceeded westward. This shifting frontier, he maintained (which had, at the time he was writing, just reached its final stage and definitive "closing," according to the U.S. census), had traced a repeated movement from wilderness to settlement to wilderness again as the continent underwent development: "Not merely an advance along a single line, but a return to primitive conditions on a continually advancing frontier line."[15] In this movement in and out of civilization, the inhabitants of the American landscape had been forged *as* Americans, different in nature and aspiration from Europeans.

Historians have pointed out that Turner's concept of the frontier was an ideological construction, built on rendering invisible the presence of Native Americans and on turning westward expansion from a bloody battle of conquest into a courageous exploration into the unknown. But this does not negate other aspects of the thesis, namely, that the Europeans, in taking the land, were forced to assimilate Native American customs in the process and come to terms with an unfamiliar and intractable landscape. Turner's is an ethnocentric vision, but it is also the vision of the conqueror who acknowledges, if simplistically, the effects of the conquered on the future of the land and its inhabitants. Moreover, in positing a movement in and out of civilization as the form of American character, Turner's conception makes the primitive "other" not a vestigial part of what it means to be an American but a dynamic, ongoing part. In doing so, it leaves room for the assimilation of other forms of difference into the dynamic shape of American identity—difference that must first enter under the rubric of the primitive but in time may "graduate" into civilization, leaving room for others to occupy the primitive space.

Turner produced his essay the same year that Freud, with his colleague Josef Breuer, published his first contribution to the psychoanalytic model of human character, *Studies on Hysteria*. In this work Freud postulated a deep structure for the self—a primitive unconscious, lurking beneath a civilized, conscious surface. To move from the unconscious "inside" to the conscious "outside," Freud argued, was to trace a developmental journey from childhood to adulthood. The same developmental journey was the central theme of the nineteenth-century novel form known as the *bildungsroman,* or "novel of growing up" (of which Dickens's *David Copperfield* is probably the most familiar example).[16] Turner's frontier thesis stands in marked contrast to these European narrative forms by proposing a very different model for the formation of character. American character, according to Turner, was not a simple matter of growing up, not a one-way journey into maturity and society, but a two-way movement, an *oscillation,* between the child and the adult self—the primitive and the civilized state of being.

Turner's thesis can be seen as a blueprint for solving the dilemma that confronted American writers and artists over the course of the nineteenth century—a way of adding movement to the American landscape without destroying it. Although Cooper, Twain, James, and other American writers had conceived of their heroes and heroines as independent spirits, they were working within an inherited literary tradition, that of the *bildungsroman,* and this meant acknowledging a society that must inevitably limit the freedom and aspirations of their characters. Cole and other American landscape painters had tried to solve the dilemma by taking refuge in the spatial coordinates of painting: "The balance between settlement and pastoral innocence, between cultivation and wilderness, has been magically frozen at a moment of perfect equilibrium," notes Simon Schama of Cole's work.[17] But when Cole tried to widen the lens and peer into the future, to add narrative to pictorial space, the result was similar to that of his literary peers: a vision of decline, loss, desecration, and death as the natural landscape gave way to the social one. Even the moving panoramas popular later in the century, which tried to incorporate the viewer into the landscape for the sheer purpose of thrills and entertainment, were still detached forms of spectacle. The gap between primitive landscape and civilized viewer was never bridged.

Turner changed the terms by which movement in landscape could be understood. Whether or not his frontier thesis is a true description of the shape of American history is beside the point. What gives his argument such power is its ability to organize American experience around the idea of a dynamic landscape, an idea that had existed as part of the American myth from its beginning. Henry Nash Smith described the dichotomy in terms of the two sides of the Daniel Boone story. Boone was at once the pioneer who led a party of settlers into the wilderness to build an empire (the image in George C. Bingham's 1851 painting *The Emigration of Daniel Boone*) and the man who fled civilization and represented freedom and primitivism (the image in Cole's *Daniel Boone and his Cabin at Great Osage Lake,* discussed earlier).[18] Turner's thesis answered the need of the nation to reconcile these two opposing images for its own use—to define American experience not as a sacrifice of one mode of living for another but as a combination of both in alternation. The Puritans began the process of coopting dissent in the defense of a self-serving ideology—reconciling an idea of spiritual mission with a drive for individual prosperity. Turner took this Puritan errand further, reconciling the dichotomy in the "facts" of the land, thus appearing to remove the issue from religious, even human connection.

Studies show that Americans still believe Turner's frontier thesis, despite efforts by historians to discredit it.[19] One reason may be the pleasure of having it both ways: it allows moral righteousness to coexist with individualistic assertiveness and ambition, and it supports an idealism that is rhetorical and naive. But a more positive understanding of the continued appeal of Turner's thesis is that it speaks to a reformist inclination in the American people. Despite the brutal facts that belie the story of a noble westward movement, Turner's ideas provide a democratic, heterogeneous country with a gradualist model for change—a workable way by which an entrenched middle class can be infused with the possibilities for greater inclusiveness and tolerance.

If Turner's thesis was a blueprint for a compelling shape for American identity, silent film was the form of its realization. The oscillation between the civilized and the primitive could find conceptual correlatives in the still and the mobile shot and in the long and the close shot, which were fundamental to the lexicon of film. Movies could translate America's dynamic relationship to landscape into a mode of representation suited to express it long after the frontier had closed.

The properties of film that would allow it to visually represent what Turner had described can be glimpsed even before the medium had its birth. In 1840, when Louis-Jacques-Mandé Daguerre was still perfecting his early version of the photograph, he produced a work that anticipates the hierarchical relationship that would exist between the still image and the moving one in the first silent films. This early daguerreotype, entitled *Boulevard du Temple, Paris,* is the first known instance of a human figure captured on photographic film. It is a

J. L. M. Daguerre *The Boulevard du Temple, Paris,* 1840 (Bayerisches National
museum; photograph provided by the George Eastman House)

scene of a Paris street and shows a man in the bottom left-hand corner of the
shot getting his shoes shined while at his feet is a blurred image, the trace of the
bootblack who is performing the service. Given the long exposure time necessary at this point in the development of the medium, we can assume that the
image of the man who is getting his shoes shined is made possible because he is
obliged to stay still and that the bootblack eludes the photograph and appears
as a blur because he is performing the service that immobilizes his customer.
Thus, the image of the one man exists at the expense of the other.[20]

With the advent of moving pictures, this parasitic relationship, in which the
moving image serves the still image, would be reversed. Although the still remains the foundation and source for the moving image, it is the nature of the
moving image to obliterate and continually destroy the still. Once the scene
Daguerre photographed is animated, the customer, instead of being the focus
of the scene, becomes the pretext for rendering the movement of the man at
his feet.

The use of the still as the foil and launching pad for movement was demonstrated in the first public demonstrations of moving pictures. One of the earliest
American film exhibitors, J. Stuart Blackton, predicated his performances on

this idea. He actually devised an addition to Edison's kinetoscope that would delay the projection of an image a few seconds longer than would otherwise be possible before having it move: "In just a moment, a cataclysmic moment," Blackton would announce, motioning to the still photograph of a train on the screen in the manner of a circus barker who is introducing a magician or an acrobat, "you will see this train take life in a marvelous and most astounding manner. It will rush towards you belching smoke and fire from its monstrous iron throat."[21] In the next second, the train would grind forward, and the audience, suitably excited in anticipation, would let out a shriek of delight. The structure of Blackton's presentation makes clear that what delighted the audience was not so much the illusion of a moving train hurtling toward them as it was the transformation of the still train into the moving train, the magical sense that the audience had of *crossing over* from representation into reality. The appeal of primitive film to its first audiences can be explained in these terms. It is the drama in which seemingly impossible feats are made possible and the inanimate becomes animate. In this sense, primitive film is not very far from the feats of circuses and magic shows, the kinds of feats discussed earlier as central to Houdini's performance.

But the addition of a narrative—a story—brought changes to the workings of the medium. Narrative obscured the shift from the still to the moving image and replaced shock with a more sustained and engrossing, though less convulsive, kind of entertainment. One of the earliest and most popular American narrative films, *The Great Train Robbery,* produced by Edison's employee Edwin S. Porter in 1903, demonstrates the change. The film features a crude western plot: a group of bandits rob a train and are chased and apprehended by the sheriff and his men. Though shot almost entirely from one distance and recirculating a small number of actors in a variety of roles, the film has a modicum of continuity and even some unusual camera techniques—pans and tilts that help add variety and urgency to the action. But what characterizes the film most of all is its breakneck speed, its compulsive need to keep moving. The only pause occurs in the final shot, after the bandits have been rounded up, in which the sheriff faces the camera and shoots his gun directly at it. The shot is said to be the first facial close-up in film history, but its purpose seems less artful than desperate. How, the filmmaker seems to be asking, is the action to end without destroying the illusion that the film has taken such pains to maintain?[22]

Primitive films had exaggerated the contrast between still and motion, counting on the audience's shriek of surprise to mark their success. Early narrative films were intent on obscuring that contrast because they had a different objective in mind. Once realism rather than thrills became the object, filmmakers worried that the spectator would deconstruct the film back to its origin in the photograph and that the illusion of the persistence of vision—the ocular effect on which the motion picture depends—would be lost. Endings posed a problem in early narrative films because they represented that moment when movement must stop and the film must declare itself a representation, a superimposition, as it were, on real life. Thus many early narrative films simply peter out or end with an act of annihilating violence. Two British films by Cecil Hepworth, *The Fatal Sneeze* and *How It Feels to be Run Over,* show the catastrophe as reaching out to include the viewer, much as Porter's *The Great Train Robbery* did, as if to say that if the film must end, it will take its audience along with it.

A corollary to the drive for action was the tendency to ignore or flatten character. In other words, the dynamic and spontaneous nature of the form made the kind of long-term development of the *bildungsroman,* in which a character experiences growth and becomes inserted into the fabric of society, irrelevant to the story. When one thinks of the first narrative films, one sees that they divide themselves predictably into the two basic genres in which movement is primary and character development, nonexistent: chases and slapstick comedies.

The first films to abandon the extremes of the primitive action film, on the one hand, and of the static theatrical film (like that in Zukor's Famous Players series), on the other hand, were westerns. The genre had the advantage of being inherently cinematic since outdoor shooting, natural to the western plots, encouraged a freer and more creative use of the camera. The introduction of landscape also added a variable to representation that could serve as a bridge between action and character. Even an early western like Edison and Porter's *The Great Train Robbery,* although it hardly takes notice of character, prepares the way for it. Some of the action is set inside the train station and the railroad car as the bandits tie up the stationmaster and shoot the payload supervisor. The rest of the film features exterior shots of the bandits, who line up the passengers outside the cars to collect their money and then ride over the hills, with the sheriff and his men in pursuit. The outdoor scenes are the best parts of the film, but their contrast with the indoor scenes is the beginning of an alternation between "outside" and "inside" that would become a major component of film syntax and help in the development of character.

As with so much else, D. W. Griffith must be credited with taking Edison's hints further. He seems to have grasped from the beginning the value of outdoor shooting both as a cheap and realistic backdrop for action and as a source of contrast with indoor scenes that would help him structure his plots around character. Even his first film for Biograph, *The Adventures of Dollie,* exploits this kind of structural contrast, although shot completely outdoors. The film shows

The outlaws run off with the money in *The Great Train Robbery*
(Museum of Modern Art)

a little girl being kidnapped by gypsies from her family's estate and placed in-side a barrel that falls off a wagon and rolls into the river nearby. The barrel then plunges over a waterfall and follows the rapids into a peaceful cove, where it is found by a group of fishing boys. In orchestrating this simple series of events, Griffith alternates between the bucolic landscape (the lawn of the country estate where the child is kidnapped), the turbulent landscape of the waterfall and rapids, and the peaceful cove where the journey ends. Two years later, in *The Lonely Villa,* Griffith takes such dynamic contrasts further by mak-ing them depend on an alternation between outdoor and indoor space, cutting back and forth between a mother and her children, under attack inside a house, and a father, outside, rushing to the rescue. The alternating spaces used in the last-minute rescue, initiated in this film, would be a Griffith trademark, refined in such films as *Fighting Blood, The Last Drop of Water, The Lonedale Op-erator,* and *The Battle of Elderbush Gulch,* all made within the next few years and all with western themes. In each of these films, Griffith crosscuts between interiors in which victims, usually women and children, are besieged by vil-lains, and exteriors in which husbands or lawmen race to the rescue within a natural landscape. These scenes not only build drama through the rhythm of shifting action (with one line of action meant to complement the other and delay the final confrontation for the purpose of suspense) but also provide additional texture through the contrast of interior space, with figures generally shot at closer range, and exterior landscape, with figures in full or long shot. In moving between interior and exterior, closer shot and longer shot, Griffith produced visual correlatives for the sense of constraint and freedom that supported the storyline of the films. These shifts in perspective can be said to correspond to Turner's ideas about civilization and wilderness as the structuring poles of American character .

Griffith's 1915 *The Birth of a Nation* contains the most famous example of the filmmaker's use of contrasting spaces and camera distances in its climactic scene, which alternates between interior, closer shots of the characters under siege in the cabin, and exterior, longer shots of the Klan, riding to the rescue. The film is also a veritable compendium of interesting renderings of landscape achieved through original camera angles, editing techniques, and camera movement. The very long shot of the battle, the panoramic shot of the countryside as the Little Colonel contemplates the effects of war on the South, and the striking iris shot used to open onto the devastation of Sherman's march are some of the more memorable instances in which landscape, presented in cinematic ways, contributes to the epic sweep of the film. Some scenes also contain still shots, momentary freeze frames that return us to the spatial coordinates of painting and photography. The most memorable is the famous still of the battlefield, strewn with dead bodies and preceded by the intertitle "War's Peace." Such moments are powerful not only as static commentaries, expressive of an unchanging, universal message, but also as dramatic pauses, soon to be swallowed up in the continued forward movement of the film. They are moments of reflection in counterpoint to action, and they contribute to the structure of oscillation between two opposing states of being.[23]

Griffith continued in his later films to contrast violent nature with pastoral settings and to set panoramic vistas against domestic interiors, particularly in *Hearts of the World* and *Way Down East*. But despite many innovative structural contrasts, his use of landscape was a generalized one, adding atmosphere and support to the melodramatic aspects of the plot rather than delineating either plot or character in a more complex way. It is this generalized relationship to landscape that may have prompted his assistant cameraman to comment that World War I was simply a "typical Griffith production on the most gigantic scale: all Europe under the iron heel of a monstrous enemy, with the rescue now coming from the massed might of America."[24] One is again reminded of Thomas Cole, whose American landscapes were informed by the heroic style of European history painting. For Griffith, landscape was the frame and dy-

The Klan ride in *The Birth of a Nation,* 1915 (Culver Pictures)

namic correlative of epic deeds; its primary function was to serve as a foil and complement to the domestic interiors, where he situated the more important, relational aspects of his films.

The figure who took landscape to another level of expressiveness, who integrated it more fully and creatively with action and character, was William S. Hart. His westerns were the first to relay cinematically the full implications of the American experience in landscape—or rather, the imaginative possibilities of that experience as they were first articulated by Frederick Jackson Turner. Both John Ford and James Cruze, filmmakers who began their careers during the silent era, were influenced by Hart and would incorporate his use of landscape into their pictures and carry it into sound film.

Hart's contribution to the western genre was a marked departure from the two western stars that preceded him on the screen: Broncho Billy Anderson and Tom Mix. Anderson had no firsthand experience with the West but had appeared in *The Great Train Robbery* and then went on to star in a number of short films that focused on gunfights and chases. Mix, an authentic cowboy transplanted to Hollywood, made films that featured stunt riding and colorful costumes. But although both performers contributed important elements to what is now associated with the western film, neither was concerned about connecting his character with the idea of landscape. The Broncho Billy films were still too short and engrossed in the miracle of movement and Mix's were too closely linked to the antinarrative tendencies of vaudeville and circus to care much about deserts and prairies.

William Hart was a new kind of screen cowboy. He approached the western not as an excuse for action or as a source of colorful accouterments but as an experience from which essential moral values could be derived. For Hart, as for Cooper and Turner, the West was a site of freedom and possibility, as well as a furnace and testing ground for character. It seems significant, if we consider these apostles of the shaping effects of American landscape, that all three could boast some degree of familiarity with the frontier but were by upbringing and experience Easterners, seeking meaning for their lives and for their nation through a western mythology. Another figure in this mold was Theodore Roosevelt, the asthmatic son of a wealthy Eastern family who felt the need to prove himself by cattle ranching in the West before embarking on a political career.

Hart's family moved West soon after his birth in 1870, when his father opened a flour mill in the Dakota Territory.[25] During the years he spent there, he claimed to have had the full range of requisite adventures: he accompanied his father on a cattle drive, saw a gunfight, met Wyatt Earp and Bat Masterson, and learned sign language from the Sioux. But this western experience, although intense, was short-lived. The flour mill failed, and the family had returned East by the time Hart was eight years old, leaving him with a residue of memory that would grow into a potent imaginative resource.

Hart began a theatrical career in his teens and succeeded modestly as an actor on the Broadway stage—his repertoire included both Shakespeare and a number of popular plays with western themes. Not until 1914 did he notice the movies, but when he did, what he saw convinced him to redirect his career. He believed film was missing the chance to relay the western experience as it really was, and he immediately determined to break into the business and improve it. Originally hired to play villains for the producer Thomas Ince, he soon began writing, directing, and starring in his own films. Hart repeatedly stated that he wanted western films to be "authentic," and he took pains to make them so. Other directors liked to wet down the ground to prevent the dust of galloping horses from obscuring the clarity of their shots. Hart abhorred the practice; he reveled in dust, wanting to be true to the real dirtiness of western life. He maintained the same attitude toward other aspects of production, casting himself, a decidedly unhandsome man in his forties, as the hero of his films, bypassing fancy costumes for authentic ones and taking for his extras real cowboys who had been thrown out of work with the closing of the frontier.

The unique intensity of Hart's films, still perceptible today, may derive from the fact that he approached filmmaking less as an imitation of western experience than as an extension of it. He was helped by the fact that Hartsville, as his studio came to be called, encompassed 1800 acres and contained several open-air stages, with complete sets of ranches and towns, meticulously designed to his specifications. He talked about filmmaking with the same language that cowboys talked about the West; he professed a devotion to his horse, Fritz, quite as intense as any real cowboy might have for his; and at the completion of each of his films, he proposed to his leading lady in earnest (only one accepted him, and they were divorced soon after he began work on a new film).

This determination to equate the real past and the cinematic present was central to Hart's ability to translate the dynamic values of Turner's frontier thesis to the screen. The conflict in his films always revolved around the nobility of a natural landscape and the degeneracy of the make-shift communities that had been erected in that landscape, that had betrayed the natural values of the West and had to be redeemed by the hero. The hero's task was thus analogous to the task Hart had set for himself when he decided to break into filmmaking—to improve the quality of the movie western.[26]

In the more notable Hart films of the teens and early 1920s like *Hell's Hinges, The Return of Draw Egan, The Testing Block,* and *Three Word Brand,* his character begins as an outlaw but is called on to save a corrupt community by infusing it with juster values. Concepts of East versus West, so basic to western fiction, are introduced but not maintained in the films since the West is likely to be as corrupt as the East, and the East is likely to bring (usually in the form of the heroine) moral attributes that inspire the rough-edged hero to reform himself. Western landscape in this context functions less as a specific locale than as a site of possibility, a geography of the second chance and the new beginning.

In the 1916 *Hell's Hinges,* Hart's most powerful and representative film of the group, he uses the camera to establish correspondences between the degeneracy of the East (an excess of civilization) and the barbarism of the West (a dearth of civilization). Early in the film we are shown a weak and corrupt minister who is surrounded by a fawning female congregation, prompting his superior in the church to worry about his values and to send him westward for moral rejuvenation. As the minister travels with his sister, we are given a panoramic shot of open land, the site of his imagined redemption. But the frontier town to which he is sent does not demonstrate the expected values. The site of saloons, gunfights, and loose women, it is a betrayal of the land on which it has been erected. We now meet Hart's character, Blaze Tracy. He is a western outlaw, but unlike others in the town he exists outside the law, not because he is corrupt or dissolute but because his character, like the unsettled land seen earlier, remains unclaimed and not yet put to a higher use. Seeing the minister's sister, he is inspired to activate his potential—to help her cause and to wreak vengeance on the corrupt citizens of the town. In the final scenes, after the town has been destroyed by fire and the minister killed by a drunken mob, Tracy and the sister go off together, presumably to found a better society. A return to a panning shot of the landscape beyond the frontier town suggests that here is the site of their future, the tabula rasa on which they will erect a meaningful community.

The plot of the film is not so very different from that of the most famous literary western of a generation earlier, Owen Wister's *The Virginian,* which also showed the union of a western hero with an eastern heroine who domesticates him (Hart had actually starred in a 1907 stage adaptation of *The Virginian* early in his career). But what distinguishes *Hell's Hinges* from Wister's novel is the absence of a nostalgic tone. Its ultimate message is not a paean to a lost West but a modeling of reciprocal values that will presumably prevail when the hero and heroine settle on land that has not yet experienced the taint of either savagery or corruption. The film places its hope in the future.

Hart did not revel in the kind of natural spectacle that figured in Griffith's films and would become so much a part of the look of the epic western. To deal in pure spectacle, Hart's films suggest, would be to compromise their intensely character-centered plots and their austere sense of virtue and sin. Instead, landscape in his films is always a correlative and extension of character and action. The most spectacular scene in *Hell's Hinges* occurs when the town is set on fire and silhouetted figures are shown in chaotic movement in front of a flickering backdrop. This is apocalyptic landscape: the frontier town become Dante's inferno.

Hell's Hinges articulates the basic relationship of the individual to landscape that would be a defining feature of American westerns, but for all its drive for authenticity it also seems at moments surreal and expressionistic and, in this sense, vaguely *un*-American. The film reveals succinctly why Hart had great initial success with audiences but why, very quickly, he lost his following to the lighter, more relaxed Tom Mix. *Hell's Hinge's* is simply too austere and intense to be taken as the prototype for the American western film. For this reason, a better film by which to gauge Hart's cinematic legacy is not the 1916

Hell's Hinges but the 1925 *Tumbleweeds,* a more seasoned work that reflects an effective melding of his own vision to existing tastes and trends. Of all Hart's films, *Tumbleweeds,* made after his popularity had declined, looks most like a conventional western (and has points in common with both Cruze's 1923 *The Covered Wagon* and Ford's 1924 *The Iron Horse*) but with a more interesting and consistent emphasis on character that makes it worthy of closer analysis.

Tumbleweeds gathers together the themes and images that had preoccupied Hart over the course of his career and gives them an epic articulation. It deals with events surrounding the 1889 land rush—the opening of the Cherokee Strip in the Oklahoma Territory, the last tract of land to be made available to white settlers. Its subject is the closing of the frontier. Hart was so intent on making the film that he underwrote its cost himself when his studio failed to support him. In 1939, he rereleased it with the addition of an eight-minute spoken prologue in which he addressed his audience directly for the first time, explaining the historical background to the plot and formally announcing his retirement from the screen (he was then sixty-nine years old and would die seven years later). The film's theme and characterizations, the way in which it is shot, and the way in which it is framed by this spoken prologue added fifteen years after the film was made and more than ten years after the advent of sound, all make it a unique artifact—a film that, more than any western I can think of, locates itself with respect to an American past and an American future.

The film interweaves two plot lines: a character-centered plot, dealing with Hart's position as a cattle rancher who falls in love with and is converted into a homesteader, and a broader, historical plot that pertains to the closing of the frontier—the end of the long cattle drives and the scramble by homesteaders to claim the land for settlement. To weave together these two kinds of action, the film alternates between foreground shots and long shots—between figures as individuals seen alone or in relationship and figures in synchrony with or encompassed by landscape. In the early scenes of the film, a series of emblematic shots establishes the situation of the protagonist, Don Carver, played by Hart. We see middle and close shots of chaotically herded cattle, a tumbleweed, a rattlesnake, a wolf and her cubs, and a pig in the mud, and these are juxtaposed to medium shots of Carver on his horse, wandering on the prairie. The impression relayed is that Carver is a loner and an anachronism: he scorns the domestic life of the homesteader but is destined to be destroyed by the closing of the frontier.

But in subsequent scenes, Carver's positioning changes. He meets a woman and her young brother, who are prospective homesteaders, and is drawn to the woman and develops a bond with the boy, both of whom he will

The arrival of the homesteaders in *Tumbleweeds,* 1925 (Photofest)

protect against the exploitation of their villainous stepbrother. Meanwhile, the film intersperses its use of close and medium shots with long shots of the landscape. In one scene, we see a trail of cattle being herded off into the distance—the last of the long cattle drives. In another, we see the homesteaders come into town, a line of wagons stretching across the horizon.

The rhythm of the camera movement, which alternates between closer shots that delineate individuals and animals alone or in relationship and longer shots that place individual elements in the context of landscape, creates contrasts and analogies based purely on this visual syntax. At the outset, when Carver stares at the line of homesteaders' wagons and the intertitle records his pronouncement, "Boys—it's the last of the west," one might assume that he is to be destroyed or driven elsewhere as a result of this encroachment of civilization (in the way, for example, that Cooper's Deerslayer becomes negligible with the disappearance of the frontier or Huck Finn has to escape being "sivilized" by heading for the territories). When, in another scene, Carver shows himself smitten with the woman, one is drawn to the opposite conclusion—that Carver will now become domesticated and lose his freedom—the conclusion that characterizes classic *bildungsroman* novels like *David Copperfield* and *Jane Eyre.* Yet a subsequent long shot that shows orderly lines of herded cattle stretching out into the distance establishes an analogy to the homesteaders' line shown earlier. And later, during the land rush scene, the homesteaders are represented like a group of stampeding cattle. These visual analogies contradict the sense of a simple tradeoff of one way of life for another. We are no longer dealing with a disorderly past and an orderly future, with Carver's independence as a rancher weighed against his domestication as a husband and homesteader, but with the idea that freedom and domestication are present in both conditions.

The film dramatizes this most effectively by counterpointing the image of the "line," an innovation of Griffith's in the long shot of the Klan march in *The Birth of a Nation,* with the idea of the "stray," a particularized rendering of

East meets West: Barbara Bedford and William S. Hart in
Tumbleweeds (Kobal Collection)

mass. As a herder of cattle, Carver must deal continually with bringing strays from the herd into line. Before the land rush begins, he is asked by his boss to go into the Cherokee Strip to capture a stray. In the process, he is mistakenly labeled a "sooner"—someone who tries to make a claim before the land is officially opened to settlement—and is taken into custody, as though he were a stray himself. The plot device brings home the film's basic premise: just as the stray cattle must be brought back into the line of the herd, so the stray individual must be apprehended as he deviates from the line of behavior deemed proper by the dominant group. But this is not a singular act of retrieval; it is one that must be continually repeated. If there were not a persistent tendency for cattle to stray, there would be no use for cowboys. And if human beings did not continually need to assert their identities and desires, there would be no stories. Carver, significantly, is both a stray and a herder in both the past and the present. His image with the orderly herds and his assignment to bring back a stray associate him with the line of the past at the same time that his courting of the girl and his eventual entry into the land rush as a homesteader (who will also bring the villains to justice) establish his place in the line of the present. The sense of movement in and out of a line—whether that line is past or present, nature or society—is the oscillation that Frederick Jackson Turner had described as proper to the American character, born out of the frontier experience.

The film's climactic scene contains a sequence of shots that expresses this idea with particular economy and power. As the land rush begins, we first see footage of the homesteaders, driving wagons, on horseback, even on a bicycle, as they rush forward to stake their claim. Then, we see Carver on his horse, foregrounded against this chaotic landscape, as he gallops across the screen with them. Finally, to emphasize his surpassing speed and determination, the background becomes a blur. All we see is a medium shot of Carver on his horse, the horse's legs moving but the image remaining fixed to the left of the screen. In Keaton's and Chaplin's films, moving stasis is a gag, a deconstructive joke about the absurdity of trying to get anywhere. But in Hart's film, moving stasis is a quasi-religious moment as the figure of the hero appears to collapse time and space and becomes a moving icon: figure merges into landscape; landscape merges into figure. The image holds for a few seconds, then breaks as horse and rider now move across the screen and arrive at the place where Carver battles the villains and stakes his claim.

The few seconds of moving stasis are important in dramatizing the continuous and repetitive aspect of film as it has evolved at this point and which Hart's understanding of landscape has helped to make possible. The film recycles the dynamic relationship between mass and line, rest and motion, close-up and long shot, and individual and landscape in order to achieve its effects. And narrative film, in its developed form, does this in a more general way. "Real" time, linear and irreversible, is, after all, belied by film, which not only denies irreversibility through its ability to be rewound, but also makes the past and the present subject to the same patterning. Without the interlacing of speech to introduce abstract meaning, film is driven by contrast and analogy, impressing meaning on images through this simple binary code.

According to this rhythm of separation and assimilation, the "values" of nature and society and of past and present are not at odds with each other but are interdependent, oscillating states of being, subject to cinematic arrangement. In an earlier sequence, Carver was shown inside the Cherokee Strip, conversing with a group of Indians in sign language. The scene established his fraternity with the Indians, who, the title cards inform us, are willing to fight on his behalf should he desire it. From a historical point of view, the scene registers an awareness of the prior existence of Native Americans on the land (they were usurped by the cattlemen, just as the cattlemen are about to be usurped by the homesteaders), but since no titles reinforce this idea, the Indian scene serves mainly to establish Carver's ability to function within other representational systems and, analogously, to show us that Hart is similarly adept (that he learned Indian signing during his boyhood days in the West). The film also draws an implicit analogy between Indian culture and film culture because silent films rely on gesture for relaying meaning. Significantly, toward the end of the movie, when Carver is about to see the heroine, who he believes has rejected him, he raises his hand to his face in an exaggeratedly histrionic pose of the kind popular in nineteenth-century theater, where Hart began his acting career. The use of this kind of gesture to denote a moment of intense emotion inserts the kind of sign we saw in the scene with the Indians into the central line of the story. Such recycling of images in new contexts (the bringing of the "stray" image into the "line") reflects film's ability to erode distinctions that might otherwise have kept experience compartmentalized.

An obvious danger in this process is its tendency to overlook or mask injustice by assimilating it in the service of something else (what Griffith did with such insidious effectiveness in *The Birth of a Nation* and what *Tumbleweeds* does insofar as it renders the condition of the Indians invisible by making it irrelevant to the syntax of the film).[27] But the assimilation of images into new contexts has the advantage of broadening the range and potential for action open to the protagonist within the film, as well as empowering the viewer who identifies with that protagonist. If life in society and life in nature can be so easily represented through the same kinds of visual and dynamic imagery, it becomes possible to see oneself as both natural and social within the same context—to move from the spirit of the cowboy to that of the homesteader and not remain fixed in either role.

These shifting affiliations, embodied by Hart's "good-bad man" persona, would be extended further and more dramatically by the great American film star of the late teens and 1920s, Douglas Fairbanks. A little more than a decade younger than Hart, Fairbanks's representation of the West diverged sharply from his predecessor. He came to his subject with a different temperament and a different family background, and the West he knew bore little resemblance to the one that Hart had known (or imagined he had known) as a boy.

Douglas Fairbanks was born in Denver, Colorado, in 1883 into a life of dysfunction and relative poverty. His mother came from a fairly prosperous Massachusetts family, had made two unfortunate marriages, and had gone West with a man who abandoned her soon after her son's birth. Like Chaplin's mother, Fairbanks's maintained her pretensions to gentility even with no money and no husband, and these pretensions eventually propelled her back to the East, where she encouraged her son to seek his fortune. Fairbanks would fail at a number of white-collar jobs before achieving moderate success on the Broadway stage, but this was only a prelude to the phenomenal success he would achieve a few years later in the movies. His early films, in which he played the genial boy-next-door, were elaborations of his stage roles, but the settings of the films were different from anything possible on stage. Landscape, which movies alone could make integral to plot and character development, were what helped turn Fairbanks from a conventional leading man into a star. The British critic Alistair Cooke, in defining Fairbanks as the first and supreme example of the American movie star, would make clear the relationship of his persona to landscape: "'Doug' could breath freely on the tops of church steeples, hanging from a mountain crag, or diving through a window pane; the only things that choke him are the scent and epigram of the boudoir."[28]

Many of Fairbanks's early films had plots that seem like wishful revisions of his father's story: an Easterner, often from a wealthy and conventional back-ground, goes West, where he meets with unfamiliar and physically taxing cir-cumstances but where he ultimately proves his mettle and realizes his romantic destiny. In his first film, *The Lamb,* made in 1915, he plays a cowardly Wall Street broker who is transformed into a fearless western hero. In *Wild and Wooly,* made two years later, he plays a wealthy New York banker's son who saves a western town from a band of drunken Indians. And in the 1920 *The Mollycoddle,* his last film in this genre before beginning his swashbuckler phase, he plays a foppish American expatriate who must return to his family roots in the West and do battle with an unscrupulous diamond smuggler. In one of the more suggestive films of this early period, the 1917 *Man from Painted Post,* a film that Fairbanks wrote himself, he plays an Easterner who has come west to revenge the deaths of his mother and sister and who eventually traps the villain and wins the girl; for good measure, he also adopts the villain's half-Indian son. (The plot recalls Fairbanks's father's marriage to a woman with children, as well as his mixed ethnicity—he was presumably part Jewish.)

These early roles gave Fairbanks an opportunity to imaginatively revise his family history while providing a new way of thinking about the relationship between East and West.[29] Although his films tap many of the same themes and settings as Hart's, they are actually satires of western adventure and of the preconceptions that Americans from the East tended to have about the western landscape. The satirical thrust may derive from Fairbanks's unfortunate family situation and the fact that life in the West held no particular glamour for him. But the satire also serves a higher or more generalized purpose. Whereas Hart was devoted to the actual scenery of the West, Fairbanks, more pragmatically, was seeking alternative ways of representing the western spirit and new sites for exercising it. His characters are often prompted to leave their jobs and homes in search of adventure, but the final lesson tends to be that a change in locale is not really necessary. What *is* necessary is a capacity for "play." Play, these films suggest, is not a fantastic exercise in timing and ingenuity, not the precinct of professional clowns, but the visible expression of youth and energy. And though a man can sometimes seem foolish in seeking an outlet for play, what is farcical in an everyday context can prove useful in emergencies.

In *Wild and Wooly,* the West that the hero finally visits turns out to be fully settled, but the townspeople, eager to please the wealthy businessman's son, put on an act to pretend otherwise. Then a real crisis develops—the town is attacked by Indians (led not by warrior chiefs but by a crooked Indian agent), and the hero draws on his resources to save the day. A comparable challenge might have occurred anywhere. Several of Fairbanks's early films take his character to a foreign setting (Europe or South America) and have him use his boyish energy and improvisational skill to solve problems or fight enemies that confound the tradition-bound natives. On some level, the films are exuberant parodies of Hart's, but they never debunk or scorn what Hart achieved; they simply translate it into a more knowing and usable form.

Fairbanks's films always acknowledge, what Hart's do not, that the frontier is gone, and though the Easterner goes west to prove himself and succeeds in doing so, the West is never the way he imagined. In *Wild and Wooly,* the opening titles make clear the distinction between the image of the wagon train, once associated with the West, and the image of the railroad, the present reality. In *The Mollycoddle,* the hero, who has been brought up in England, tells the heroine of the rough and tumble life he believes exists in New York City: the film dissolves to show gunfighting on the streets of Manhattan (what he imagines goes on), then dissolves again into a traffic jam to show what the city is really like.

In other early films, Fairbanks directs his satire in the opposite direction, revising the landscape of urban life to conform with the western idea. Nineteenth-century dime novels had depicted the city as the site of sin and corruption, a place one must carefully navigate to avoid the material and sensual traps that are lying in wait. By the turn of the century, however, a new attitude toward urban space had begun to develop. This attitude, encapsulated in the City Beautiful Movement, took its inspiration from the design of Washington, D.C., with its symmetrical arrangement of radial boulevards and planned groupings of public buildings. Washington stood as a symbol, as one historian has put it, "of what the future promised for the entire country, which, like the capital city, remained unfinished but which boasted of boundless energy, optimism, and natural resources."[30] In other words, Washington, and by extension all American cities, now shared the mythic potential that had been associated with the western landscape.

Fairbanks's ability to see East and West as interchangeable sites—to envision an East as delightful and challenging as the West—was very much in the spirit of the City Beautiful Movement. It was also a way to extend Hart's theoretical articulation of this idea into more concrete terms. In one film of this kind, *The Matrimaniac,* Fairbanks plays a young man in love with a girl whose father wants to marry her off to someone else. He engages in a round of fantastic stunts to rescue her and manages, in the end, to achieve his goal by climbing up a telephone pole and having the marriage performed in a three-way call involving the minister, the woman, and himself, suspended on the wire between them. The telephone wire has assumed the role of the modern horse. Toward the end of another early Fairbanks film, *Till the Clouds Roll By,* the hero performs his stunts on the top of a speeding train. In *Wild and Wooly,* the fusion of eastern and western landscapes occurs in the concluding scene in which Fairbanks and the girl, both dressed in elegant riding clothes, descend the stairs of an opulent mansion, open the fancy doors, and proceed into an unsettled western landscape where their horses are waiting.

In the next decade, Fairbanks took what he had done in the teens to another level, extending the heroic landscape to encompass history and legend—coopting the past, so to speak, to American use. These swashbuckler films of the 1920s are extravaganzas, the grandiosity of the sets recalling those of Griffith's *Intolerance*. But whereas Griffith's are essentially impressive backdrops, Fairbanks's are dynamic spaces, tailored arenas for action—what Alistair Cooke termed a "disguised gymnasium" in which trellises, walls, and rooftops all seem to be waiting to be made use of. Fairbanks's fascination with retrofitting the landscape of his films to the stunts he wanted to do increased throughout the 1920s: chair legs were sawed off, special holds were built into the sides of buildings, and technical tricks were used to make athletic feats appear to be both more astonishing and more graceful. Among the most ingenious set features of this period was the placement of a child's slide under the massive velvet curtain draped across the palace wall in *Robin Hood,* making it possible for the hero to swoop down its folds in a smooth, continuous movement. A similar device is used in *The Black Pirate* when Fairbanks slices through a sail with a knife to arrive with grace and speed from the top of the mast to the deck. Obviously, the aim of such highly orchestrated feats was to make Fairbanks look as physically impressive as possible, but they also served the grander purpose of bringing the character and the landscape into harmo-

Douglas Fairbanks, eluding his pursuers in *The Mark of Zorro,* 1921
(Museum of Modern Art)

nious conjunction, establishing a heroism not of effort but of ease and integration. In this sense, Fairbanks's films are the fulfillment of the quest by nineteenth-century American writers to fit the self to an environment that seemed to be hostile to it. (Fairbanks's true heir in this respect was Fred Astaire, who would display a comparably dazzling integration with his environment, which in his case functioned as a disguised dance floor rather than a disguised gymnasium.)

Some critics have found fault with the later swashbucklers, maintaining that the Fairbanks persona, so delightfully emphasized in the teens and early 1920s, was now smothered in costumes, props, and elaborate sets. *Robin Hood,* which makes generous use of long shots to relay the massive scale of the castle (then the largest interior set ever built), does at times dwarf its star and make it hard to distinguish him from the other heavily costumed players. But this also makes more dramatic those moments when Fairbanks, performing a particularly spectacular athletic feat, suddenly springs into relief like an organic eruption of the landscape itself. In these films, the "real" frontier, as authentically recreated by Hart, gives way to a wholly imagined one, perfectly tailored to its hero, made real through the expenditure of enormous sums of money and the deployment of armies of skilled craftsmen and designers. Hart's landscapes were the testing ground for character; so are Fairbanks's, but his are also spaces where the movie actor as "star" can find a context fitted to the scale of his fame and, symbolically, to the scale of American aspiration for the century.

Fairbanks's swashbucklers were part of a general tendency in the 1920s to replace or enhance natural landscapes with something more exotic. We see this in the movies of Rudolph Valentino and John Barrymore and in the large-scale spectacles of Cecil B. DeMille. These films seem to be the extreme realization of what the cultural critic Anne Hollander has called "the American form of romance," in which effects are created through the imaginative revision of the country's geography. Hollander traces this esthetic back to Cole and Bierstadt and attributes it to a uniquely American need "to keep pace with overwhelming facts, to enlarge to meet them."[31] The cinematic trend in monumental imaginative landscapes also connects to a more general architectural trend during this period to reimagine the city according to new ideas of space and mass. One of the most striking urban designs of the late 1920s, the *Metropolis of Tomorrow* by Hugh Ferriss, though never built, was a subject of extensive discussion and debate in architectural circles.[32] The plan, which featured a massive skyscraper city in an urban space that had been thoroughly razed of all previous construction, could well have been inspired by the set design of a DeMille epic or a Fairbanks swashbuckler.

Set for *The Thief of Bagdad,* 1924 (Museum of Modern Art)

Business Centre, from Hugh Ferriss's *Metropolis of Tomorrow,* 1929 (Avery
Architectural and Fine Arts Library, Columbia University, City of New York)

Fairbanks's films of the 1920s were also significant in that they gave new expression to the alternating movement between constraint and freedom that was basic to the western plot. Each of the swashbucklers calls for the protagonist to break away from an established order within which he occupies a prominent role and to fight for justice under the cover of a new identity. Having once achieved his end, the hero assumes his mainstream position of wealth and privilege, though not without reserving the right to return to his other identity if the need arises (a return realized in the sequels to *The Mark of Zorro* and *The Three Musketeers*). These plots exhibit the same structure as Fairbanks's boyish plots of the earlier decade and are versions of the good man–bad man plots that Hart had pioneered. The difference is that the hero is now possessed of a noble pedigree and exists in an epic historical context—a European past that film magically makes accessible to the resources of the valiant American spirit. Mark Twain had tackled the idea of the brash and savvy American who entered the past to save it in *A Connecticut Yankee in King Arthur's Court,* but his treatment was satirical, in keeping with the skepticism and insecurity inherent in the American literary tradition.[33] Fairbanks's satire, however, is always cheerful and uplifting, never skeptical or insecure. He carries himself with unshakable confidence; all obstacles are to be laughed at and leapt over ("I was disappointed in the Grand Canyon," he is quoted as saying, "—I couldn't jump it"). The result is a kind of colonization in reverse of historical fact, a molding of an imagined European past to the shape of the American myth. This idea is what lends point to Robert E. Sherwood's famous witticism about Fairbanks's performance in *The Three Musketeers:* "When Alexandre Dumas sat down at his desk, smoothed his hair back, chewed the end of his quill pen, and said to himself, 'Well, I guess I might as well write a book called *The Three Musketeers*,' he doubtless had but one object in view: to provide a suitable story for Douglas Fairbanks to act in the movies." The joke plays on the time reversal that Fairbanks's films of this period suggest—that the past, including the literature of the past, is waiting to be reanimated and reclaimed by the American movie star.[34]

We see the idea dramatically enacted at the end of *Robin Hood.* The Fairbanks hero (Lord Huntingdon in disguise as Robin Hood) returns to the king's court, where he is acknowledged by the king himself to be the superior personage: "Until now I never bowed my head to man," declares King Richard. In the last scene the king is banging on the door of the room into which Fairbanks and his bride have escaped from their wedding party; he is still waiting for the door to open as the movie ends. The string of identities that leads from Lord Huntingdon to Robin Hood and from Robin Hood to Douglas Fairbanks leaves us with the final impression that the British king is waiting for the American movie star to grant him an audience. The image would be supported in life by Fairbanks's popularity with the most venerable aristocratic families of Europe, many of whom treated him with the admiration and deference of starstruck fans.

Robin Hood and other Fairbanks swashbucklers adapted the international theme that Henry James popularized in his novels to a cinematic context, producing a different outcome. The theme pertains to the clash of American and European values. In James's novels, it leads to tragedy: the innocent Americans inevitably lose to the wily Europeans because they lack the social and linguistic tools needed to overcome the sophisticated strategies of the Old World. But in Fairbanks' films, the guilelessness of the American, instead of thwarting him, frees him to act heroically. He has only to climb through a window, flash a 100-watt smile, and dash off with the heroine across the ramparts of the castle. In silent films, the hero and heroine run no risk of compromising themselves through speech, and the vista for action that opens through a spectacular, manipulated landscape makes words superfluous.

Finally, Fairbanks performed the greatest possible gymnastic feat of all: collapsing the idea of the American landscape into the singular space of his own person. The best demonstration of this occurs in *Don Q, Son of Zorro,* the sequel to *The Mark of Zorro,* in which he plays the son of the character he played in the original. Throughout the film, the son, Don Pedro, announces that his father is "the greatest man in America," and in a delightful scene toward the end of the film, father and son, both played by Fairbanks, are shown dueling with the villains side by side (an effect obtained with split-screen projection). In playing both father and son (a casting idea Valentino would repeat in *The Son of the Sheik*) and by drawing attention to his own celebrity at the same time, Fairbanks expanded the epic nature of his cinematic persona, suggesting not only his ability to transform himself in space (from fop to hero, from nobleman to leader of the people) and to inhabit different roles in historical time (Robin Hood, D'Artagnan, and Zorro) but also to inhabit different spots of time within the space of one film: to time-travel not just from film to film but also within a single film and to perform the ultimate epic feat of self-regeneration.

A figure of sublime cheerfulness and play, Fairbanks came to embody for his nation and for the world those elements of freedom, individualism, and changeability that Turner had associated with the American West. His character was always in a state of alternation between boyishness and manliness— boyish in the act of everyday life, manly when heroic action was called for. Though he gave these attributes heroic scope in his films, he also extended them into more realistic contexts in his daily life. He preached, through self-help books and interviews, that to be boyish was to be spontaneous and fun-loving and that to be heroic was to work hard and win at tennis. His shifting identification with the boy and the man in himself was a version of Hart's oscillation between the stray and the line, but by translating the rigorous moral categories that defined Hart's persona into a lighter context, he made this dynamic ideal available for imitation by a mass audience. In a 1924 introduction to one of Fairbanks's many self-help manuals, a spokesman for the Boy Scouts of America lists the kinds of advice Fairbanks offers to young readers: "he talks in a friendly fellow-to-fellow way about such things as success, keeping fit, tolerance, on making a start, on advancing, on the inspiration of the sunrise."[35] This is advice capable of speaking to and potentially influencing anyone, regardless of educational background; economic status; or religious, ethnic, or political affiliation.

Turner had written optimistically that although the frontier had closed, the American spirit would not be satisfied with staying put: "Movement," he wrote, "has been [the] dominant fact [of American life], and, unless this training has no effect upon a people, the American intellect will continually demand a wide field for its exercise."[36] Silent film presented such a field. Movement in film is, of course, very different from movement across land: one is representation, the other is real. Yet silent film had the unique capacity to erode that distinction. Through its ability to represent experience by dynamic images, it opened to the American populace a new frontier in the mold of the original as Turner had conceived it. It schooled its audience in a way of thinking in which the concepts of self and society, past and present, and reality and artifice, which literature had made mutually exclusive, could be reconciled. This new way of thinking is embedded in the "farewell to the screen" that William S. Hart appended to *Tumbleweeds* when he re-released the film in 1939. It is worth quoting much of this spoken prologue to demonstrate how completely Hart, the father of the American movie western, had entered into the spirit of his films but how awkward and unconvincing his cinematically derived values became once they were articulated in words.

As the prologue begins, Hart, dressed in his cowboy clothes but looking decidedly old and frail, walks forward with his horse and addresses the camera:

> The story of *Tumbleweeds* [he pronounces in slow, highly enunciated tones], marks one of the greatest epics of our American history. It tells of the opening of the Cherokee Strip in the year 1889. Twelve hundred square miles of

Cherokee Indian land . . . were thrown open by our government to those seeking good earth on which they could make their homes. . . . The story of *Tumbleweeds* is entwined, bound up in this great American epic . . . that mad rush of destiny . . . was indeed a sight to behold. [Here the camera moves in closer, Hart removes his hat, and a lachrymose western melody begins to play in the background.] My friends, I love the art of making motion pictures. It is as the breath of life to me. . . . The rush of the wind that cuts your face, the pounding hooves of the pursuing posse . . . the clouds of dust through which come the faint voice of the director: "OK Bill, OK. Glad you made it. Great stuff, Bill, great stuff. And say, Bill, give old Fritz a pat on the nose for me, will ya?" Oh, the thrill of it all. You do give Fritz a pat on the nose and when your arm encircles his neck, the cloud of dust is no longer a cloud of dust but a beautiful golden haze through which appears a long phantom herd of trailing cattle. At their head, a pinto pony, a pinto pony! With an empty saddle. And then, a long, loved whinny—the whinny of a horse so fine that nothing seems to live between it and silence—saying: "Say boss, what you riding up there with the drag for? Why don't you ride point with me? Can't you see, boss, the saddle is empty. The boys up ahead are calling; they're waiting for you and me to help drive this great round-up into eternity."

We tend to think of silent film as struggling to produce the effects of speech through images. This sequence shows the opposite. Hart is trying to approximate in words the use of long shots, close-ups, even intertitles. It is speech here that seeks to approximate the syntax of the dynamic image.

Hart's words in this prologue are devoid of irony, and although he is stiff, he is not self-conscious. He is "inside" his story, a character in a narrative at the same time that he is an actor, speaking lines. We see this in the way he segues from the history of the American West to his own life in pictures. He means to equate one experience with the other and to mark a passage from a distant past, when the frontier was open, to a more recent past, when movie making became the new frontier, showing the two experiences to be continuous and interchangeable. He then draws a new analogy and appends it to the temporal progression he has sketched—that of himself riding off into the sunset toward death—and we see to what extent cinematic values have come to dominate his way of structuring experience. It is the same kind of effect that occurred inside the film with his use of sign language: the signing was an enactment of an antecedent Native American culture and was used again later in the film to represent the protagonist's "genuine" emotion; it crossed various systems of meaning and historical time frames, erasing boundaries of past and present, real and staged. But when the same kind of boundary crossing is attempted in language, as it is in this prologue, the effect seems hokey and embarrassing (though endearing, I admit, in its very awkwardness[37]). Distinctions and discriminations, instead of falling easily into a new line, are anchored in place by the stubborn singularity of speech. Gone is the fluid, analogical effect that was possible with moving images liberated from words.

Hart's prologue to *Tumbleweeds* is an extreme of vocal ineptness. His voice was trained for the stage, in an earlier theatrical style at that, and he had had no practice speaking in a film. By using his prologue as an example, I have therefore exaggerated the distinction between silent and sound films more than is warranted. Good cinematic speech is more fluent and natural; one might even say that it aspires to the condition of images, though I would argue that no matter how integrated it is, it always makes for compromise, for a "fall" from the purer visual dynamism of silent films.

The medium of silent film brought about a fundamental change in how we see the world in which we move. It took landscape from its traditional representational role as a backdrop for action or object for contemplation and gave it a complex, dynamic connection to the human subject that was operating within it. The vitalization of landscape in the service of character was one of the great innovations of silent film. Sound films would never be able to deny that legacy; they would never entirely efface the shifting relationship between figure and ground as the imaginative form for American experience.

4

GRIFFITH, GISH, AND THE NARRATIVE OF THE FACE

"**B**ILLY, move in! Get that face! That face—*get that face!*"[1]

The frantic direction was delivered by D. W. Griffith to his camera-man, Billy Bitzer, during the making of *Way Down East,* as Lillian Gish, the film's star, struggled to maintain her footing on an ice floe in the middle of a storm-tossed river.

For Griffith, the success of the filming clearly depended on capturing his heroine's face in close-up. And indeed when we watch the movie today, Gish's face, quivering in fright and desperation, is crucial to the effect, lifting the scene above mere action and giving it an epic human dimension. Because of that face, we watch not simply to see what happens next but also to revel in the beauty and intensity of the character whose life seems, momentarily, entwined with ours.

To understand what Griffith achieved with Gish's face in *Way Down East,* I would like to backtrack in time and look at two descriptive passages from two novels by Henry James. Each passage introduces us to the central character from that novel but uses a different technique to achieve the introduction. Taken together, these passages can help explain how the face would eventually be used to portray character in film.

The first passage is from James's 1875 novel, *The American,* and it intro-duces the protagonist, Christopher Newman, by minutely describing his face:

> He had a very well-formed head, with a shapely, symmetrical balance of the frontal and the occipital development, and a good deal of straight, rather dry brown hair. His complexion was brown, and his nose had a bold, well-marked arch. His eye was of a clear, cold gray, and, save for a rather abun-dant moustache, he was clean-shaved. He had the flat jaw and sinewy neck which are frequent in the American type.[2]

The description of Newman presents him as a specimen: the quintessential American man. It draws on phrenology, a popular fad in nineteenth-century America, which included careful classification of skulls, noses, and jawbones as a means of assessing character.[3] The eugenic implications of this type of think-ing are plain and can be connected to the large number of new immigrants into the United States at the time the novel was written, an influx that seemed to many, including James, to threaten the purity of a national type. By the same token, the urge to produce a physical blueprint for the typical American can also be seen more positively—as an effort to realize Whitman's brash pro-

Preceding page: Lillian Gish in *Way Down East,* 1920 (Museum of Modern Art)

nouncement: "Writing and talk do not prove me, I carry the plenum of proof and every thing else in my face." Books, customs, monuments—all the stuff of European greatness, Whitman's line suggests—can be contained in the richness of a single human physiognomy.

Such a statement makes clear why the country might be concerned with delineating a face that could, again in Whitman's phrase, "contain multitudes." And if Christopher Newman is meant to be emblematic of his country's population, he can also be seen as the condensed expression of his country's geography. The adjectives used in the description of his face—"symmetrical," "straight," "dry," "clear," "cold," and "flat"—suggest a return to the simple, elemental forms associated with the western prairie where Newman grew up and made his fortune. As with the American body, noted earlier, the prototype for the American face was the face of Lincoln, whose plainness was connected to the harsh but ennobling facts of American life: "Certain faces in the crowd are recognized at once as American faces" notes the historian James Mellon, "that is, faces which America alone has made possible. In Lincoln's face, as in the story of his life, every American sees something made of his country's toil, something atavistic, for Lincoln remains the nonpareil example of the American character as it formed, and sought to define, itself."[4] Newman, in this context, is a fictional counterpart of Lincoln, presenting to the reader the same kind of atavistic, self-creating identity.

Now consider a second passage, one that contrasts the first and adds another dimension to an evolving sense of national character. This is the description of the American heroine, Isabel Archer, in James's 1881 novel, *Portrait of a Lady:*

> She had a great desire for knowledge, but she really preferred almost any source of information to the printed page; she had an immense curiosity about life and was constantly staring and wondering. She carried within herself a great fund of life, and her deepest enjoyment was to feel the continuity between the movements of her own soul and the agitations of the world. For this reason she was fond of seeing great crowds and large stretches of country, of reading about revolutions and wars, of looking at historical pictures.[5]

If, in describing Christopher Newman, James was attempting to describe a latter-day Lincoln, a man whose face "America alone has made possible," in describing Isabel Archer he was trying to show the spirit that complements the face. The gender difference is important here insofar as James saw the female as the proper support and complement to the male (and he often decried the breakdown of that complementarity in modern American life).

The spirited, restless quality that James attributed to his American heroine was actually given a clinical name during the nineteenth century. Nervousness —or "neurasthenia," as it was more fashionably referred to—was dubbed the "American disease" and had acquired a native expert in the Yale-educated physician George M. Beard, who connected it to the American myth. Beard maintained that it was America's great promise and its urge to fulfill that promise that caused the nervous debilitation of so many of its most creative citizens.[6] To experience such symptoms was therefore to be the best sort of modern American and to reflect what Henry James might call a "finer sensibility." (James, along with his sister and his older brother, was a well-documented neurasthenic; a less creative, younger brother suffered, more prosaically, from alcoholism.) The idea of the American disease had existed in nascent form as early as Tocqueville, who had devoted a chapter of *Democracy in America* to the question: "Why Americans are so Restless in the Midst of their Prosperity." He concluded that restlessness was a function of the greater competition that exists among a democratic people who cannot be satisfied with having less than their neighbors.[7] Beard had added his own, decidedly idiosyncratic theories on the subject. He argued, for example, that neurasthenia was more commonly seen in young women and was connected to the "phenomenal beauty of the American girl." This, he explained, was because the stimuli associated with female upbringing in such a rapidly developing country produced a "fineness of organization" not seen elsewhere (his terminology, it might be noted, could just as well be applied to the superior produce of the American farmer).[8]

The description of the neurasthenic as it evolved in nineteenth-century American culture borrowed a great deal from the description of that other psychological condition, hysteria, that was generally believed to be comparably epidemic among women, although here the incidence was more documented in Europe than in America. The physical attitudes and facial tics of the hysteric were first reported by the French physician Jean-Martin Charcot, who greatly influenced the early work of Freud. Photographs from the Salpêtrière clinic in Paris, where Charcot staged "performances" by resident hysterics, show women with contorted bodies and faces, the pictures affixed with titles that relate the expressions to emotional states like "amorous supplication," "ecstasy," and "eroticism."[9] The photographs put one in mind of the dramatic poses that actresses like Sarah Bernhardt made popular and which were disseminated on postcards and displayed on placards in theater lobbies.

But although neurasthenia, being characterized by restlessness and hypersensitivity, had much in common with hysteria, it was also a kind of inversion of hysteria. As commonly understood, the neurasthenic patient was always try-

ing to express more than the tools available would allow: "When a neurasthenic describes his pains," explained Freud, "he is clearly of opinion that language is too poor to find words for his sensations and that those sensations are
something unique and previously unknown, of which it would be quite impossible to give an exhaustive description. For this reason he never tires of con-
stantly adding fresh details."[10] Whereas the hysteric, one might say, is expressing too much feeling, the neurasthenic is seeking to express more—seeking, as
it were, a form adequate to a highly complex and tumultuous inner state. This
is the crux of the 1892 story, "The Yellow Wallpaper," by the New England
writer and early feminist Charlotte Perkins Gilman. The story describes a
neurasthenic wife whose husband, a doctor, denies her access to the creative
activities of writing and socializing in an effort to keep her calm. But this repression only worsens her condition. The more she is deprived of a creative outlet,
the more desperate she becomes, until, at the end of the story, she finally goes
mad—moving, as it were, from neurasthenia to hysteria.[11]

If we return to the descriptions of Christopher Newman and Isabel
Archer, we see that James is drawing, if unconsciously, on some of the imagery
and references I have discussed. The first portrait is of a head in its concrete,
quantitative details; it is the American as an assemblage of physical features.
The second portrait, lacking physical details, is of personality and spirit; it is
about interior rather than exterior space, and it represents a young woman
who is reaching to express and encompass what always seems to remain out of
reach. The one is a static pose; the other, a dynamic movement. One, we could
argue, is associated with photography, the other with film.

During the height of his success in business, Christopher Newman might
well have had his portrait taken in a studio owned by the famous midcentury
photography entrepreneur Mathew Brady. At that time, Brady was making a
fortune as a portrait photographer and had exhibited his Imperial Prints
(twenty-four inches by twenty inches), as well as his full-length portraits of famous and prosperous men (including many of Lincoln) in a string of galleries
in New York and Washington.[12] By the 1870s, however, the decade in which
James sets Newman's retirement from business and his trip to Europe to acquire culture and a wife, photographic portraits of the famous no longer drew
crowds. Brady's fall from favor, what the historian Mary Panzer attributes to
the emergence of new cultural values (a change that James may have sensed in
depicting his hero's change in goals), can be explained as a shift from the stolid
face of Christopher Newman to the more elusive, restless face of Isabel Archer.
In photography, this shift was expressed in the public's loss of interest in grand
portraits of famous men and its increased interest in smaller, more personal-

Mathew Brady's photograph of Abraham Lincoln, 1864 (Culver Pictures)

ized portraits for family albums. As Panzer notes, "The family album allowed everyone to construct a private gallery and construct a different kind of national narrative."[13] One might also connect this shift in values to what Tom Gunning describes, in his discussion of the increased use of the "mug shot" in police work, as an abandonment of the phrenological notion of general criminal characteristics for the idea that each criminal is unique: "Only the unique body," notes Gunning, "imprinted with its particular, inherited physiology, and especially, its unconscious habits and adaptations to the life it has led could betray an identity which has become the produce and residue of a life history."[14] The change, then, was toward a more mobile, more individualized, and more intimate conception of character.

Film would dramatically realize this change through its clear preference for intimacy over monumentality in its representation of the face, with only the film cowboy remaining attached to the style of Brady's Imperial Portrait. It should be noted that the shift from the monumental to the intimate was in some sense a shift from the male face to the female, and I have already suggested that the face in film was primarily associated with women. A corollary to this was the emergence of the kiss as the modern expression of love. As the French critic Edgar Morin has explained, the kiss "is the triumphant symbol of the role of the face and the soul in twentieth century love."[15] Clearly, the kiss achieved this symbolic role through film's tendency to associate the facial close-up with the woman, whose conventional link to romance made kissing an inevitable part of the plot.

This gender division was certainly not absolute. Just as there were many important men, like Henry Adams, Owen Wister, Woodrow Wilson, Theodore Dreiser, and Henry and William James, who suffered the "American disease" of neurasthenia, so there would be many important male stars, as I shall discuss, whose faces would be central to their success. Nonetheless, facial expressiveness was most closely identified with women in silent films (and has continued this identification into sound films), where it complements the bodily expressiveness of men.

It is a unique attribute of film that it allows us to gaze at a face in motion for a prolonged period of time—to see the restless energy of thought and feeling play over the features. Although we look closely at each other's faces all the time, until the advent of film we did so only insofar as we were personally involved with the faces in question. Film was a revolutionary means of providing intimacy without involvement, the opportunity to gaze closely at a face without its registering awareness of being looked at. This effect can be staged (the actor knowingly performing for the camera) or it can be real (the camera hidden and the subject captured unaware). Film also has the ability to capture the mobile faces of children and animals, unique subjects who register the camera without knowing its meaning. We see this effect very early in the history of film in the Lumières' 1895 *Feeding Baby*—a disarming bit of footage, sometimes referred to as the first home movie, in which a baby, being fed by its parents, holds out its biscuit to the camera and smiles.

Perhaps the only precursor to the cinematic approach to the face can be found in the gaze directed at Helen Keller, the blind and deaf woman who became an international celebrity at the end of the nineteenth century.[16] Keller's disability placed her in the unique position of presenting a face to the world that could be looked at close up without looking back. This may account for why her performances extended beyond lecture halls and vaudeville houses to drawing rooms and other more intimate settings. The public had read about

Helen Keller, 1913 (Culver Pictures)

Keller's courage and determination through the many newspaper and magazine stories written about her, but they were not satisfied with stories; they
wanted to see her, and if possible they wanted to see her at close range.

Keller's face offered viewers the novelty of the "electric play" of her features, which would be precisely what film would routinely offer its viewers:
"The invention of printing gradually rendered illegible the faces of men,"
maintained Béla Balázs. "At present a new discovery, a new machine is at work
to turn the attention of men back to a visual culture and give them new faces."
The camera's scrutiny of the face produced "a new field of action," said Walter
Benjamin, and this was capable of creating "an entirely new formation of the
subject."[17] Both Balázs and Benjamin saw the cinematic rendering of the face
as the basis for a new conception of character.

These critics' forward-looking perspective was correct in one respect at
least: the revelation of facial expressiveness marked a definite departure from
earlier notions of representation. It challenged the centuries-old claim of litera-

ture and theology that appearances deceive, and it made possible a new vocabulary for the self based on physical performance. Paintings and even photographs had seemed to freeze the self and distill certain generalized elements of character—elements that the sitter wanted to relay (hence the idea of the "pose,"—the mannered self-presentation for the camera). And theatrical representation, though it added the element of movement, could only take physical performance so far: the face in its intimate expressiveness was out of range for most of the audience, making duplicitous behavior hard to distinguish from truthful behavior (Edmund in *King Lear* would appear to us as he appears to his brother were it not for the rhetorical devices of the aside and the soliloquy, which *tell* us what he really feels and thinks). But film could bypass these linguistic revelations and *show,* through a character's facial expression, what characters inside the film could not see. The silence of early film was crucial in establishing this effect, for the medium was forced to take advantage of the close-up in its effort to render cinematically what novels and plays had been able to do through language. Had simultaneous sound existed in films from the beginning, it is possible that this particular component of storytelling might not have developed as it did, and our notion of the relationship between character and facial expressiveness might have been different.

The first great master of the facial close-up was D. W. Griffith. Working at almost the beginning of narrative film, he created a dramaturgy for the face that is embedded in our cultural memory and has been drawn on by filmmakers ever since.

Griffith did not invent the close-up; the technique had existed since the very earliest days of the medium. *Fred Ott's Sneeze,* made at Edison's Black Maria studio in 1893, was an extended close-up. A 1902 American Mutoscope film called the *Magnifying Glass* goes haywire with close-ups as a little girl carries her magnifying glass around the house, peering at objects and people. Edison and Porter's *The Great Train Robbery* in 1903 contains that surprising shot at the end in which the sheriff faces the camera and aims his gun directly at the audience. Yet even fifteen years into the development of the medium there was still no consistency in the use of the close-up, and the technique was discouraged by early producers under the assumption that audiences paid to see the whole actor, not just his head. It took an evolution in perception, akin to the evolution that introduced perspective painting during the Renaissance, to revise this thinking and to change the facial close-up from a gimmick to an integral part of film syntax. Griffith was among the first to adopt this syntax and the first to develop from it a new, cinematically derived conception of character.

We can see Griffith laying the groundwork for a meaningful use of the close-up in his 1908 one-reel film, *After Many Years.* A man is shipwrecked on an island and looks at a locket with his wife's picture in it; the film then cuts from the island scene to a shot of the wife, waiting for her husband at home (a near duplication, taken at slightly closer range, of the earlier shot in the film of her waving good-bye to him). The scene is innovative not only as an early example of cross-cutting but also because it suggests that the image of the wife can relay more emotional meaning than an intertitle or a picture from a locket and, moreover, that emotional meaning is as central to the film's visual success as the fact-based images that make up the story.

By 1910, Griffith was making short films that had his characters communicating through looks: men staring appreciatively at women; women shyly averting their eyes or smiling slightly. By 1913, in *The Mothering Heart,* he had moved beyond the use of simple marker or single-reaction shots to an extended display of facial expressions in close-ups. Lillian Gish, who played the role of the betrayed wife in this film, recounts the running commentary that Griffith fed her during her performance: "You feel that you've been humiliated by your husband in public. You think that he doesn't love you any longer because you're carrying his child. You're afraid that he wants to get rid of you."[18] One can see by the form of this verbal instruction that facial expression was functioning rather like a Shakespearean soliloquy; it had begun to carry some of the narrative content of the film.

In *Judith of Bethulia,* made later the same year, Griffith inserted a series of shots in which Blanche Sweet as Judith looks out of the window at her suffering people, who have been trapped by an enemy siege within the walls of the city. Her face is shown first in dreamy contemplation and then in beseeching prayer. When she leaves the window and descends into the city below, her face moves from an expression of concern and anxiety to one of beatific revelation as she decides what to do. The next scene shows her preparing to seduce and kill the enemy leader, Holofernes. This narrative of facial expressiveness is an early example of how Griffith tried to make us "see [his characters] thinking"— as one fan of the period put it. "He puts his camera near the subjects and the lens and you see what is passing in the minds of the actors and actresses," commented a reporter for *Moving Picture World* as early as 1909. Griffith himself explained his aim succinctly: "The near view of the actors' lineaments conveys intimate thoughts and emotions better than can ever by conveyed by the crowded scene."[19]

In developing a dramaturgy for the face, Griffith borrowed from the two principal schools of acting that existed at the turn of the century, both of which he knew from his earlier experience on the stage. The more old-fashioned, "histrionic" school favored exaggerated, declamatory gestures—actors beating their breasts to denote grief or clenching their fists high in the air for anger. By the end of the nineteenth century, this style had become associated with low-brow tastes and figured in the cheaper theaters. It was carried over into early films, partially because the nickelodeons and store-front movie houses drew a largely uneducated audience familiar with this style and partially because the simple, coded gestures could be easily adapted to a primitive, silent medium. During the same period, however, a "naturalistic" school of acting was developing for the stage, informed by the detail and fluidity of everyday life. This style was suited to the work of more modern playwrights like Ibsen, Chekhov, and Maeterlinck and reflected a general trend toward a more quotidian realism in the arts at the end of the nineteenth century.[20]

As Griffith began to use the close-up with more logic and consistency, he discovered that the standard histrionic gestures were unnecessary and, indeed, hindered the effect that he wanted. But his response was not simply to replace histrionic with naturalistic acting. Instead, he invented a new style that took many of the elements of the naturalistic school (the tendency to modulate gestures, keep arms closer to the body, and add everyday details to the action) and wedded them to an amended version of the histrionic school as it applied specifically to the movement of the face.

What Griffith was after was the representation of intense private emotion, a goal that he had inherited from the nineteenth-century domestic novel. The novel was able to take its readers inside the head of a character and describe the private emotions and thoughts lurking there. The later scientific advocates of montage like Kulechov and Eisenstein would react against literary form by closing the faces of their actors to the expression of emotion, constructing meaning through the pure juxtaposition of images. But Griffith's aim was different. He wanted to turn the literary into the visual—to find objective correlatives for what literature could do. This constitutes his place in an American tradition associated with Emerson and Whitman, authors who had suffered under the burden of a language and literature inherited from Europe and had called for a more natural, native form of expression capable of representing the complexity of human character. The close-up was the means through which Griffith reconciled a literary concern for the subtleties of feeling and thought with a medium that favored action and spectacle.

What allowed Griffith to achieve an intensive representation of emotion was his choice of a singular type of actress, one who conformed to George Beard's definition of a specifically American psychological type: the neurasthenic girl. Griffith's heroines were all very young, some no more than fifteen or sixteen when they joined his company. But youth was not enough. He also specified that he wanted his actresses to be "nervous"; that is, he wanted them to be emotionally fragile, their feelings close to the surface and ready to spill out at the slightest provocation. Being both young and nervous, they were also, of course, enormously susceptible to the shaping influence of their director.[21]

From Griffith's first entry into filmmaking in 1908 until his forced retirement in the early 1930s, he gathered around him a group of young girls who displayed different facets of his neurasthenic ideal. Some were pixies, some were frail flowers, some were nervous butterflies; all were young and small (with the exception of the more voluptuous Blanche Sweet), with delicate features and quick expressive faces. They were enough alike to be in constant rivalry for roles, a competition that Griffith encouraged as a means of keeping them on edge and solicitous of him. Yet eventually one emerged as the fullest representation of the type and the most closely identified with him. Of all the actresses in the Griffith stable, none embodied his female ideal more completely than Lillian Gish.

Gish's personal history reads like that of many other early stars. She claimed to trace her ancestry back to before the Revolution, but her actual upbringing was a life on the edge of want and dislocation. Her father, an apparently charming ne'er-do-well, was never able to support the family. She spent her earliest years with her grandparents in Ohio, then moved to New York City after her father definitively abandoned the family, where she began a career as a child actress in theatrical touring companies. Often she toured the country alone since her mother and sister might have engagements with other companies elsewhere. She was never formally schooled and spent long and arduous hours memorizing lines and in rehearsal. In her autobiography, she claimed that her father's unpredictable behavior and his failure to make a living produced a lifelong insecurity, which she viewed as "a great gift": "It taught me to work as if everything depended on me." It also, one might add, gave her the nervous energy and desire to please that would mesh so well with Griffith's notion of the ideal film heroine.[22]

Lillian and her sister, Dorothy, were first made aware of the advantages of a film career by their friend Mary Pickford, whom they had known on the theater circuit as Gladys Smith and who had gone on to achieve prominence in Griffith's company as "the girl with the curls." Pickford explained that a movie could be a source of easy money between theater engagements and that it had advantages over the theater in allowing for a more settled existence. She arranged an audition with Griffith for her friends, and he hired them both on the spot.

Eventually, Lillian Gish would become the most valued of Griffith's actresses. Though his philosophy was to treat his performers in the same way and cast them interchangeably, she became the first among equals. He sought her advice and even allowed her to direct some of his films.[23] But her principal value for him lay in her ability to perfectly embody what he wanted on screen.

Gish was the consummate "gaga girl," as the Biograph actresses referred to the saccharine female ideal they were expected to play. She was small and fragile, with large dewy eyes, bow-tie lips, and copious blond hair. Griffith would emphasize these physical characteristics by having her dress in layered, unfashionable clothing (shawls and aprons, funny hats, and little buttoned boots); arranging her hair with romantic unkemptness; and filming her with soft lighting (in the late teens, he assigned to her her own photographer, Henrik Sartov, who developed the soft focus, "Lillian Gish" lens). But more than her appearance, Griffith came to value her physical intelligence. She moved well and seemed to understand, better than anyone else, the physical effects he was after—how a flat-footed walk or an angular arm could project guilelessness and pathos. No other actress could be quite as gracefully graceless as Lillian Gish. Most important, she had a wonderful plasticity of facial expression that Griffith would increasingly draw on as they worked together.

Gish remained with Griffith for ten years, from 1912 to 1922. Although she went on to have an extraordinarily long career, much of it on the stage, her reputation remained tied to his. This seems to have been as much a function of her own self-conception as it was imposed on her by the public and the media. The title of her autobiography, *The Movies, Mr. Griffith, and Me,* suggests a profound symbiosis that is confirmed in the reading. What the book makes clear is that the formative years Gish spent with Griffith established the shape and tenor of her personality ever after. She never married; she remained devoted to her mother and sister; and by all accounts, she never acted meanly or inappropriately, though she suffered betrayals, abuses, and losses, much as she did on the screen. Reading about Gish's life, it is impossible to determine where the characters she played left off and she herself began, which is entirely the effect that Griffith aimed at in his use of the close-up.

The effect was not achieved overnight. Griffith realized Gish's dramatic potential only gradually, as he extended and refined his use of her face. He had initiated the facial close-up in his early two-reel films, but when he moved to full-length features with *The Birth of a Nation* and *Intolerance,* the personal elements were subordinated to larger historical and philosophical themes. In *The Birth of a Nation,* Gish plays the Northern daughter, Elsie Stoneman, who, like the Little Sister (Mae Marsh) in the Southern Cameron family, is meant to dramatize Griffith's views about post–Civil War society. Despite the expressiveness of Gish's face in the scene in which she is threatened by the villain (a scene that thematically parallels the pursuit and death of the Little Sister earlier in the film), our attention is directed to the villain's abusiveness and the ramifications that follow from it; her emotion, like the Little Sister's death, is designed to justify the image of the Klan march at the end. In *Intolerance,* Griffith avoided a close-up of Gish altogether. She appears as a mother, rocking a cradle (the intertitle: "out of the cradle endlessly rocking" is from Whitman), shots of which are spliced throughout the film as it moves from one historical narrative to the other. They are middle-distance shots because their message is generic rather than particular.

But with the failure of *Intolerance,* Griffith could not afford another epic, and if only by default, his attention shifted to more circumscribed, domestic themes. *Hearts of the World,* filmed in Europe to support the war effort in 1918, spends more time focusing on the emotional state of the characters and the minutiae of their interaction than on the larger concerns of World War I that loom in the background. *Broken Blossoms,* made a year later, is also primarily a drama of private emotion. The plot centers on the pain suffered by a young girl who is abused and finally killed by her drunken father, although this focus is diluted by the subplot of the socially ostracized Chinese man who temporarily rescues the girl (a subplot that suggests that Griffith was still awkwardly seeking amends for the racial intolerance of *The Birth of a Nation*). Finally, in *True Heart Susie,* made later in 1919, all political and exotic trappings have disappeared. The balance of values has shifted entirely from the epic to the domestic. The panoramic long shot has been superseded by the close-up.

True Heart Susie is a provincial tale of the events that separate and eventually unite a young girl and boy. At the heart of the very simple, even simplistic, plot is the drama of the heroine's private emotion, made accessible to us through the artful use of the close-up. One of the first and most dramatic examples of Griffith's method in this film occurs as Gish, in the role of Susie, moves her face up to the boy (Robert Harron), expecting a kiss, while he, moving toward her at first, veers away at the last minute. This failed kiss will be repeated several times in the course of the story until it is finally consummated in the last scene. Although it has almost the quality of vaudeville business (the two heads drawing together, hovering a moment, but never quite meeting), it draws a laugh only the first time, when the characters are presented as children, com-

Lillian Gish and Robert Harron, after the failed kiss in
True Heart Susie, 1919 (Museum of Modern Art)

ing home from school. In its subsequent appearances, the failed kiss ceases to
be funny and becomes deeply moving. The emotional effect of this facial business lies in the way it dramatizes the thwarted desire of Susie as we have come
to understand it through the plot and as it is reinforced for us in the image of
the pale, quivering face and pursed lips, straining forward. No one inside the
film can see the face as we, the audience, do. No one but us can follow the repeated disappointment in not realizing that kiss.[24]

Something of the same effect is achieved in *Broken Blossoms,* which also
features a bit of business focused on the face. Gish, in the role of the abused
daughter, pulls up the corners of her lips with two fingers to appease her brutal
father when he demands that she look cheerful. This artificial smile is repeated
throughout the film and is the heroine's final gesture as she dies from her father's beating at the end. (The gesture became so famous that people greeted
Gish with it on the street, and Buster Keaton parodied it in his 1925 film *Go
West.*) As with the unconsummated kiss in *True Heart Susie,* it is the intensity of
Gish's face, given in close-up, that lifts the gesture out of the realm of theatrical
business and makes it expressive of an individual soul in pain.

Way Down East, made in 1920, was Griffith's last successful film and stands
as an extraordinary coda to the Griffith-Gish partnership. I can think of no film

Lillian Gish, reacting to the death of the baby in *Way Down East*

that approaches it in drawing so much meaning from the human face. The story is structured in two parts. In the first part, Gish's character is tricked into a false marriage by a lascivious playboy who abandons her when she tells him she is pregnant. She gives birth alone, and in a harrowing scene midway through the film, she sits in a vigil over the baby, who is sick and finally dies. *True Heart Susie* contains moments of intense emotion but does not build to an emotional climax; it simply leads us to the end of the film, where the narrative is resolved in the final, long-delayed kiss. But in *Way Down East,* the face in this central scene becomes a sustained "field of action" on which an emotional narrative slowly and deliberately unfolds. Gish is first shown in a madonna-like pose, holding her baby on her lap, fondling and kissing its little hand so that only the upper portion of her face is exposed. As the scene progresses, we see her face fully and watch it pass through a series of nervous expressions—eyes darting, mouth moving anxiously—until she sees that the baby is dead. The realization penetrates slowly: she is immobilized for a second; then her mouth opens in what looks like a macabre laugh but which turns into a silent scream; she then shakes convulsively and, finally, throws her head back in a faint.

As I describe this facial narrative, it may sound like a cartoonish demonstration of emotion—a simple throwback to the histrionic school of acting (as the failed kiss and the upturned lips in the earlier films seem to be when taken out of context). But although histrionic elements certainly figure in the scene, the effect, far from being artificial, seems excruciatingly real. By the same token, although Gish's behavior actually corresponds quite closely to clinical descriptions of hysterical fits, nothing about the scene suggests that we are watching a textbook case of hysteria.[25] Her responses seem neither artificial nor clinically formulaic but intensely private and original. In other words, the scene is moving not because it corresponds to some known idea of what intense grief is like but because it traces a narrative that seems inextricably connected with Lillian Gish, to whose face, in all its mobile distinctiveness, we have been given special access through the close-up.

The facial drama that unfolds in this scene does more than represent intense personal emotion; it also traces a journey into the full meaning of character. Griffith turns what, for a novelist, would be a descent into the self through descriptive language, into a visual performance. The face moves from half exposure to full exposure; from hysterical disbelief to horrified belief; and finally comes to rest, stripped bare of all complacency, false hope, and innocent wiles. This final state of revelation is epitomized by the character's fall into literal unconsciousness. In early silent films and in nineteenth-century stage productions, the fainting heroine was a standard shorthand for profound emotion. But Griffith's use of the convention changes it by placing it at the final point of a dramatic sequence focused on the face. It marks the moment when the actress, having exhausted her reactive repertoire, can no longer represent herself. Gish faints in *The Birth of a Nation, Hearts of the World, Orphans of the Storm,* and in an earlier scene in *Way Down East* when her seducer reveals to her that they are not married. She does one better and dies in *Broken Blossoms.* In each case, the faint (or death) comes at the end of an intense drama of facial responsiveness.

In staging such scenes, Griffith takes the idea of the still, which he employs intermittently in dramatizing the facial narrative, and extends it to its logical conclusion. The still, when used in a motion picture, is a moment that reveals the medium's source in photography. But whereas the photograph offers only one frozen moment, emblematic of an essential, enigmatic self, film's entire drive is to provide context for the still and hence make it expressive of something in particular. This was the rationale behind Lev Kuleshov's famous experiment in film montage, in which he alternated the image of a man's expressionless face with that of a bowl of soup, a corpse in a coffin, and a child with a toy.[26] Audiences concluded that the face looked hungry after the soup, sorrowful after the coffin, and joyful after the child. When the heroine faints or dies in a Griffith film, one could say that this marks a moment when the narrative play that is demonstrated by the Kuleshov experiment stops—when we are forced to abandon contextual meaning and are back on the level of the isolated photograph. When Gish faints in the film, she stops reacting (or being interpreted as reacting) and a bridge opens between the representation associated with the role and an extranarrative space beyond it. This is the space of the viewer's own meaning. It is also what we call reality.

When the real father of the baby in *Way Down East* saw his baby's "death" on screen, he responded by fainting himself, meeting Gish, as it were, at this point outside of the coordinates of the film—outside of representation. This incident may remind us of Freud's statement about neurasthenia—that it reflects a struggle to express "something unique and previously unknown, of which it would be quite impossible to give an exhaustive description." In the scene of the baby's death, Gish seems to be acting out the limit of neurasthenic expressiveness, pointing the spectator to a space that is purely personal and imaginative: "Facing an isolated face takes us out of space," wrote Balázs in what could also be a gloss on this scene, "our consciousness of space is cut out and we find ourselves in another dimension: that of physiognomy." Roland Barthes, in a similarly apt passage about the effect of the face in silent film, refers to "that moment in cinema . . . when one literally lost oneself in a human image as one would in a philtre, when the face represented a kind of absolute state of the flesh, which could be neither reached nor renounced."[27] One might translate this as saying that at such moments the face becomes an iconic essence, something akin to that monumental, all-encompassing idea of physiognomy embodied in Brady's Imperial Print (the same static idea that James, in a light-hearted way, had tried to suggest in his description of Christopher Newman).

Gish's character will faint one more time in *Way Down East*—during the ice floe sequence toward the end—but its purpose will have changed. It will now serve to place the burden of her rescue on the hero (Richard Barthelmess), who has entered the story midway through for this express purpose. The second half of the film is a countermovement to the scene of the baby's death: a conventional melodramatic plot takes over to make possible a happy ending— to bring the heroine back from the abyss of reality to the safe port of cinematic representation.

In the sense in which the narrative of the face leads out of representation to a place where actress and audience meet, one can see how Griffith, who of all the early directors worked hardest to maintain an anonymous group of repertory performers, probably did more to further the development of the star system than anyone else. The close-up, which he took beyond the simple locating and reaction shot into the realm of existential exposure, caused audiences to believe they knew the actress on the screen better even than she knew herself. It is the sense of such privileged knowledge—of intimacy gained by simply following the visual narrative of the face—that lies at the heart of the fanaticism and presumption of the fan.

Lillian Gish, rescued by Richard Barthelmess in *Way Down East* (Kobal Collection)

By the 1920s the facial narrative that Griffith pioneered had become associated with a number of male stars, Rudolph Valentino being the supreme example. Valentino's face not only came to mean something quite specific for its audience but also became an object of fanatical devotion. No male face has ever come close to producing its effect.

Where did Valentino come from? His background was vague (and was kept so intentionally by publicists), but sources suggest that he was born to an Italian family of modest means ("the beautiful gardener's boy," his detractors would later dub him), had emigrated to America while still in his teens, and had begun his career as a paid partner at one of the dance halls that were popular early in the century.[28] Such dubious occupations fed readily into the movies, and one of Valentino's first screen appearances was, appropriately, as a gigolo in a Griffith picture. Griffith did not cast him in larger roles because, he explained, "women are apt to find him too foreign-looking."[29] Yet it was a woman, the screenwriter June Mathis, who recognized his appeal and had him cast in the 1921 *Four Horsemen of the Apocalypse* for Metro, in which the famous tango scene remains an enduring Valentino moment. One tends to think of that scene in terms of Valentino's undulating body, but equally striking are the shots of his face in profile, gazing smoulderingly down at his partner. The scene launched his career, but it was not until later the same year, having moved from Metro to Paramount, that his face was used to fullest advantage in a swash-buckling orientalist fantasy entitled *The Sheik,* which turned him into a star.

Valentino's dramaturgy of the face ranks with Gish's for its charm and mesmerizing power. In *The Sheik,* he even seems to be borrowing elements from Gish's performance to suit his own. For Gish, the hair, the shawls, and the funny little hats bring into relief the intensity of her face; for him, the head-dress, the cape, and the cummerbund serve the same purpose. Gish tends to cover her lower face with her hand; Valentino smokes a cigarette, creating a haze over his delicate features. Just as she is taken over by jumpy, awkward ges-tures and facial expressions in moments of profound emotion, so he undergoes radical changes of expression at critical points in the action. Early in *The Sheik,* when he approaches the heroine (Agnes Ayres) after kidnapping her, his face suddenly takes on a look of wolfish passion and violence, eyes popping and mouth exaggeratedly leering. Whereas Gish's face is wracked with grief,

Rudolph Valentino in *The Sheik,* 1921 (Museum of Modern Art)

Valentino's is wracked with lust—evidence, the film seems to say, of the foreign and threatening side of his nature. In the end, however, he harnesses these impulses and does battle on behalf of the heroine against the rival, "bad" sheik. He succeeds in the encounter but is brought back wounded and unconscious. As with Gish in the climactic moment of the baby's death in *Way Down East,* Valentino's narrative of the face reaches its apotheosis in this final scene of unconsciousness. The heroine gazes down on his unconscious face and learns his true identity from his friend: though raised by Arabs, he is really the son of English and Spanish aristocrats. The lustful sheik and the well-bred nobleman—the alternating poles of savagery and civilization that defined the American character according to Frederick Jackson Turner—are reconciled in the unconscious figure. Ego and id, so to speak, come together where representation stops.

Most of Valentino's films incorporate a comparable scene in which he lies sick or wounded in a state of unconsciousness. The ultimate such scene occurred on the occasion of his sudden death from a perforated ulcer at the age of thirty-one. By dying, Valentino extended the facial narrative of his films, literally, into life. It seems altogether in keeping with the power of his image that his funeral featured an open casket and that his face in death was reproduced in magazines and newspapers throughout the world, unleashing an avalanche of emotion from his female fans. Mass faintings and even suicides were reported. Like the baby's father in *Way Down East,* Valentino's fans were meeting him in the extranarrative space—that "other dimension of physiognomy"—that he had helped to forge.[30]

With the coming of sound, it became possible to make the voice an adjunct to the face in the representation of character. Bogart and Brando, Hepburn and Mae West were characterized in part by the quality of their voices: the raspiness, the slurred speech, the exaggerated enunciation, and the strident nasal whine each helped to constitute a distinctive star persona. The uniqueness of the voice supported the sense that a real person occupied the role. One could even argue that the school of Method acting, as it developed in the 1940s and 1950s, carried the legacy of the silent era back to theater and from theater back to film; that is, Method speech severed all ties to the declamatory, content-oriented style of traditional theater and emphasized instead the nonlinguistic accompaniments to speech: the movement (or lack of movement) of the face and body and the unique sound and cadence of the voice. Lee Strasberg, the father of the Method in America, explained that "the actor need not imitate a human being. The actor is himself a human being and can create out

Valentino, unconscious, with Agnes Ayres and Adolphe Menjou in
The Sheik (Museum of Modern Art)

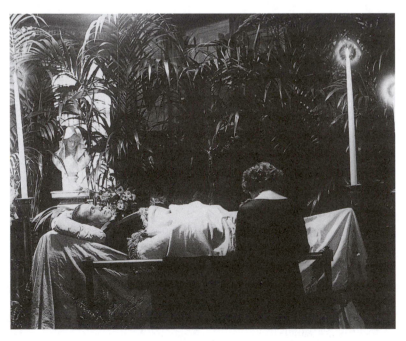

Valentino, dead, with unidentified mourner, 1926 (Kobal Collection)

of himself."[31] This philosophy gave the voice a more personalized role in representation.

But if sound expanded some aspects of the emotional effect bred out of images, it also repressed others, and it is here that so much of the pathos associated with the end of the silent era lies. Before sound, facial expressiveness evolved into a necessary part of storytelling. Griffith had concentrated on women as the vehicle for a narrative of character, following the lead of the female-centered Victorian novel, but he did not neglect male expressiveness either. Henry Walthall, Robert Harron, and Richard Barthelmess all give wonderfully moving performances in his films, and Barthelmess made several films after Griffith that focus on the expressiveness of his features in the grip of profound emotion. The most notable, *Tol'able David,* plays like a male-centered *Way Down East.*

The relationship between men and emotion would never be the same after the silent era. Valentino died before he became obsolete, but John Gilbert had to suffer the indignity of obsolescence. His celebrity had rested on his ability to speak his character through his face—for this reason, *The Big Parade* is the most intimate war movie ever made—and his failure in talking pictures had less to do with the quality of his voice than with the fact that his facial expressiveness was too extreme to accommodate sound. Less facially expressive actors like Ronald Colman and Gary Cooper were able to make the transition.

Yet despite the loss of facial expressiveness that came with sound, the dramaturgy of the face, pioneered by the silent film, remains an essential part of our inheritance. We now assume, as Griffith taught, that the face can portray the truth of character. The smile, the scowl, the smirk, the fleeting look of panic—all do more to define a presidential candidate being televised than anything in his spoken words. We may not believe the words, but we tend to believe what we see on the face as the camera captures it in its unguarded (or seemingly unguarded) moments. In movies, some facial expressiveness is still required to move the plot forward. Even the toughest contemporary male stars like Clint Eastwood and Harrison Ford are expected to show feeling on their faces in the course of their films; if they don't, we won't accept them as heroes.

By giving us access to facial expression and then developing a dramaturgy of the face, silent films gave concrete physical form to what had otherwise been seen as accessible only through language. D. W. Griffith was both the pioneer and the greatest practitioner of this dramaturgy, and Lillian Gish was the vehicle through which he worked his greatest effects. Together, they extended the "field of action" in which film operated to include the psychological and emotional terrain that had been previously demarcated from it. In doing this, they staked a claim that film would never relinquish. The sense that we can, if we pay attention, know everything about our movie stars, our politicians, and each other—that their hearts and minds are potentially available to our understanding—has its roots in the cinematic practice of the close-up, which taught us that we could know people by simply gazing at their faces.

5

THE BIRTH OF THE
STAR SYSTEM AND THE
SHAPING OF THE MODERN SELF

Why I like my favorites? I like Joan Crawford because she is so modern, so young, and so vivacious! Billie Dove is so beautifully beautiful that she just gets under your skin. She is the most beautiful woman on the screen! Sue Carol is cute 'n' peppy. Louise Brooks has her assets, those being legs 'n' a clever hair-cut. Norma Shearer wears the kind of clothes I like and is a clever actress. . . . My day-dreams instigated by the movies consist of clothes, ideas on furnishings, and manners. I don't day-dream much. I am more concerned with materialistic things and realisms."

Twenty-two-year-old college senior, 1933[1]

W HAT constitutes the self? What causes it to undergo elaboration and revision in a culture? "In or about December 1910, human character changed," Virginia Woolf pronounced in 1924.[2] She was alluding to the postimpressionist exhibition held in London on that date, suggesting that it had a far-reaching influence on those who saw it. The statement reflects the ironic vigor characteristic of Woolf's style: she uses hyperbole to emphasize both the importance of the event and its limited public appeal. But she would not have had to engage in this kind of satirical overstatement had she slightly amended her dates, crossed the Atlantic, and referred to something else as the basis for the change she had in mind—say, to the first publicity stunt surrounding a motion picture actress (Florence Lawrence in March 1910) or the first mention in print of the phrase "motion picture star" (Florence Turner in June 1910) or the first appearance of a movie star's photograph on the cover of a magazine (Mary Pickford in December 1911).[3] Had Woolf been referring to the birth of the American star system rather than to a European exhibition of highbrow art, she would have seemed less culturally refined but more accurate in connecting the event to a new shape for human character.

Admittedly, many developments—political, economic, and cultural—can be used to explain the paradigm shift that Woolf had in mind. But the rise of film and the related phenomenon of the film star represent a particularly powerful nexus for understanding the emergence of a new kind of character—the "modern" self as we tend to think of it—for the twentieth century.

Preceding page: Clara Bow, the "It" girl (Photofest)

A premodern idea of the self in Western culture can be connected to a long-standing distrust of visual appearances. Plato had maintained that what we see is a distortion of what is real and that only philosophy—reason and contemplation—can provide access to the ideal forms outside the "cave" of sensory perception. Both Judaism and Christianity supported the Platonic division of a higher, spiritual world and a lower, sensory one: "The true, literal image is the mental or spiritual one," wrote the twelfth-century Talmudic scholar Maimonides; "the improper, metaphorical image is the material shape perceived by our senses, especially the eye."[4] Even the Christian effort to connect God with material nature ("the flesh made word"; "nature as God's book") assumed that the world perceived by the senses was a temporary vestment to be cast aside or a coded language to be deciphered.

In keeping with these views, human character was traditionally believed to reflect a disjunction between worldly appearance and spiritual reality. The soul—the essence of the self—lay within and was garbed or obscured on the outside by material concerns and by the flesh. With the decline of spiritual authority in the eighteenth century, a more secular view of the self began to emerge, but it remained attached to a structure that separated "inside" from "outside." The British philosopher John Locke acknowledged that sensory experience had a direct bearing on the shape of thought, but he nonetheless retained the belief that the mind, in its highest state, could produce "ideas of sensation" and thus carry on its creative operations more or less removed from the material world.[5] Locke's emphasis on the mind in both filtering and, to some extent, imitating sensory perception made it possible for his contemporary John Addison to argue for the superiority of literary description over direct visual experience: "[W]ords, when well chosen, have so great force in them that a description often gives us more lively ideas than the sight of things themselves. The reader finds a scene drawn in stronger colors and painted more to the life in his imagination by the help of words than by an actual survey of the scene which they help to describe."[6] One sees the legacy of this thinking in the Romantic poets, who, though they glorified nature and granted an important role to sensory experience, also maintained the Lockean hierarchy, reserving their highest praise for the human imagination, the source of creativity, which alone could "build up greatest things/From least suggestions."[7]

With the rise of the novel, these ideas were applied more directly to human character. Just as imagination was seen to replace divinity as the animating force in the representation of nature for the Romantics, so individual psychology was seen to replace spiritual essence as the source of meaning in the delineation of character for their literary successors, the great nineteenth-century novelists. Characters in the work of Dostoevsky, Tolstoy, Balzac, Flaubert, the Bröntes, Dickens, and George Eliot become significant selves, not through what they do (which in an earlier, epic tradition had connected to a higher, spiritual set of meanings[8]), but through the complex, hidden motives and emotions that determine their actions. Thus Eliot's 1860 *The Mill on the Floss,* a novel that exemplifies the *bildungsroman* tradition, is a meticulous chronicle of how the developing inner life of its heroine, Maggie Tulliver, shapes her destiny. Were it not for the novel's exploration of what lies beneath the surface, Maggie's decision at the end to abandon a man who loves her in favor of her brother, whom she knows will condemn her, would seem to be simply perverse; with it, the decision becomes comprehensible and even heroic. Eliot's technique resembles Freud's, who also sought to explain the surface (or symptoms) of his patients by plumbing their depths (or unconscious), using talk and interpretation as a means of connecting inside and outside.

With the rise of film, however, the distinction between inside and outside finally gave way, and a new model for human character emerged. Film was revolutionary in emphasizing the surface of things, not as a source of duplicitous, fragmented, or coded meaning, but as a site of complete and unambiguous meaning, a place where to see was to know: "We don't 'talk' about things happening, or describe the way a thing looks: we actually show it," Griffith had boasted of movies, connecting the medium to what he called "the good old American faculty of wanting to be 'shown' things." Showing without talk meant that the image had meaning in itself and, indeed, that its meaning was purer in not having talk get in the way: "We see truth in silence," Griffith concluded.[9]

Whereas the literary representation of an internalized self had linked it to the past (since what was buried was invariably what had been constructed or implanted before), the visual dynamism of film placed a new emphasis on the self as immediate and forward-looking, formed in the "here and now," a value in motion. This change in conception corresponded to the shift that Emerson had called for when he encouraged his readers to move from static "being" to dynamic "becoming." And this change, as Emerson had anticipated, was uniquely attuned to the strengths and deficiencies of the American nation at the beginning of the twentieth century—its technological expertise and energy, as well as its lack of a usable past.

A wide array of forces and events were involved with the shift I am describing, from the popularity of John Singer Sargent's portraits of the wealthy to the development of national surveying techniques and the advent of buying on credit. But as the pressure to live in appearances and the ability to do so became greater for Americans, the movie star acted as a uniquely influential guide and impetus. Many of the changes that are associated with the 1920s—the loosening of sexual mores, the rise of the New Woman and the Corporate Man, the new interest in leisure and play, and the increased emphasis on consumerism and stylishness—can be attributed in some part to the role of the silent movie star in shaping and promoting a new, more plastic, more outer-directed sense of self.

To clarify the difference between a nineteenth-century self and a twentieth-century one, it helps to differentiate the movie star from previous forms of celebrity. Individuals have existed as objects of awe and reverence since the beginning of history, but the nineteenth century saw a new, more intensive fascination with those who had distinguished themselves in the public arena. Sarah Bernhardt, the doyenne of the Paris stage, was besieged by fans when she toured America toward the end of her life, although she had already grown old and feeble and had lost a leg to gangrene. Vaudeville and musical comedy stars Lillian Russell and Anna Held, known for their voluptuous physical appearance and the outrageous stories of their private lives, were also subject to extravagant attention, as were the boxers John L. Sullivan and Jim Corbett, who parlayed their fame into appearances on the stage after their careers in the ring were over. Helen Keller became an enormous star through the promotion of her life's story (and took to the vaudeville circuit herself), and Houdini, as the world's greatest escape artist, became the preeminent live performer, able to sell out the most prestigious theaters in New York, London, and Paris as soon as his bookings were announced. Even Teddy Roosevelt might be added to this list of nineteenth-century matinee idols: he was able to turn the presidency into a star vehicle through the circulation of colorful stories of his heroism and "bully-boy" personal style. Roosevelt may also be the first celebrity to have inspired a spinoff product, the Teddy bear, which can boast a more extended name recognition than the individual it was named for.[10]

Although the stars that emerged from the new medium of the movies had elements in common with these celebrities, they were also different in important ways. The earlier figures were larger-than-life objects of hero worship, glorified for what they had done or could do—for courage, talent, grace, or beauty. No one wanted to be Helen Keller or Houdini or Theodore Roosevelt—or even Lillian Russell—they simply wanted to share in the aura projected by their presence.[11] But the star system as it developed for movies was not about heroes and heroines but about role models and friends: "You look like my sister but she is not so pretty," wrote one fan to one of the earliest stars, Florence Lawrence, articulating quite succinctly the sense of the star as a kind of idealized family member.[12] Stage and vaudeville stars were never known by their first names: it was Miss Keller, Madame Bernhardt, Miss Adams, and Mr. Drew. But movie stars were known, as soon as they *were* known, by familiar nicknames and diminutives. Broncho Billy, Buster, Fatty, Charlie, Doug, and Little Mary are the names of beloved intimates, pets of the public imagination. (One may speculate about why the practice mutated after the coming of sound, with stars now referred to by their last names—Cagney, Bogart, Gable, Dietrich, Lombard, et al.—a form of address that suggests good pals more than emotional intimates.)

We can begin to understand the relationship of the movie star to the creation of a new kind of self if we consider how the star system evolved. As many film historians have noted, movies did not immediately generate stars. At its inception, the medium's appeal lay not in the performers but in the novelty of movement and special effects. Primitive film was a "cinema of attractions" that drew crowds for the shocks and surprises that it delivered to a mostly working-class audience, untutored in the character development that novels and "legitimate" theater offered. Thomas Edison simply commandeered his handyman, Fred Ott, to sneeze for the camera in his first film, and for his early narrative film, *The Great Train Robbery,* he circulated a handful of actors in multiple roles. Even after the advent of the nickelodeons, films were marketed for their production values and for a certain predictability in the variety of short subject matter in the program. A slapstick sketch, a chase, a boxing match, and a newsreel event like a fire might reflect a typically rounded program during this period. Before 1909, most film performers were simply hired by the day and paid a pittance for the work. They shied away from being identified in films, either because they came from such lowly backgrounds that the idea of visibility hardly occurred to them or because they came from the stage or vaudeville and saw the movies as a disreputable way of making easy money between legitimate engagements.[13]

Yet the public desire to know the performers emerged and grew steadily until, by 1910, something akin to the star system had begun to take shape. The root of the change can be traced to the advent of films in which a consistent character could be viewed over a more or less sustained period of time. The first of such films were in the western and comic categories. Max Aaronson, his name changed to William Anderson, launched the Broncho Billy series of one-reel westerns in 1910, and John Bunny, a comic precursor to Arbuckle and Chaplin, made a series of "Bunny films" during the same period. Both of these early stars used titles (e.g., *Broncho Billy and the Baby* and *Bunny's Birthday*) that identified their presence in the films.

A more elaborated sense of character began to emerge a few years later with the advent of serial films, which became popular in 1912. These were conventionalized adventure or mystery stories, generally adapted to run alongside weekly newspaper serials. They featured an active protagonist who suffered the requisite trials and tribulations before solving the mystery or saving the day. Serials like *The Adventures of Kathlyn* with Kathlyn Williams, *The Hazards of Helen* with Helen Holmes, *The Virtues of Marguerite* with Marguerite Courtot, and most famously, *The Perils of Pauline* with Pearl White, were notable for casting female leads in the action role (the IMP detective series, starring King Baggot as Detective King, was an exception) and for using the real names of the actresses for the names of the characters they played. In the case of Pearl White, the best known and most long-lasting of the "serial queens," the real and the serial name don't quite match, but the similarity between "Pearl" and "Pauline" is close enough to suggest the kind of analogical correspondence between the real and the fictional that would appear with increasing frequency in the ensuing development of the star system. It seems fitting that White was the first figure in movies to publish an autobiography.[14]

Like serials, series and specials films produced during the early teens also helped create a sustained idea of character. A series was a group of films that featured a particular actor or actress and was marketed to exhibitors as a package. Pickford's enormous stardom was built from the Little Mary series that was developed for her when Adolph Zukor gave her her own label, Artcraft, in 1913, and marketed her films independently from the rest of the Paramount program.

Specials were multiple-reel films that were exhibited over a period of days or weeks under the assumption that the public would be unwilling to watch more than one reel on one subject at a sitting. Like the serials, the specials kept a consistent character in view and were associated with a single performer. Specials, like serials, functioned in the way that serialized novels had functioned in the nineteenth-century, producing something of the same combined frustration and expectation that had made the serialized novels of Dickens so popular. But they added to the desire for more plot a desire for more image—a hunger to *see* more of a particular actor or actress.

Serials, series, and specials were piecemeal ways of giving an individual characterization a more sustained life than was common in the otherwise one- or two-reel program format. What would prove to be the more effective way of establishing a unique, recognizable character was to abandon the program format altogether and to replace it with the longer, feature-length film. When Adolph Zukor imported the Pathé production of *Queen Elizabeth,* starring

Sarah Bernhardt, in 1912 and exhibited it on its own at the fashionable Lyceum Theater, charging theater ticket prices, he hoped that the advantages of length would lure a more respectable and moneyed public to the movies. That showing, along with a similar independent showing of the Italian epic *Quo Vadis?* the same year, inspired Griffith to make *Judith of Bethulia* in four reels in 1913 (which Biograph, failing to comprehend the direction of the market, withheld from release until 1914). Finally, in 1915, having left Biograph, Griffith definitively broke the length barrier with *The Birth of a Nation,* which ran twelve reels and had ticket prices running as high as $2. The enormous, unprecedented success of *The Birth of a Nation* was proof to producers, distributors, and exhibitors that the feature film was destined to replace the one- and two-reel program package as the standard form for the medium.

The advent of the feature film solidified the star system. The earlier multi-subject programs had been designed to be shown only once before being replaced by new programs, thus giving audiences less of a chance to associate performers with particular roles. (Serials and series, as the exceptions, were unsurprisingly the site of the first stars.) Feature films stayed for as long as a week and could be viewed again and again. They also provided the time necessary for a distinctive character to be delineated. A simple action narrative like *The Great Train Robbery* conforms to a simple cause-and-effect plot: first the bandits rob the train; then they are pursued and arrested by the sheriff's posse. So formulaic are these events that the actors are interchangeable in the roles. But a longer film like *Judith of Bethulia* uses character to help precipitate action, and hence the distinctiveness of the portrayal becomes important. Judith does not simply cut off the head of Holofernes to free her people, she also pines, rants, flirts, and looks tortured with ambivalence before that culminating act. Character, in other words, is developed in the interim space between cause and effect, as we watch not only how things lead directly to a given end but also how they delay or digress from that end.[15]

When Zukor launched his Famous Players in Famous Plays series in 1912, he permitted the introduction of more complex narratives, but his series ignored the fact that the most salient feature of theatrical narrative—spoken language—was missing in silent films. With their fixed cameras and minimal editing, the Famous Player productions were mere records of stage plays. Griffith's innovation was to look to novels rather than to theater for clues to storytelling and to translate these into visual and dynamic form. His use of cross-cutting found its equivalent in novelistic shifts in scenes ("Doesn't Dickens write that way?" he asked his critics), and his use of the close-up might be compared to the literary use of description to establish character or setting. Even in his two-reel films for Biograph, Griffith placed characters in a more central position, cultivated distinctive behavioral tics (the nervous drumming of fingers or swinging of a foot), and exploited the close-up to dramatize the important role of emotion in driving the narrative forward. Audiences singled out Biograph films during the nickelodeon era largely because of what Griffith was able to do with character in twenty minutes or less.[16] In his longer films, these techniques were elaborated, establishing a centrality for character that was impossible to ignore. It is not surprising that although Griffith opposed the star system in theory—and Biograph was the last of the studios to identify its players—his films were the greatest initial impetus to the public's recognition of stars. Mary Pickford was identified by the public as "the girl with the curls" while she was working for Griffith at Biograph, and Florence Lawrence, Blanche Sweet, Mae Marsh, and Norma Talmadge had their initial impact and character delineation under Griffith, although they would go on to other studios to be promoted and to develop their identity as stars.

Movie reviews and advertisements began to mention the idea of movie acting at around 1910 (before that, actors were said to "pose" for their roles), and the star system developed at the point at which the public began to see the figures on screen as skilled performers.[17] Yet to see a concern for acting as central to the development of the star system is to miss the extent to which the audience saw the screen character as a personality that transcended or bypassed the idea of the staged performance. It was precisely the public's impression, helped by the close-up, that it had special access to the figure on the screen that constituted the star's unique appeal and that still constitutes what we think of as star power.

But if acting was not at issue in the emergence of the star system, neither was the opposing idea: that stars merely projected their "real" characters onto the screen, cutting through the flimsy packaging of the role by the unique forcefulness and distinctiveness of their personalities. This argument, still popular in some circles, assumes that an antecedent self exists behind or beneath the role. But if this were so, why did it take fifteen years after the birth of the medium for the star system to emerge? And why did so many of the great figures of nineteenth-century culture like Bernhardt, Buffalo Bill, Houdini, Isadora Duncan, and Helen Keller fail to be compelling on screen although they existed as forceful, well-delineated characters in life?

Far from being formed characters in the sense that these cultural celebrities were, most of the early screen stars were very young and unformed. Robert Harron had been an errand boy when Griffith began casting him in leading roles, and Mae Marsh was a telephone operator. Gish and Pickford began their careers when they were only sixteen, pushed into movies or onto the stage by their mothers and showing themselves to be uniquely pliable not only to maternal influence but also to the will of authoritarian directors. Fairbanks and Hart both had little experience or education before beginning careers in theater, from which they moved to film, and Chaplin and Keaton had been in music halls and vaudeville since childhood as the prelude to their film careers. These stars, in short, were not forceful characters, existing "behind" their roles; they were tabula rasae on which their roles imprinted themselves. Indeed, many stars floundered in diverse roles and genres before being helped to the characters and kinds of films for which they became known. Gloria Swanson, whose mother put her in movies at the age of fifteen, tried comedy unsuccessfully under Mack Sennett before being hired by Cecil B. DeMille, who cast her as the incarnation of glamour and gave birth to her enduring image as the ultimate "clothes horse." Harold Lloyd tried a number of variations on the Chaplin persona before Hal Roach finally fashioned him into the energetic go-getter in tight suit and glasses, in which guise he surpassed Chaplin in popularity during the 1920s. John Gilbert began his career as a frightened extra in a William S. Hart western before emerging, through a felicitous series of casting decisions, in the role of the passionate lover that would make him the highest paid star in 1926.[18]

These cases suggest that the most prominent stars to emerge during the silent period were possessed of an unusual plasticity of character and that they followed the cues of public response to shape themselves along the lines that the public wanted. Almost all had come from relatively poor backgrounds, had had no settled homes or consistent influences, and had lived from an early age in the public eye. Although the same might be said for many stage stars, movies were uniquely designed to cast these performers in roles that reinforced a particular structure and style for their personalities, and which allowed the public to fix on them a sustained and intensive gaze.

Given the fact that the stars began to be produced as individuals through their films, the public's desire to know their private lives must be set in its proper context. Although the press that sought such information is often characterized as muckraking, the truth seems to have been somewhat different. Gossip columns and in-depth profiles emerged only at a certain point in the development of the industry, and even these were less about digging *beneath* a surface than about elaborating *on* a surface.

The development of personal information on the stars was, like the movies themselves, a gradual movement to narrative form. The Kalem Company was the first to begin the identification of performers by exhibiting their photographs in the nickelodeon lobbies. Soon postcards of popular performers were being circulated, and photographic portraits, identified generically with a given studio (e.g., the Biograph Girl, the Vitagraph Boy, the IMP Girl), were publicized in trade journals and advertisements. From here followed the release of names (Edward Wagenknecht, in his nostalgic evocation of the silent era, recalls the jolt of first seeing the name of Florence Lawrence publicized with a picture title[19]), and along with names came abbreviated commentary on the personalities, kept to platitudinous adjectives like "beautiful," "winning," and "lively." A turning point in this evolution was the publication of anecdotes, or mini-narratives, involving the presumed private lives of the stars. The first, or at least the most famous, example was the false report in 1910 of the death of Florence Lawrence soon after she was lured from Biograph to IMP by the scrappy and promotion-minded Carl Laemmle. Laemmle circulated the story that Lawrence had died after being hit by a streetcar, then announced that the accident had not occurred and that Lawrence was alive and well and about to begin employment as the IMP Girl. The promotional gambit is a crude example of the way in which analogy would work in linking the private and public aspects of the star image. In this case, the "private" death and resurrection of Lawrence corresponded to what Laemmle wanted to portray as her "public" death and resurrection in the move from Biograph to IMP.[20]

In 1911, the first fan magazines were launched as the forum for a "star discourse."[21] Initially, the stories in these magazines were little more than press releases from the studios, as flat and conventionalized as the films of this period. Before 1915, for example, *Photoplay* refused to answer questions about the personal lives of the stars. But as movies grew longer and incorporated a more elaborated sense of character, the magazines loosened the parameters of their reporting, opened themselves to letters and inquiries from fans, and evolved narratives for the private lives of the stars that could be compared and contrasted with the narratives on the screen. In other words, as the film narratives grew more complex, they were correspondingly able to support more complex private narratives, which were linked to them through the creative exercise of analogy.

One of the earliest stars to connect a private narrative to her screen role was the first of the screen vamps, Theda Bara. Born Theodosia Goodman, the daughter of a Jewish tailor from Ohio, Bara had had a lackluster career in the theater before being hired by William Fox in 1914 for exotic roles like Cleopatra, Salomé, and Madame de Pompadour. In other films for Fox, Bara played a more generic sirenlike female who enticed men away from their jobs and homes into a life of sexual debauchery, then discarded them after their careers and reputations had been destroyed. For the male viewer, the moral of these films was unambiguous: avoid temptation or risk ruin. What was not so clear from the films was how the vamp herself suffered for her sins. This may account for the fascination Bara exerted over her audience despite the formulaic quality of her femme fatale roles. To capitalize on this fascination, a private narrative was constructed for her: her name was promoted as an anagram for "Arab Death"; she was given an Egyptian mother and a French father (Egyptian for mystery and exoticism, French for sophistication and sex); it was publicized that she practiced black magic and that she distilled perfume as a hobby. Also part of Bara's off-screen persona was her outspoken championship of women's rights: "The vampire that I play is the vengeance of my sex upon its exploiters," she explained. "You see, I have the face of a vampire, but the heart of a feministe."[22] It is not clear whether such remarks were generated for her or whether she came by them herself, but certainly there was no attempt to censor them. The vampire and the feminist were perfectly compatible role identities and therefore acceptable to fans and publicists alike.

Theda Bara, "Arab Death." (Photofest)

Little Mary, "America's Sweetheart" (Photofest)

A more important star who would develop more complex analogies between her screen roles and her private life was Mary Pickford. Like so many of the stars of this early period, Pickford had started on the stage as a child, encouraged by an ambitious mother and a family in need of financial support after her father's death.[23] She began working for Griffith at Biograph in 1909 when she was barely sixteen and remained with him, playing typical Griffith-style Victorian heroines, until 1911, when she was briefly lured to IMP, then Majestic, then back to Griffith, and then back to the stage before finally signing with Adolph Zukor at Paramount in 1913. In the course of these changes in employment, Pickford had begun to develop a profile as Little Mary and "the girl with the curls," but it was not until she began working for Zukor that her character took on a clear outline and she emerged as "America's sweetheart."

On a first view, Pickford seems to be the simple antithesis of the exotic seductress Theda Bara, mirroring the familiar contrast between nature and society that had been central to Turner's frontier thesis, explicitly linking the one to
the innocent American and the other to the sexually corrupt foreigner. But
Pickford's image was actually more complex than this, or perhaps one could
say that it was more in line with the more complex dialectic of Turner's thesis.
Pickford, though admittedly not sexual by any stretch (Alistair Cooke called
her the girl that every man wants for a sister), was no passive goody-goody either. Her defining role was the spunky mountain girl in the 1914 *Tess of the
Storm Country;* in the film, her friend gives birth to an illegitimate baby, and she
helps the friend by pretending that the baby is hers. The role gave Pickford the
opportunity to push beyond conventional moral boundaries without overstep-
ping them, and many of her subsequent films would follow in the same pattern:
they show her standing up for the weak and dispossessed, often at the cost of
her reputation, safety, or financial security.

Tess of the Storm Country catapulted Pickford to stardom and prepared the
public for the story that broke the same year about her negotiation with Zukor
for the highest salary in Hollywood. That negotiation had actually begun a year
earlier when Pickford was reported to have sidled up to "Papa Zukor," as she
called him, and disingenuously raised the issue of salary: "You know, Mr.
Zukor," she is reported to have said sweetly, "for years I've dreamed of making
$20,000 a year before I was twenty. And I'll be twenty very soon now." No di-
rect mention was made of the fact that her mother had overheard Zukor's sales-
men boast that they need not worry about other Paramount films because they
could be "wrapped around Mary's neck" (i.e., sold as part of a package that included hers), but as this knowledge somehow got relayed, she received her
$20,000. In 1914, after the success of *Tess,* she again demurely negotiated a
salary, this time of $104,000 a year, "more," as the newspapers ecstatically put
it, "than the President." A few years later, her fame even greater, she was
wooed by Albert E. Smith of Vitagraph for close to a million a year but backed
out at the last minute. She was offended that Smith wanted to finish the contract before showing her his new baby: "Then I'll never see it," she is said to
have pronounced, closing the door on the deal. The plot of *Tess of the Storm
Country* and these negotiations over salary, without having any similarity in
content, were analogous in form: both dramatized Pickford's willingness to risk
social approbation in battling for what she wanted while also showing her
readiness to abandon self-interest if it clashed with higher, human values.[24]

By the late teens, Pickford had established a private narrative that the public accepted and admired: she could control her own financial affairs, write a

weekly syndicated column, support female rights, and generally promote an image of energetic self-sufficiency. At the same time, she continued to be photographed in pinafores and curls, chaperoned by her mother. Unlike Theda Bara, whose independent opinions and actions were the byproduct of her "deviant" screen role, Pickford's independence was derived from her image on the screen as a feisty, mischievous, but morally upright girl-woman. "We are our own sculptors," she boasted at one point of her ability to direct the course of her career, while in the same breath extolling clean living and chastity as an extension rather than a contradiction of this idea: "No woman can be a success on the screen if she dissipates even one little bit. The slightest excess, the least giving away shows unmistakably in the face and its expression. . . . I cannot remain up at night and have my face clear and shiny."[25] Such words, which combine career savvy with a traditional concern for propriety and moral rectitude, were precisely the kind of mixed message that the public had been conditioned to expect from Little Mary.

If Pickford projected an image of femininity on the screen that found analogous expression in a private narrative, Douglas Fairbanks did the same with an image of masculinity. The practical jokes and exuberant energy that characterized Fairbanks's movie roles—first as the frenetic boy-next-door in the comic spoofs of the teens, then as the costumed adventurer, marauding through history, in the swashbucklers of the 1920s—were extended into his personal life with a completeness and intensity that would never be rivaled. Fairbanks seemed to live his life for the pleasure and convenience of the reporters and photographers who besieged him wherever he went. He was continually performing stunts or engaging in vigorous exercise of the kind featured in his films, and he embroidered his image by writing a stream of articles and books, giving interviews, hawking products, and making live appearances throughout the United States and abroad. Fairbanks was also able to rewrite his own past, concocting a history for himself that simply extended the plots of his films backward into his life. He claimed to have attended Harvard and gave himself family connections and credits that find no verification in the hand-to-mouth experiences that had brought him to the movies.[26] It seems in keeping with the constructed nature of his character that he was actually remembered by his mother as a sullen boy who "learned" to smile when he fell off a roof and saw it draw a reaction from the anxious faces of onlookers. He made the learned smile the motor of his career (the antithesis of Keaton, who learned *not* to smile in order to get more laughs). In Fairbanks's 1917 book, *Laugh and Live,* one of a series of self-help manuals that he wrote (or had ghostwritten for him to support his image), he articulated his behaviorist philosophy succinctly: "to laugh is to be happy."[27]

A particularly interesting example of the way Fairbanks's movies helped define a direction for his private life is the way in which he dealt with the color of his skin. It was far darker than that of the conventional leading men of the period and might have led scrupulous biographers to research his background and uncover the fact that his father was half Jewish. In his early roles, he simply used makeup to lighten his complexion. (In his first film, *The Lamb,* the makeup people, in a practical joke, applied the white foundation so thickly that he looked like he had been dipped in chalk.) But in his swashbucklers, he circumvented the problem more creatively by setting the films in exotic locales like South America, Spanish California, and the Middle East, where his darker appearance was in keeping with his roles. In many of these later films, his character assumes an illicit persona in which his dark skin has a costume-like effect that loses its prominence when he returns to a more establishment image— Zorro is "really" a Spanish aristocrat; the Black Pirate, a British nobleman; the Thief of Bagdad, a spiritual knight—and different clothes, lighting, and makeup help to dramatize the return. Thus, in each case, the darker "other" is employed but assimilated to something more conventionally acceptable. In his private life, Fairbanks reduplicated the dynamic of the roles by popularizing the suntan, using his dark skin to suggest that lighter skin existed underneath. Tanned skin, which he helped to make an international fad in the 1920s, became a way of normalizing a look that would otherwise have marginalized him in mainstream culture.[28]

Both Pickford and Fairbanks were adept at controlling the relationship between their screen image and their private image, but the control they exhibited was not shared by all stars. It seems fitting that just as the star system began to solidify, a crisis would erupt that would highlight difficulties inherent in its mechanism. The general view has been to see the scandals that swept the industry in the early 1920s as reflections of the hypocrisy of Hollywood image making. Yet when examined more closely, one sees that these scandals were not so much revelations of a reality behind the movies as logical spinoffs or byproducts of the movie narratives themselves. It was not that the scandalous stories jarred with the star images on the screen but that they coincided with them too closely—they set up analogies that put a new and unpalatable spin on the screen roles.

Three incidents form the nexus of the crisis: Fatty Arbuckle's alleged rape and murder of the starlet Virginia Rappe in 1921; the murder of the director William Desmond Taylor in 1922, whose name was linked with the ingenue Mary Miles Minter; and the death of the popular leading man Wallace Reid, as a result of his morphine addiction, in 1923.[29]

In the case of Reid, the addiction was the result of a dependency that developed when he injured himself during production and was given the drug by a studio doctor to keep him working. Reid was not an addict who was posing as an actor but an actor who, to function, had become an addict. What was illicit about his persona was not beneath his movie roles but was a part of the mechanism that made it possible for him to appear in a new feature every seven weeks over a seven-year period.

As with Reid, the scenario of the Arbuckle case was profoundly entwined with the fact of his movie making. Vulgar and unruly behavior was the very basis of Arbuckle's comedy, and his wild parties were extensions of his on-screen antics. Even the method in which Rappe was supposed to have been killed (her bladder ruptured as a result of his massive weight) was echoed in his films, where he often used his huge belly as a battering ram, throwing his female costars backward or crushing them under him.

Mary Miles Minter's involvement with William Desmond Taylor is another case in which the film narrative directed the private narrative. Both Minter and the comedian Mabel Normand (coincidentally, Arbuckle's frequent costar) had been linked to Taylor romantically, but Minter's involve-

Fatty Arbuckle in a typically rambunctious scene (Photofest)

ment was more shocking because she played such a demure character on the screen. But, then, her devotion to Taylor does not seem incompatible with that image. Only a year before the murder, she had been featured in *Photoplay* under the title "The Lonely Princess," which had described her as a "pure, lonely, spartan girl."[30] Minter's love for Taylor, as expressed in letters and signed photographs, was yearning, sentimental, and naive, very much in keeping with the image of innocent and lonely beauty that was projected in her films and in the fan magazines; only now, it appeared, the object of her devotion was a compulsive womanizer, drug taker, and liar (after the murder, rumors circulated that Taylor had deserted a wife and child before coming to Hollywood and that he had been carrying on simultaneous affairs not only with Normand and Minter but also with Minter's mother).

Behind the outrage at the Taylor scandal was a general sense that sexual promiscuity was rampant in Hollywood and that the confusing tangle of romantic alliances surrounding Taylor and, by extension, Minter were evidence of a gross and profound degeneracy. Again, however, it must be noted that the star romances were largely reflections in the private sphere of the movie narratives in which the stars appeared, which moved them through a continual mill of romantic plots. William S. Hart, as already noted, had the habit of proposing to his female costar at the end of each production, and when one accepted him, she remained his wife only until he began work on a new picture with a new leading lady. To change partners—or to carry on simultaneously with more than one partner—was merely to follow the cues of the films themselves.

But if the film narratives helped to suggest acts of impropriety that scandalized the public, they could also reframe and diffuse acts traditionally viewed as improper if the context happened to be right. Before the Arbuckle scandal, Fairbanks and Pickford had announced that they were divorcing their respective spouses and would marry each other. Divorce was still viewed as morally unacceptable in 1920, but in the case of Doug and Mary the expected opprobrium failed to materialize. Mary, so often entrapped by foul villains in her films, was able to depict her former husband (actor Owen Moore) as an abusive drunk and to portray Fairbanks, always the heroic boy-next-door, as her savior. Fairbanks, on his side, was seen as escaping from the restraints of a society marriage into the lively, more democratic company of Little Mary. Viewed in this way, the public not only accepted the divorce but also applauded it. *Photoplay* even featured an admiring account: "The Pickford-Fairbanks Wooing, the story of filmdom's greatest real life romance with moonlight fade-out."[31] Helping, of course, was the fact that Pickford and Fairbanks were stars of equivalent stature with complementary images. They were each too valuable

Fairbanks and Pickford on their honeymoon in a characteristic pose, 1920
(Museum of Modern Art)

alone to be cast opposite each other in the same film (though after their marriage their films were often timed for simultaneous release), but nothing could
seem more proper and inevitable than their pairing off screen.

The public's acceptance of Mary Pickford's romance and its rejection of
Mary Miles Minter's demonstrates that the crisis that swept Hollywood in the
early 1920s was less a crisis of morals than of narrative coherence. Pickford's divorce and marriage to Fairbanks were rendered unobjectionable when framed
within the master narrative of her films; Minter's involvement with Taylor, far
from being diffused by her films, threatened to assimilate them to it—to under-
mine their sunny and romantic message by incorporating a darker, more
predatory one. What the star system represented was a drive for continuity and
consistency, which supported the essential tone and moral structure of movies.
Although audiences appeared to be hungry for what lay beneath the surface,
thus encouraging fan magazine articles that promised "the truth," "the inside
story," "the most revealing interview," and so forth, their interest ultimately
was in a comforting rather than a disruptive sense of analogy between public
and private narratives. The idea of Wallace Reid's drug addiction not only

jarred with his all-American boy image but was also an uncomfortable reminder of something untoward in the sheer number of films he had made during the height of his popularity. The idea of Fatty Arbuckle's crushing of Virginia Rappe was too close to the iconography of his films to be redeemable by a jury verdict of innocence. And the unsavory romantic entanglements of the Minter-Taylor case were too suggestive of what might logically follow if one cast young women in romantic roles with predatory older men as their love interests or their directors.

In the wake of the scandals, a new organization, the Motion Picture Producers and Distributors of America (MPPDA), was formed to serve as a homeostatic mechanism for the industry: to maintain an acceptable continuity between the star narratives and the private narratives that were generated from them. Will Hays, a former postmaster general and leader of the Republican party, was chosen to head the organization, and he made as his first publicized acts the banning of all Arbuckle films (despite the fact that Arbuckle had been acquitted of all charges), the insertion of morality clauses into movie contracts, and the institution of limits on the duration of the screen kiss. If stars were to behave better off the screen, they were also to provide less of a resource for projection while they were on.

The MPPDA (also called the Hays Office) provided a formal means of enforcing continuity between public and private narratives that related to the film star. A more indirect means of enforcement was through star photography as it evolved during the 1920s.[32] The publicity photographs of stars in a variety of settings expressed the idea of a public-private continuum that the Hays Office was designed to enforce. The *still shot,* taken at the studio, usually on the set of the film in progress, associated the star with a particular vehicle. The *glamour shot,* showing the star in a characteristic pose, associated him or her with the movies in a more general way. The *posed shot* in a living room or kitchen established a link between the star's life on the screen and the narrative of life at home, thus reinforcing the idea of a sustained and continuous self. And, finally, the *candid shot,* often taken at a nightclub or restaurant, showed the star ostensibly captured unaware but still extending the narrative associated with a given personality into another realm—the world of parties and relationships that spring from stardom. All of these photographs displayed trademark characteristics that asserted their relationship to one another; the smile, the stance, even the style of clothing was similar from shot to shot, though tailored to the different contexts involved.

These photographs reversed the relationship between the still image and the moving image that existed at the origin of film. Initially, the still was the launching pad for the moving image; now, it referred back to the moving image or, rather, to the narratives produced through the moving image that had produced the star. In the same way, the idea of "posing," the term first used to describe acting in early movies, now emerged as the product of the movies themselves. In the 1920s, as an expression of this idea taken to its logical conclusion, stars began to pose *inside* their films, as if placing themselves in italics for the audience: Fairbanks, standing with his sword drawn and his hand on his hip; Valentino, staring pensively, with the smoke of his cigarette curling in front of his face; Barrymore, in magnificent profile, gazing off into the distance; Garbo, glowering enigmatically. In such cases, the poses encapsulated the entire range of narratives that had become associated with the stars, elevating them above the particular vehicles that had made their reputations. Each new appearance on the screen thus automatically referred back to an already existing image while reinforcing, or "thickening," that image in the process. The stars' self-reflexive poses within their movies also made clear their evolution into what Richard Dyer has called "intertextual constructs": they were now associated with a range of cultural practices—newspaper interviews and columns, product testimonials, special "appearances," and home movies, as well as screen roles—and these practices, far from splintering their image, unified and solidified it, producing a kind of extended multimedia text.[33]

Another development in the industry that helped make Hays's work much easier was a loosening of the parameters of acceptable behavior as a result of changes in the film plots themselves. As films grew longer and more atmospheric in the course of the 1920s, the correspondence between the movie narratives and the private narratives of their stars grew accordingly more complex and circuitous, pressing the boundaries of the idea of character into more ambiguous moral terrain. As William Everson has noted, the 1920s heroine merged the once clearly separated character types of the vamp and the good girl into a new kind of hybrid.[34] Clara Bow was an unabashedly sexy and provocative heroine, who, unlike the demonic Theda Bara, was the fortunate purveyor of what Eleanor Glyn called "It"—a euphemism for sex appeal—and this sanctioned her behavior as the party girl of Hollywood. When Adolph Zukor stated that Bow "was exactly the same off the screen as on," his remark betrayed the latitude with which the industry was willing to look on her off-screen antics.[35] (Bow's immunity to criticism would not be sustained into the sound era, when her Bronx accent became more jarring to her reputation than any of her earlier romantic improprieties.)

Very different from Bow but projecting an equal capacity for moral turpitude was Greta Garbo, another star of the 1920s who can be said to have

Greta Garbo and John Gilbert in *Flesh and the Devil,* 1927 (Photofest)

emerged as film narratives grew capable of accommodating a more complex view of character. Garbo's morally ambiguous film roles directed and sanctioned her tendency in life to attach herself to a series of leading men without ever committing herself to any one man. John Gilbert, with whom she was linked most closely, was correspondingly her most important costar, and her jilting of him at the final hour before their marriage coincided wonderfully with the mysterious capriciousness of her behavior on the screen (most notably, in her powerful, duplicitous role opposite Gilbert in the 1927 *Flesh and the Devil*). Gilbert, on his side, exhibited personal behavior equally in keeping with his roles: "The paths he followed in his daily life," remarked the director King Vidor, "were greatly influenced by the parts that some scriptwriter had written for him. When he began to read the publicity emanating from his studio which dubbed him the 'great lover,' his behavior in real life began to change accordingly." When Garbo jilted him, his melodramatic response (including a punch to Louis B. Mayer for a disparaging remark about his intended) was just the kind of thing he did regularly on the screen.[36]

The most noteworthy example of the kind of personality that came to be sanctioned with the advent of longer, more "artistic" film narratives was Valentino. It was originally imagined that Valentino's reputation might suffer from the accusation that he was "woman-made"—beginning his career as a paid dance partner, discovered for the movies by a woman screenwriter, and

The two faces of Valentino in *The Sheik* (Museum of Modern Art)

twice married to women of aggressive and allegedly lesbian tendencies. But such accusations, far from detracting from his popularity, supported it by being so compatible with the quality of romantic interaction in his films. Consider, for example, the moment in *The Sheik,* the film that made his reputation, when his character, threatening to rape the heroine, is suddenly overwhelmed by her disgust for him and shrinks away like a wounded dog. This pattern repeats itself again and again in Valentino's films: aggressive desire is shown to be the defensive manifestation of a morbid sensitivity. With the films built around such characterizations, the "pink powder puff" name-calling that was used to try to discredit Valentino with his fans had no effect: it complemented rather than contradicted his image on the screen. Of course, the most effective private act to correspond to Valentino's film narratives was his death, which one is tempted to ascribe to an inspired press agent. By dying, he took to its limit a passive receptivity to female desire, inspiring an international paroxysm of grief. Valentino had been wildly popular before his death; when he died, he was propelled into the stratosphere of eternal stardom.[37]

When the public's relationship to the stars is discussed, the tendency is to represent their fans as naive and ignorant. A theatergoer is said to bring a sophisticated understanding of role playing to the viewing experience, but a moviegoer, lacking in education and cultural sophistication, is believed to confuse fiction and reality, to lose himself or, more stereotypically, herself (since so much of the work on movie spectatorship has concentrated on female viewers) in the play of images on the screen.[38] But the distinction between the naive and the sophisticated seems to be the wrong one to use in comparing a theater and a movie audience. It would be more correct to say that theater and film generate different kinds of responsiveness not because one allows for a "truer" response to reality than the other but because the idea of the self is changed in moving from one medium to the other. Gaylyn Studlar's study of fan magazine discourse has shown that fans did not passively accept the images of the stars they liked but actively critiqued and helped to construct them, giving advice to their favorites on dating, appearance, and decisions about roles. And far from seeing the constructedness of the stars as an impediment to their pleasure, the fans acknowledged that it served their pleasure. As one fan put it in articulating her perspective on Mary Pickford, "I want Mary Pickford to stay just the way she is even though I know she really isn't a little girl. I don't want her to take the little girl away—that child is a comfort and a friend."[39]

What movie fans seemed to understand was that the stars were constructed personalities—"made" selves in a uniquely American, democratic sense. The idea can be traced to the country's pioneer history, where to move west was not so much to have room to be oneself as to have resources to re-create oneself, to reimagine oneself in accordance with the new conditions of the land. William James, who in 1875 moved from the chairmanship of Harvard's physiology department to the chairmanship of its psychology department (a succinct reflection of the American sense of proximity between body and mind), would elaborate on Emerson's notion of "becoming" in a way that seems especially relevant to the conception of life as represented by film. For James, the self did not contain a secret, hidden structure or meaning but was instead plastic and always in the process of being made. To divide experience between inside and outside, between knower and known, was, for James, the dualistic fallacy of previous (European) philosophy:

> [T]he paper seen and the seeing of it are only two names for one indivisible fact. . . . The paper is in the mind and the mind is around the paper, because paper and mind are only two names that are given later to the one experience, when, taken in a larger world of which it forms a part, its connections are traced in different directions. *To know immediately, then, or intuitively, is for mental content and object to be identical.*[40]

James's theory anticipates the operation of film, in which outward forms would correspond to inward states, or to be more accurate, where the distinction between inside and outside would cease to have meaning. In this context, the "real" self of the star does not reside in some artificially partitioned private space but is part of a continuum that runs from the movie narrative to the so-called private narrative and back again. Both, in short, are part of the "flux of experience" that constitutes the subject.

In this respect, the movie star was a new kind of role model. Again, William James, in his specifically American brand of psychology, provides a helpful gloss when he introduces the notion that feeling is the result of the expression of feeling, not the other way around: "The more closely I scrutinize my states, the more persuaded I become that whatever moods, affections, and passions I have, are . . . constituted by . . . those bodily changes we ordinarily call their expression or consequence."[41] In this respect, film was the ultimate school for the expression of emotional "states." It offered the opportunity to teach feeling through the modeling of the physical expression of feeling. Béla Balázs made this idea explicit in his championship of film as a redemptive medium: "If we look at and understand each other's faces and gestures, we not only understand, we also learn to feel each other's emotions. The gesture is not only the outward projection of emotion, it is also its initiator."[42]

But film stars were role models in a different sense as well. They offered lessons not only on how to feel but also on how to be. Previous celebrities had achieved renown through heroic actions or extraordinary talents: Teddy Roosevelt triumphed over asthma and battled outlaws in the Dakota Badlands; Helen Keller overcame the most severe physical handicaps and went on to write books and tour the world; Houdini, a poor and uneducated immigrant, engineered miraculous escapes and achieved international fame; and Bernhardt, even when old and lame, was acclaimed wherever she performed for her astonishing feats of dramatic interpretation. Movie stars, however, became famous through a generalized idea of behavior as it was distilled through a circuit of narratives. No particular action or specific talent conferred meaning on the movie star; he or she acquired meaning through the accumulation of expressions and gestures that supported a *style* of being. Daniel Boorstin, who has written on this shift in the nature of celebrity, has located the change purely in the realm of publicity. The old celebrity, he argues, was known for heroic acts; the new celebrity "is known for his well-knownness."[43] Unsurprisingly, he sees this as a loss for culture. But his analysis misses the new aspects of the self that publicity brings into view. He fails to acknowledge the values and meanings encoded in visual *style*.

Style is character that is expressing itself outside the goal of a particular action; it is the promise of action during a lull in action. Before film, such interim expression was confined to language. The most stylish characters in the theatrical tradition are Shakespeare's Beatrice and Benedict (and their successors in the works of Oscar Wilde and Noel Coward), characters who relay their personalities through the give-and-take of words. In prose fiction, Jane Austen translates the idea best; her characters are stylish to the degree that they can engage in witty repartée on the dance floor or in the drawing room. In silent films, however, where language was not available as a means of self-presentation, style became associated with visual display. It became a matter of gesture, appearance, and a relationship to physical things.

Because movie stars expressed style through visual means, elements of their style could be appropriated by their fans. This helps to explain why a modern consumer society and the phenomenon of the star system evolved together. Women, who had already been conditioned to conceive of themselves in visual terms, were obviously most susceptible to a consumerism linked to self-image, and it is not surprising that clothing, accessories, and makeup should figure among the more highly visible products derived from the star system. But many products were also associated with male stars and directed at male consumers. Douglas Fairbanks not only popularized the suntan and, with it, more vacations to tropical climates, he also brought into vogue the sports jacket and made marketable the wardrobe and implements to go with a variety of leisure sports. Cigarettes, automobiles, wine, and dining out in were all promoted through movies as expressions of style that both men and women could choose to imitate. Even divorce became a stylish commodity, available for a suitable price, once Doug and Mary had bought one.

One does not need to be a Marxist to see the lust for things that the star system helped to promote as a potentially shallow and egregious thing. America at the beginning of the twentieth century, one critical view maintains, was transformed into "a society preoccupied with consumption, with comfort and bodily well-being, with luxury, spending, and acquisition, with more goods this year than last, more next year than this."[44] Another critic has argued that movies by the 1920s had betrayed their original working-class interests, focusing on the pleasures of consumerism to divert attention from "the deadening world of production" in which the majority of the audience was mired.[45] Certainly, if we judge such a culture at face value, it may seem that the Emersonian ideals of quest and becoming that critics like Vachel Lindsay had associated with film's promise had been betrayed, reduced to escapist fantasy, shallow posturing, and an insatiable drive for more things.

But the consumerism that grew out of the star system does not require such a negative reading. For one thing, the stars were not mere placards for the display of commodities but also the embodiment of the public's deepest desires and fears, so that what the stars wore and surrounded themselves with became invested with these feelings. Mary Pickford, for example, was singled out by audiences and encouraged to cultivate her "Little Mary" persona very early in her career. She was virtually forced by her fans to maintain her long hair and little-girl dresses into her thirties. In 1925, after two less than successful pictures in which she played adult roles, she put out an "appeal" to *Photoplay* readers, asking advice on the future of her career: "I know the magazine is read by two million five hundred thousand people every month . . . and that these constitute the essence of picture patronage. So I'm taking this direct route to ask for suggestions as to the type of stories I should do." The public answered overwhelmingly that it wanted Little Mary back, so Pickford made *Little Mary Rooney,* "the tomboy of the tenements," one of her most successful films. (When, in a subsequent fit of independence, she finally bobbed her hair, her career went into definitive decline.) Douglas Fairbanks's case was similar. He was "not a cultural knick-knack handed down from above," as Alistair Cooke put it, "but an actual creation of the audience, a copy of their liveliest impulses."[46]

At a certain point, of course, studios sought to make stars, but the effort worked only if the image resonated in the public imagination. Sometimes the effects were unpredictable and hard to trace back to the studio's original intention. Joan Crawford, one of the most successful of the studio-made stars, is especially interesting in this regard since her appeal seemed to rest on a complex analogy between her status as a "made" star and the narratives of her films. In roles like *Our Dancing Daughters* and *Our Modern Maidens,* MGM promoted her as a stylish "Jazz Baby" who, after misbehaving for most of the film, finds happiness in the end in a "proper" marriage. These films are about a young woman's search for an authentic self—very much an underlying anxiety during this period, in which women were experimenting with various forms of liberation—and although in the end the heroine settles down, these movies nonetheless leave the viewer with a lingering sense of her wildness. It is as though the films were capitalizing on the very constructedness of their star's persona, raising implicit questions about the relationship between reality and artifice, freedom and constraint, even while giving ostensible support to a conventional moral code.[47]

To the extent that the stars were shaped by public consensus, the products that derived from their movies were not so much foisted on the public as recognized by it as distillations—totemic symbols—of what people wanted to be. Star iconography, as I have argued, never lost its link to the film narratives from which it was generated. Although a Jane Austen character might be a witty and charming conversationalist, this did not guarantee that he or she had a good character; on the contrary, in Austen's world, stylish repartée was often a cover for caddishness or villainy.[48] But in film, the relationship between style and character is much closer. Unlike literature, there is no place for the self to hide; as a surface medium, there is no "inside," and what you see is generally what you get. The image of the star is coded, therefore, for both style and conduct, form and content. Mary Pickford was not just a girl with golden curls but a good girl with the courage to stand up for her convictions; Clara Bow was not just a sexpot but a vital presence who could inspirit others; Valentino was not just a handsome gigolo but a passionate man susceptible to tender and benevolent feelings toward women. Not all of the star narratives were conventionally or stereotypically moral, as I have shown, but in each case the image was linked to a comprehensible notion of conduct—each was, above all, vibrantly human. With these narratives behind the images of the stars, the fans made a judgment in choosing to buy products associated with them. The choice of lipstick or of hairstyle became a metonymic choice—a choice that was coded for lifestyle, that denoted a relationship to love, to family, and to self.

Joan Crawford in *Our Dancing Daughters,* 1928 (Museum of Modern Art)

The distilled, visual nature of the star thus provided a pool of concrete elements, translated into commodities, by which the public might construct a style of self-presentation that was connected to a narrative of character. A number of feminist critics, taking a revisionary view of fan culture, have argued that fans were discriminating in their relationship to star styles, adapting what they liked about their favorites to their own personalities and budgets. The knowing tone of the fan magazine discourse suggests that its readers understood what was going on and could deconstruct the product or style under discussion even as it was sold to them. Thus a *Photoplay* piece on Gloria Swanson's new hairstyle begins: "We suspect Gloria Swanson of a conspiracy with the hairdressers. This is her newest bob. The effect is obtained by cutting the top shorter than the rest and curling it over in a soft wave." An ad in the same issue presents the case as very much in the hands of the consumer-reader: "What with wigs and cosmetics, any woman can be anything she desires to be." And another article proclaims, "It isn't what you wear, it's how you wear it."[49] In this view, the star, far from being a fetish or an escapist ideal, becomes simply a useful resource, "only relevant," as one critic puts it, "in so far as [she] relates to the spectator's own identity."[50]

In this context, the department store, where aspects of the star style could be purchased, became the equivalent for the public of what the movie screen was for the stars. The store became the site of self-creation within the parameters of a public consensus. As with so much else that film helped to inspire, the results of this consumer orientation were also incorporated back into the movies themselves, whose plots began to laud the idea of creative consumption. In a trio of enormously successful films from the late teens, *Old Wives for New, Don't Change Your Husband,* and *Why Change Your Wife?,* Cecil B. DeMille launched a new genre of romantic comedy in which men and women make themselves over through the acquisition of new clothes, an exercise regime, or a more sophisticated style of behavior. The idea in these cases is that the careful purchase and knowing use of things can redirect and reanimate the course of a life. DeMille was a master at dramatizing these stories through lavish sets and costumes (Swanson, his favorite star, was known for her wardrobe and invariably had at least one scene in a deluxe bathroom).[51] Toward the end of the silent era, films like *The Crowd* and *Sunrise* would touch on the dangers of a consumer culture, but even these films are not generalized critiques; they continue to suggest that "things," although deceptive and dangerous in some contexts, can play a positive, even redemptive role in others.

The consumerism generated by film was of special value to Americans in the first three decades of the twentieth century. A large immigrant population had deluged the cities and, lacking the skills necessary to express themselves in words, were seeking alternative routes to becoming American as quickly and efficiently as possible. Women were also poised on the brink of changing roles, and the consumerism they learned from films gave them a leverage in the marketplace that would help them to gain the vote. The stars operated as representatives and guides for these groups. In conformity with the principles of democracy, the larger the public consensus in the creation of the star, the more the star had influence over the public, and the more the public in turn asserted its expectations of the star. The result was a powerful system for both enforcing and revising values—for producing a durable and coherent national identity.

6

THE TRANSITION TO SOUND

In a film, that which we hear remains, for good or worse, inextricably fused with that which we see ... whereas, on the stage, the spoken word makes a stronger rather than a weaker impression if we are not permitted to count the hairs in Romeo's mustache.

Erwin Panofsky

One of the revelations of the talkies is the fact that the most beautiful nose in the world isn't much of an asset to an actress if she talks through it.

New York *Evening Post*[1]

FROM THE beginning, of course, silent film was not silent. First, there were the narrators who stood alongside the screen, introducing the moving images as a circus barker might introduce a fire-eater or a contortionist. Then, as narrative film developed, along came the music—the single piano accompanist or, in the movie palaces, the organ or full-scale orchestra. Given the obvious contradiction between the existence of music and the designation of "silent film," it is no wonder that a fanatical enthusiast like Vachel Lindsay would see musical accompaniment as a violation of the purity of the medium. But though purists might argue otherwise, it is hard to enjoy silent films without music; this fact alone suggests a basic disequilibrium in the system and indicates that the medium would eventually incorporate more extensive and varied kinds of sound. The door into the future had been opened from the beginning.

But music in silent films was also a bridge back in time, a link to the antecedent physical era of vaudeville. Live piano accompanists were positioned near the screens and operated in real time. They could impose their own extemporaneous scores on what they saw and make the quality of the film experience rely on the skill and imagination they brought to their playing. With live accompaniment, the films were never complete or closed works but open to that always variable element of the musician's mood and inspiration.[2]

But as the silent era progressed, music ceased to be spontaneous, and eventually it ceased to be live. It became, instead, another element that the filmmaker and the studio could control. When *The Birth of a Nation* opened in 1915 in Los Angeles, it featured an elaborate score performed by a seventy-

Preceding page: Al Jolson in *The Jazz Singer,* 1927 (Museum of Modern Art) piece orchestra. When the film was distributed throughout the country and the world, it was accompanied by printed versions of the score that had been arranged for smaller orchestras, for trios, and for solo pianos. In the 1920s, the new movie palaces were installed with "mighty Wurlitzer" organs that could perform the symphonic scores that had been written for individual films and could also produce cued sound effects: footsteps, gunshots, knocks, bells, and so on. In the mid-1920s, Warner Brothers began experimenting with the Vitaphone sound system in which long-playing records were coordinated with the length of a reel of film. In 1926, it released, with Vitaphone music, a series of shorts, newsreels, and the feature film *Don Juan*, starring John Barrymore. Finally, a year later, Warners produced *The Jazz Singer*, the film credited with ending the silent era. Since *The Jazz Singer* was "less of a 'talkie' and more of a 'singie,'" in Andrew Sarris's words, it supports the argument that sound film grew out of musical accompaniment.[3]

As the changing relationship of music to image indicates, the silent film was a fleeting moment in the history of representation that could not have been expected to endure. Walter Benjamin wrote that every art creates a demand that can be satisfied only by the development of a new art. The silent film demonstrated his thesis: its evolution plotted a course that eventually led to its own obsolescence and the triumph of a new form.[4] Late silent films, viewed retrospectively, have mannerist properties: they are slower, more pictorial, and more self-consciously artful than their predecessors. Films like Stroheim's *The Wedding March* and Murnau's *Sunrise* invoke a European artistic tradition with a directness not seen earlier. These films, brilliant though they are, also have a saturated feel, as though they had realized the full extent of their medium and were waiting for something to shake them up.

But although simultaneous sound may seem retrospectively inevitable, its delay seems so as well. A new relationship to physical reality that was proper to a democratic way of life had to develop before the addition of a more potentially elitist element could be allowed to intrude. In this scenario, silent film waged what Christian Metz describes as an "attack on speech" in order to do its work.[5] And the American public, by failing to respond to Edison's early efforts to produce talking pictures, made sure that this attack was successful. Sound films arrived only after silent films had taught the public to "see in pictures" and had created a homogeneous audience from a huge and diverse population. Sound, in this sense, was not so much a contrast or counterpoint to silence as it was an elaboration of silence. Indeed, some theorists have argued that sound film merely solidified cinematic practices that had been laid down in the silent era so that "by 1933, shooting a sound film came to mean shooting

The apotheosis of silent cinema: F. W. Murnau's *Sunrise,* with
George O'Brien and Janet Gaynor, 1927 (Museum of Modern Art)

a silent film with sound."[6] This seems an overstatement; the introduction of
sound transformed the medium, dictating the development of a new subject
matter and style. What *is* true is that the use of sound, as ingenious and sophisticated as it might be, would always remain secondary to the visual and dynamic
properties of the medium. Even today, these properties still define our sense of
the movie experience.

Given the priority of the moving image in film, it is nonetheless logical to
think of technological innovation as progress and to conceive of sound in film
as an enhancement to meaning. Only if we know silent films can we appreciate
how the addition of sound involved a loss, as well as a gain—that where meaning was extended and amplified in some areas, it was curtailed and flattened in
others. Mary Pickford, characterizing silent film as the refinement and distillation of a complex art form, pronounced that "it would have been more logical
if silent pictures had grown out of talkies instead of the other way round."[7] Indeed, there were effects of great wit and dramatic power that had to be abandoned. It is impossible, for example, to sustain in a sound film the kind of visual pun that happens in the opening shot of *Safety Last,* where Harold Lloyd

faces us on the screen, apparently prepared to be hung on the gallows, only to have the camera pull back and reveal that he is waiting for a train. It is similarly impossible to stage the kind of romantic stare—the hero virtually on top of the heroine without her knowing it—that is a hallmark of Valentino's films and makes him such an extravagantly romantic figure.

With the coming of sound, Lillian Gish's violent facial expressions became dated overnight; Mary Pickford could no longer play a little girl (she might otherwise have continued playing those parts into her fifties); and Keaton's career evaporated, having lost what William Everson described as the definition of his character—his inability to communicate with the rest of the world. Both Richard Barthelmess and John Gilbert, beautiful male stars, had their careers cut short by sound because no voice could do them justice, and Douglas Fairbanks ended his career as a swashbuckler because how could an aristocrat masquerade so well as a pirate if he had to speak? In Fairbanks's last silent film, the 1929 *The Iron Mask* (which actually appended a short spoken prologue and epilogue), the four musketeers all die and strut off into the sky together—a symbolic enactment of the end of the kind of heroism, optimism, and freedom that silent films had represented so well.

In the same year, Fairbanks made his first talking picture, *The Taming of the Shrew,* with his soon-to-be ex-wife Mary Pickford. It was the first, and last, film in which they performed together (discounting her cameo appearance as the Virgin Mary in his 1927 *The Gaucho*). Perhaps Fairbanks chose this vehicle for his sound debut because he hoped to use Shakespearean language as a protective cover, a shield against the exposure that contemporary speech might inflict on a character that had been born and enhanced in silence. But if he wanted to ease the transition into talking pictures, the effort was not successful. Much has been made of Pickford's difficulty with the Shakespearean dialogue in the film; the performance so demoralized her that it effectively ended her career, as well as her marriage. But the figure of greater pathos, to my mind, is Fairbanks. Speech weighs down his character. Though he speaks his lines well and shows energy and enthusiasm in the role, there is a heaviness to his presence that had not been there before. The easy oscillation between states of being and the sense of infinite possibility and unrestricted action are gone; for the first time in his career, he looks his age. It is as though the specter of a European literary tradition that had been temporarily exorcised from American films had returned (and Shakespeare, even with "additional dialogue by Samuel Taylor," brings the point home). Indeed, one could say that talking pictures not only saddled Douglas Fairbanks with a mortality that, in silent films, he had seemed to exist without but also extended that mortal coil to the country for whom

Fairbanks and Pickford in *The Taming of the Shrew,* 1929 (Museum of Modern Art)

Fairbanks had served as the embodied symbol. It was as though America had finally acquired the burden of history that it, too, for so long had seemed to exist without.

Fairbanks would declare that the "romance of movie-making" ended with the coming of sound, but his remark significantly avoids the issue of cause and effect.[8] Was it a technological change that precipitated a conceptual change or a conceptual change that made necessary a technological one? It is impossible to say; the two go hand in hand. The silent era coincided with what F. Scott Fitzgerald christened "the Jazz Age"; its termination was marked by the stock market crash, when a new kind of austerity and realism pervaded the nation. One of the last films of the silent period was King Vidor's *The Crowd,* a wistful evocation of the sacrifices and suffering that the new, urban culture had brought into being. *The Crowd* is as depressing in its tone as *The Birth of a Nation* is uplifting (that is, when it is not insulting), as if, along with the death of the child that marks the end of optimism for the young couple in the film, it were also mourning the end of an era in which such painful realities were excluded from representation. Yet if we turn to the first "breakthrough" talking picture, *The Jazz Singer,* we see the aggressive ambition and gritty social realism, which

The Crowd had made a source of tragedy, transformed into a source of energy and delight. It is a truly new beginning.

The Jazz Singer is an extraordinary film. Whereas most early talkies are dull exercises in sound, this one is vibrant and engrossing, still somehow capable of relaying the electrifying effect it had when first shown. The film is really only a partial talkie, and perhaps this is the source of its power. It begins as a silent film, then moves into speech and song, then moves back into silence, and so on, re-creating again and again its position on the cusp of two worlds.[9]

In moving between silence and sound, between the past and the future, the film also weaves its plot into its form. The movie is about an immigrant Jewish boy, expected to follow in his father's footsteps as a cantor, who runs away to pursue a career as a jazz singer on the vaudeville stage. The film matches its shifts from silence to sound with the two alternative worlds that were competing for the boy's allegiance. The sequences that involve his life in his family are mostly silent, with intertitles; the sequences that take place in the clubs and vaudeville halls are synchronized for talk and song. "Who will own Jakie Rabinowitz?" the film seems to ask—or, put another way, "Will the boy's voice be silent in American culture or will it speak and sing as an American?" The first time Jakie bursts into song (he's still a kid in this early scene and has snuck into a neighborhood speakeasy), we can feel the shock of sound as it rips through the fabric of the film. In the next sequence in which he sings, this time as the

Al Jolson in blackface, torn between worlds: his mother, Eugenie Besserer, and his girlfriend, May McAvoy in *The Jazz Singer* (Everett Collection)

adult "Jack Robin," he responds to the applause with the historic lines "Wait a minute, wait a minute, you ain't heard nothin' yet," and we know that the choice has been made, both for the character and for the medium.

One understands why, with the release of this film, there was no turning back. In its dramatic framing of sound by silence and in the staccato pulses of the sound when it comes, syncopated so wonderfully with the movement of Jolson's limbs and features, the potential for a new kind of expressiveness is too dramatically rendered to be denied. One feels that the film is not simply adding sound but also giving birth to it. Jolson is as awkward in his energy as Fairbanks was graceful; he has a face that is odd and overeager, not beautiful and polished like the silent stars, but his bursts of talk and song seem due less to technological innovation than to some inner compulsion to break out of silence, much as his character feels compelled to break out of his father's household into a larger, freer life. Robert E. Sherwood, the cultural critic always ready with a pithy comment on the mood of the moment, described Jolson's effect as the triumph of energy over beauty: "[W]hen Al Jolson starts to sing . . . well, bring on your super-spectacles, your million-dollar thrills, your long shots of Calvary against a setting sun, your close-ups of a glycerine tear on Norma Talmadge's cheek—I'll trade them all for one instant of any ham song that Al cares to put over, and the hammier it is, the better I'll like it."[10]

The Jazz Singer is about the Jewish immigrant who is taking the next lurch forward. Houdini broke with his father's world through the athletic use of his body; the immigrant entrepreneurs Laemmle, Fox, and Zukor made the break by producing moving images; now, Samuel Warner, one of a group of entrepreneurial brothers, did so with language and song. Sound was the means that Sam Warner used to get an edge on the more entrenched competition. Born in America and brought up in Youngstown, Ohio, he was more comfortable with the language of American life than the ghettoized immigrants who created the industry. For him, it was not enough to look American; one had to sound it too.[11]

The use of sound as an expression of the hero's drive to assimilate is supported by his use of blackface at pivotal moments in the film.[12] Jack Robin sings in blackface when he has finally made it into a Broadway show. These numbers bring him acclaim from the public and the love of a non-Jewish girl; by putting on the face of the black outsider, he becomes an insider. The maneuver recalls Fairbanks's popularizing of the suntan as a way to normalize his appearance, of suggesting that he was "whiter" beneath the tanned surface than he actually was. But the cases are also different. The blackface mask is an artificial disguise, whereas the suntan is a fashionable and seemingly natural extension of the self. The putting on and taking off of blackface makeup is shown in the film as a messy and time-consuming process, whereas blackface for Fairbanks is artfully blended into his persona. The difference brings us back to the difference between moving images with sound and moving images without them. Whereas in the silent film, characters could move seamlessly from one state to another, in the sound film, meaning becomes less fluid, more fully anchored in place. Jakie Rabinowitz must break with the past to become Jack Robin; the oscillation that Fairbanks and William S. Hart made possible between two sets of loyalties can no longer be sustained. Moreover, with the coming of sound, film itself acquired a history through which it could reerect the dualities of past and present, inside and outside, that silent film had been able to erase. The sound film abandons the silent film in the way Jake abandons his ethnic identity, but the earlier form still resides like a palimpsest behind the later one in the way Jack's Jewishness resides behind the cover of his blackface mask. By acquiring a history, the sound film ceases to exist in the present to the extent that the silent film did. It no longer fulfills as completely the Emersonian dream of flux and becoming that had been possible when moving images were wordless and free of the past.

Much of the charm of *The Jazz Singer* lies in its awkwardness. Despite its clear opting for the future, it remains tied to the past. This awkwardness of divided loyalty would remain during the early sound era as films continued to be made as part sound and part silent ("goat glands," as the public called them) or as silent films with sound affixed later. Even after the transition was complete and theaters had been thoroughly wired for sound, there was a period in which difficulty with the technology entailed a less mobile camera and a predilection for static "teacup dramas."[13] Favored genres were courtroom dramas and musicals, and these were often hardly more than filmed theater productions, throwbacks of a sort to Zukor's Famous Players series. One notable exception in the area of screen musicals was the work of the choreographer and director Busby Berkeley. Though theater-trained, Berkeley went to work for Samuel Goldwyn in 1930 without ever looking back. His musical spectaculars, which used extreme camera angles and wildly elaborate montage sequences, reflect how, even in so sound-dominant a genre, visual elements could gain predominance when the filmmaker thought in cinematic terms.[14]

One of the paradoxical aspects of the early sound film was the way it made use of America's minorities, groups who had been absent from or at least undiscernible in silent films. Ethnic types with accents, particularly Jewish, Italian, and Irish, were soon used in bit parts to lend local color and humor. What is unclear is the degree to which "giving voice" to minorities helped or hindered their progress in mainstream America. Since they tended to occupy the secondary, character roles and to exist in simplified, often buffoonish guises, it could well be argued that these roles merely reinforced or, worse, elaborated negative ethnic stereotypes and made it harder for those who spoke with an accent to be taken seriously. A dubiously positive result of these films may have been their inspiration to ethnic groups to improve their English vocabulary and elocution; elocution lessons were popular in the late 1920s and 1930s not just for silent stars who were trying to make the transition to talkies but also for first- and second-generation Americans who wished to rise in the workplace. As has been discussed, the desirability of moving out of a ghettoized identity into a mainstream, assimilated one was hardly questioned during this period, and even the lovable stereotypes—the affable Jewish merchant or Irish cop— were present in films to mark a place that ethnic viewers were seeking to put behind them.

For blacks the case was more complicated. African Americans were hired for roles as maids and butlers and for specialized song-and-dance numbers. (The influence of African-American music had penetrated all facets of the American musical scene by this period.[15]) But film as a visual medium could not ignore or erase the characteristic of color, and, indeed, the advent of Technicolor films only made this fact more inescapable by lending discernible gradations to the idea of blackness. Blacks had been largely unrepresented in mainstream silent films—either absent from the story, and thus left undefined, or played by whites so that the artifice of their representation was clearly visible and need not be taken too seriously. This has always struck me as a mitigating factor in the horrendous representation of blacks in *The Birth of a Nation*: the black villains are so clearly *not* African American. With the appearance of black performers and the addition of their voices in sound films, the illusion of reality was more vivid and the insidious effects on a gullible audience that much greater. The most popular black star of the early talkies was Stepin Fetchit, who portrayed the comic black stereotype derived from the minstrel tradition that had featured whites in blackface. The stereotype was of a cunning simpleton whose laziness was both natural and highly self-serving. The contradictions in the stereotype tell something about the multiple ideological functions that the African American was expected to play in the culture. But for all the obvious broadness and paradox of the characterization, Fetchit looked like a genuine expression of racial character by being a "real" black man, speaking with his own "real" voice. Historians of race consciousness have recently begun to excavate the feelings that that representation evoked in the African-American community—its enduring legacy of shame alongside the sense, never entirely lost to black audiences, that Stepin Fetchit was a brilliant if tragic performer.[16]

Sound also produced a strange mix of panic and elation with respect to an international audience. For some, the prospect of sound meant the end of film as a universal language and the destruction of its potential as an art form. Opponents to the talkies were legion, including not only silent stars and directors but also European critics and intellectuals like Rudolph Arnheim and Béla Balázs, who found their theories of visual representation undermined by the addition of this new, unwieldy element. The most visceral negative reaction may have come from the British writer Aldous Huxley, who made clear his sense that sound was a vulgarizing addition to the medium: "My flesh crept as the loud speaker poured out those sodden words, that greasy, sagging melody."[17]

For others, however, the addition of sound merely extended the universal language of cinema to include American English: "In as much as the introduction of American films into Europe has resulted in Europeans wearing American hats and shoes and almost everything else," stated the producer brother to Cecil, William C. DeMille, "so we may be sure that in a couple of generations from now, all Europeans will be speaking English so that they may continue to see and understand American films."[18] Though deMille's statement has been proven largely correct, the initial efforts of the industry were less to foist American English on a world audience than to retrofit the American product by creating multiple language productions—that is, filming with actors who could speak several languages or refilming a Hollywood movie abroad with native actors. When multiple language productions proved financially unsustainable, the industry took to dubbing and subtitling.

It must be said, however, that the advent of talking pictures, at least for the short term, curtailed rather than extended American influence abroad. Sound created a new impetus for the growth of national cinemas that had been unable to compete with the high production values and broad appeal of American silent films. What is interesting here is the way in which many European countries, especially France, were able to use sound as a means of striking out against American cultural imperialism and as a rallying cry for their own sense of cultural superiority. French critics formed a League of Silence, which proclaimed that "Americans should not imagine that in addition to having to swallow their films we will have to put up with their language or be forced to learn it if we are to understand their new movies." (If the French have since reversed themselves and helped to produce an appreciative literature on classic Hollywood cinema, the same basic sentiment continues to be expressed in their opposition to McDonalds and EuroDisney.) British opposition was characteristically less sweeping, but there was concern from the beginning that the British public would have to be subjected, as one critic put it, to the "nasal twang of the Yankee" and that Americanisms would infect the language.[19]

Here, then, was a curious illustration of the evolution of American influence. In the nineteenth century, Europeans had scorned the American "nasal twang" (or what Whitman more poetically termed its "barbaric yawp") but had seen its effect on them as negligible. Now, with the power of the movies behind it, that "yawp" seemed truly threatening and required the mobilization of sophisticated forms of resistance to keep it at bay. It seems ironic that it was now language that would bring European intellectuals to the fore to fight film as a debased form of cultural expression. During the silent era, movies were believed to know their place, not presuming to invade the verbal and literary arena traditionally occupied by European high culture. With the advent of sound, they were encroaching on the precincts of theater and literature and, according to the intelligentsia of other countries (and to some in America as well), demeaning that legacy in the process.

The integration of speech into film had its own evolutionary history. In the early 1930s, there remained a tendency to favor a fast-talking, staccato style of speech—talk proclaiming itself to be talk and seeming to race against the moving image—that we associate with early Warners' sound stars like Lee Tracy, James Cagney, and Pat O'Brian. Eventually, however, what Erwin Panofsky termed "the principle of coexpressibility" was achieved—an integration in which "the acoustic component is not detachable from the visual."[20] Panofsky saw coexpressibility as the ideal, but in the best sound films, it seems to me, there is always a certain tension between speech and dynamic image that makes us vaguely conscious of the artifice of the connection. The result is a kind of Brechtian distancing: we "hear" the film being constructed, the sound being affixed to the dynamic visuals, but we suspend our disbelief in part out of respect for the artistry involved in the construction. This is true in Preston Sturges's films, where the dialogue is faintly suggestive of theater dialogue without ever crossing the line and seeming theatrical; in Hitchcock's films, where talk has an oddly inflected quality that makes us remember that Hitchcock began in the silent era and might be evoking the music that accompanied moving images of that period; and in John Ford's films, where the slightly stilted quality of his characters' speech produces a sense of both elemental expression and crafted scripting. In most talking pictures, however, Panofsky's ideal of coexpressibility has perhaps been too well achieved, and the result seems more natural but less artful, as though the films were engaging in a too-complete repression of their past. One of the wonderful things about the silent film was that it never allowed its audiences to forget its artifice. It was a different world; one crossed a threshold to enter it. The sound film encourages us to forget this.

Of course, it is always possible to struggle against such forgetfulness. An alert media observer can see the fissures and seams in even the slickest representation and can glimpse the outline of the past civilization that was silent film in many present forms of cultural expression. Video games, with their frenetic movement and repetitive musical accompaniment, are reminiscent of the early silent chases. Television advertising, with its reliance on compact visual messages and intertitle-like promotional inserts, carries the skeleton of a silent esthetic. American comedy continues to emphasize physical stunts, with Jim Carrey a postmodern hybrid of Harold Lloyd and Buster Keaton. And the American action film invariably contains long sequences of action without words. It is worth noting that the heir to the American action hero may now be an Asian star, Jackie Chan, whose stunts are more extravagant and whose talk more parsimonious than that of his American counterparts. Poor dubbing or even no dubbing at all hardly impairs the effect. Is Jackie Chan the new Douglas Fairbanks? China is certainly poised for global power in the way America was at the turn of the twentieth century, and Chan's films may be the harbinger of a shift in control of the medium.

Yet despite the focus on action over words in many contemporary films, even the most visually stunning and action-packed cannot relay the effect of a silent film. In a sound film, silence is always framed by talk; we know that silence marks a passage of special intensity and that an explanation will be forthcoming eventually. Even if we don't understand or particularly listen to the explanation—as is the case in so many routine action films—the sound of voices in conversation punctures the illusion and brings us back to a more workaday world. When film was made without spoken language, this did not occur and the film was sustained at a higher emotional pitch.

It is an attribute of silent films that they look odd, primitive, and uninviting until one grants them full attention and gives them time to do their work. Once that occurs, the effect is intensely compelling. These films are strange and familiar at the same time. They produce the impression of something one may have known or seen already but forgotten. I think this is because silent films are our cultural unconscious. The dynamic combination of body, landscape, and face may now be overlaid with words, but these elements were the raw materials for the realization of the American myth on the screen and for the forging of an American self off it. However our sense of national and personal identity

Douglas Fairbanks in *His Majesty, the American,* 1919 (Museum of Modern Art)

Jackie Chan in *Rush Hour,* 1998 (New Line Cinema, Kobal Collection)

may since have been revised or critiqued, the silent film was the communal starting point. Like America itself, it seemed to be a new beginning.

This is what makes the recent availability of silent films on videotape so exciting. I can think of no other representational form once so fundamental to a culture that disappeared so entirely and then so magically appeared again. Although we may discover lost stashes of paintings or musical scores or books by neglected authors—whole traditions such as those of nineteenth-century women's novels or early twentieth-century African-American poetry—in each case we are dealing with fragments of a larger cultural tradition with which we are already familiar. But the silent film was a lost world, complete and self-sufficient, and to suddenly have it appear like Atlantis from the waves is to have recourse to a part of our cultural past that had been available to us nowhere else.

Vachel Lindsay, in lauding the democratic potential of the silent film, asserted that it penetrated into all manner of lives—the wild and the sedate, the quick and the dull: "There is not a civilized or half-civilized individual in this land but may read the Whitmanesque message in time, if only it is put on the films with power."[21] We can add to Lindsay's idea of the medium's influence across space an idea of its influence across time. Silent films can now penetrate into their own future if we, who are their future, care to look.

EPILOGUE

CROWDS LINED THE STREETS and the rooftops as a magnificent cortege carried the coffin, strewn with flowers, across the city. As the world mourned the loss of one so young, so beautiful, and so beloved, reports on the minutest details of the death continued to dominate the news for weeks, even months, afterward. It was, one commentator noted, "the most widely witnessed event in history." "It changed the emotional landscape," pronounced another.[1]

No doubt readers of this book will assume I am referring to the death in August 1926 of Rudolph Valentino. That funeral featured a twelve-car cortege with a motorcycle escort down Broadway, with crowds crying, "Good-by Rudy!" while battalions of patrolmen and mounted police lined the curb to prevent "grief riots." Across the world, the public wept, fainted, and even attempted suicide: in London, a housewife killed herself, clutching a sheaf of Valentino photographs; in Japan, two girls held hands and jumped into a volcano.[2]

But the death I have in mind did not take place in August 1926 but in August 1997. The funeral was not for Rudolph Valentino, the Hollywood star of *The Sheik,* who was "catnip to women," but for Lady Diana Spencer, Princess of Wales, descendent of an ancient lineage and mother of the heir to the British throne. With seventy years, an ocean, and a vast class divide between them, the scenes following their deaths were basically the same.

The striking resemblance between these two events will round out and finalize my thesis. It has been my contention that silent films, by dynamically combining the images of body, landscape, and face, made possible the triumph of the American myth of self-creation in the twentieth century and that these films' ability to dramatically represent and disseminate that myth affected not just Americans but people everywhere, including America's progenitors and rivals, the Europeans. "By the time of her death, [Diana] was a subject of intense fascination because of the woman she had become on her own," declared *Newsweek* reporter Barbara Kantrowitz. "Through Diana, [the people] saw their own troubled selves in a quest for self-improvement," wrote Warren Hoge of the *New York Times.* "Diana is an excellent role model as to how women can empower themselves and not be browbeaten," pronounced a British broadcaster.[3] What must strike us in such a statements is how fully they accept the desirability of the American myth as the right one for everyone, in-

Preceding page: Valentino funeral, New York City, August 1926 (Kobal Collection)

cluding British royalty. Even a princess, these statements suggest, should be able to pursue her own desires and shape herself according to her own needs.

Diana Spencer's short life in the public eye can be seen as an extension of the photograph discussed at the beginning of this book. That photograph, taken in England in the 1920s, features Douglas Fairbanks and Mary Pickford with their British aristocratic friends Lord and Lady Mountbatten (this is the same Lord Mountbatten, by the way, whose death fifty years later at the hands of Irish Republican Army terrorists so devastated his favorite grandnephew, Prince Charles, that it propelled him into his too-hasty marriage to Diana[4]). In discussing that photograph, I postulated the beginning of a change in traditional notions of precedence. The surface elements associated with the stars—their easy grins, their agility in performing the stunt, and their stylish appearance—gave them an appeal missing in their aristocratic hosts.

What I saw as a graphic hint in the photograph would spread and overtake the royal family in ways they could hardly have anticipated. Diana did more than imitate an American movie star's stunt; she adopted an entire way of being that American movie stars had helped to define and popularize. In doing so, she eclipsed her husband, the future king of England, and came close to toppling the institution of the British monarchy itself. Diana's life and untimely death encapsulated the shift from a past based on inherited ideas of propriety and tradition to a present in which energy, enthusiasm, and style were paramount values. It seems perfectly in keeping with this shift that the commemorative song at Diana's funeral, written by her friend, celebrity songwriter Elton John, should be a revision of a song originally written about that consummate American movie star, Marilyn Monroe.

Princess Diana seems an especially apt figure to conclude this study because she possessed so many of the characteristics of the great silent stars. More than the movie star today, more even than Monroe, whose sexy voice was so much a part of her image, Diana's persona was built out of visual elements with intertitle-like accompaniments (photo spreads with captions or film footage with voice-over commentary). Her effect was very much a function of the dynamic interplay of those elements of body, landscape, and face that were so central to the silent film. Her tall, lean figure, draped in fashionable outfits, was a constant source of fascination to the public ("a few thousand tourists watched the changing of the Guard at Buckingham Palace," observed a British journalist; "a whole world watched the changing of Diana's clothes"[5]), and the scrutiny of her body was even greater in light of claims that she had suffered from anorexia as part of the depressive effects of her marriage. She was continually shown posed or moving within suitably dramatic landscapes—extrava-

Princess Diana, a contemporary silent star, 1985 (Photofest)

gant royal settings on the one hand and hospitals, refugee camps, and other sites of suffering or deprivation on the other (candid shots of her "off-duty" life showed her in blue jeans, relaxing in the British countryside). Most of all, the camera loved her face. Close-ups of her melancholy side glances and wistful smiles made the public feel it knew her better than her husband did.

Like the silent stars, the images that film and photography afforded Diana allowed her to incorporate multiple, seemingly contradictory roles. Her ever-changing wardrobe reflected both her enjoyment of traditional notions of feminine beauty and her independence as a creative consumer and promoter of her nation's fashion industry, a role that Gloria Swanson had pioneered in De-Mille's films three-quarters of a century earlier. Her appearance in alternating landscapes of opulence and deprivation projected a connection between rich and poor and strong and weak that recalled the oscillating landscapes of the Fairbanks swashbuckler. The sense that her natural habitat was unsullied nature gave her the kind of moral force that William S. Hart had brought to his roles. Finally, her face in its vulnerability was reminiscent of the nervous expressiveness of Lillian Gish while also following in the tradition of Mary Pickford, whose fragility had belied a steely determination to stand up for what she wanted—and Diana's mother-in-law was an antagonist quite as formidable as Adolph Zukor.[6]

In the end, the huge outcry that paparazzi might have caused her death can be compared to the sex and drug scandals that hit Hollywood during the early 1920s. Then, the movies that had helped to forge a shared public morality were condemned for being immoral. Now, the media that had made Diana into "the people's princess" through their intensive coverage of her trials and tribulations was condemned for unseemly prying. The crisis in both cases was related less to content than to form. It reflected a need to recalibrate the relationship between public and private, to reassert the compatibility of democratic consensus and individual self-assertion that are the twin strands of the American myth. Far from discrediting the myth, the death of Diana merely dramatized its pervasive acceptance by the world at large. For it is now assumed to be society's responsibility to assist the individual in the act of self-creation, even if it means jettisoning one thousand years of British royal tradition in the process. The frontier now extends into the halls of the royal palace. Just as the movies had been charged to do a better job of guiding the public after the scandals of the 1920s, so the media, that outgrowth and expansion of the movies in the postmodern age, has been charged with the same task after Diana's death. The promise that Diana embodied and that her death publicized so extravagantly was the promise of the American myth, still very much alive, to which silent films first gave dynamic visual form and disseminated to a mass audience.

NOTES

Introduction

1. *Mountbatten: Eighty Years in Pictures,* 106.

2. Much of the best material on the American silent film was written two or more decades ago, some by writers who experienced the era firsthand. These include Terry Ramsaye, *A Million and One Nights;* Lewis Jacobs, *The Rise of American Film;* Benjamin B. Hampton, *History of the American Film Industry from its Beginnings to 1931;* the chapters on American film in Paul Rotha and Richard Griffith, *The Film Till Now: A Survey of World Cinema* (Rotha's portion originally published in 1930); Daniel Blum, *A Pictorial History of the Silent Screen;* Kevin Brownlow, *The Parade's Gone By . . . ;* William K. Everson, *American Silent Film;* and part I of Walter Kerr, *The Silent Clowns.* Everson's and Kerr's books are especially intelligent and readable. Kerr draws eloquently on personal recollections of the era, as does Edward Wagenknecht in *The Movies in the Age of Innocence* and James Card in *Seductive Cinema: the Art of Silent Film.* Wagenknecht, a literary critic by vocation, is a delightful stylist, and Card is interesting in being so cranky about professors who have "viciously savaged" old movies—who "bat the texts around, toss them like a cat destroying its prey, breaking their spines, tearing out their throats and leaving their corpses alone after the blood stopped flowing" (297). His words have been a warning to me while writing this book.

For more recent scholarship on the era, see the first three volumes of *The History of Cinema* series (Berkeley: University of California Press): Charles Musser, *The Emergence of Cinema;* Eileen Bowser, *The Transformation of Cinema, 1907–1915;* and Richard Koszarski, *An Evening's Entertainment.* Each volume is exhaustive in all aspects of its subject and contains extensive notes and bibliography. Another recent treatment of the era is Jeanine Basinger's sprightly *Silent Stars.*

The amazing growth of film in America is dramatized by the attendance figures some of these books report: 1905 saw the emergence of the first nickelodeons; by 1910, 10,000 were in operation, attracting up to 80 million patrons a week. The figures showing the dominance of American films worldwide during the teens are even more dramatic: by 1915, 60% of American films were made in Hollywood; by 1918, 80% of the world's films were made there.

3. R. W. B. Lewis, *The American Adam,* 5. Note that the values promoted by Crève-coeur and Jefferson were also expressed in a more lively and personalized way by the most successful of the country's early diplomats, Benjamin Franklin, a man of wit and practical know-how who exuded a simplicity, sometimes bordering on clownishness, that supported his unique identity as an American for a European audience. See Robert Jay Lifton, *The Protean Self,* 34, on Franklin's American qualities and on American "proteanism"—his term for the American myth.

4. Alexis de Tocqueville, *Democracy in America,* Vol. 2, 80–81. For the classic discussion of the American myth, see, along with Lewis, *The American Adam,* Henry Nash Smith, *Virgin Land* and Leo Marx, *The Machine in the Garden.* For more recent critical views on the subject, see Philip Fisher, *The New American Studies* and James R. Grossman, *The Frontier in American Culture.* Fisher's more recent *Still the New World,* which argues that the creative destruction of difference is a driving force in American culture, seems to come closer to my view, although he is more critical than I am of this national drive. I will discuss the disparity between older and newer approaches to the myth later in the introduction and in chapter 3 with regard to Frederick Jackson Turner.

5. V. I. Pudovkin, *On Film Technique,* 16.

6. Siegfried Kracauer, *Theory of Film,* 303. Walter Benjamin, "The Work of Art in the Age of Mechanical Reproduction." See Irving Singer, *Reality Transformed,* for an interesting analysis and synthesis of the formalist/realist debate.

7. Vachel Lindsay, *The Art of the Moving Picture,* 315–16. Élie Faure, "The Art of Cineplastics"(1920), in *Film,* ed. Daniel Talbot, 8–9. Also see Gilbert Seldes's aptly titled *The Movies Come from America,* 3, in which he states that "the moving picture corresponds to something fundamental in American life—America has always been on the move and has kept moving."

8. Quoted in David E. Shi, *Facing Facts,* 96. For background on the "rise" of the image with respect to the word, see W. J. T. Mitchell, *Iconology* and Mitchell Stephens, *The Rise of the Image and the Fall of the Word.* Judith Mayne, *Private Novels, Public Films,* connects the change to a shift in the sphere of representation from private reading to public moviegoing. Also relevant here is the paradigm shift from the monocular perspective of the camera obscura to the binocular perspective that underlies photography and film, as explained in Jonathan Crary, "Modernizing Vision" in *Viewing Positions,* ed. Linda Williams. Finally, see Miles Orvell's insightful *The Real Thing* for a discussion of the role of the photographic image in the shift in values from imitation to authenticity in American culture.

9. Poe and Holmes are quoted in Alan Trachtenberg, *Reading American Photographs,* 15, 19; Morse is quoted in Barbara Novak, *American Painting in the Nineteenth Century,* 198. See also Robert Taft's classic *Photography and the American Scene, 1838–1889.*

It is worth noting as well that the American museum became an important site of image collecting and exhibiting in the nineteenth century. Among the most memorable of the early museums was the Western Museum in Cincinnati, which Frances Trollope helped to promote as a mix of circus, vaudeville, and spiritualist emporium (see Don-ald Smalley's introduction to Trollope's, *Domestic Manners of the Americans*) and Scud-der's American Museum retrofitted by P. T. Barnum in 1841 with everything from per-forming fleas to landscape panoramas—a veritable compendium of precinematic popular entertainment (see Neil Harris, *Humbug*.)

10. The shift from creator to spectator might also be related to the well-docu-mented shift during this period from an economics of scarcity, stressing production, to an economics of abundance, stressing consumption. See, for example, John Kenneth Galbraith, *The Affluent Society* and Stuart and Elizabeth Ewen, *Channels of Desire*, Ch. 3.

11. Quoted in Trachtenberg, *Reading American Photographs,* 29.

12. See Kerr, *Silent Clowns,* 10, on film's ability to kill nostalgia, and Christian Metz, *Film Language,* 9: "Because movement is never material but is always visual, to reproduce its appearance is to duplicate its reality . . . the strict distinction between ob-ject and copy . . . dissolves on the threshold of motion." Melville's reference to the American drive for "more reality" is from *The Confidence-Man,* 215–16.

13. See Ralph Waldo Emerson, "Beauty" (1860), in *Essays and English Traits,* 309: "All the facts in nature are nouns of the intellect, and make the grammar of the eternal language."

14. The classic psychoanalytic theories of film are those of Jean-Louis Baudry, Christian Metz, Stephen Heath, and Laura Mulvey. Also see David Miller, *American Iconology,* 276–288, for a discussion of an assortment of countervailing views of the im-age.

15. Erwin Panofsky, "Style and Medium in the Motion Picture"(1934) in *Film,* ed. Daniel Talbot, 24. Lindsay, *Art of the Moving Picture,* 61–63.

16. Quoted in Brownlow, *Parade's Gone By,* 654. See Wagenknecht's Introduction, *Movies in the Age of Innocence,* for reactions by filmmakers, stars, and himself to the com-ing of sound.

17. Walt Whitman, *Complete Poetry and Selected Prose and Letters:* "Song of My-self"(1855), 50; "A Song of the Rolling Earth"(1856), 46; "Song of Myself," 52.

18. Lewis, *American Adam,* 1.

19. Charles D. Chapman, "Providing Yourself with the Proper Period," 64–65.

20. René Clair, "The Art of Sound," *Film,* ed. Richard Dyer MacCann, 40. For more on the pervasiveness of the English language, including a nod to the influence of Hollywood film, see H. L. Mencken's "The Future of English," 86–90. "Uncle Sam's Adopted Children," 68. Lindsay, *Art of the Moving Picture,* 94.

21. Fisher, *New American Studies,* vii.

22. This is a central point in the landmark essay that challenges the myth-symbol school—Bruce Kucklick, "Myth and Symbol in American Studies" (1972), in *Locating American Studies,* ed. Lucy Maddox—which, in turn, has given rise to a host of qualifica-tions and counterarguments since its original publication. I can defend myself against the literary fallacy that Kucklick points to in Leo Marx's book but am probably guilty

of other errors that he enumerates. But, then, as he says, his critique is "mainly negative" (86). Although there is value in the kind of empirical history he calls for, there is also value in a less empirical study like mine, if only to provide a template that the empiricists can fiddle with and correct.

23. Richard Dyer, *Stars,* 28. Dyer uses the example of a *Gidget* film to show how the most seemingly conformist vehicle can contain subversive elements.

24. See Michael Rogin, *Black Face, White Noise: Jewish Immigrants in the Hollywood Melting Pot* (Berkeley, Calif.: U. of Calif. Press, 1996) and his "'The Sword Became a Flashing Vision': D.W. Griffith's *The Birth of a Nation*" in Fisher, *New American Studies.* A similar thesis is argued for the Jewish adaptation of black music in Jeffrey Melnick, *A Right to Sing the Blues.*

25. See Jane Gaines, "*The Birth of a Nation* and *Within our Gates:* Two Tales of the American South," *Dixie Debates,* ed. Richard H. King and Helen Taylor. For a discussion of the reception of *The Birth of a Nation,* see ch. 7 of Janet Staiger's, *Interpreting Films.*

26. See George N. Fenin and William K. Everson's discussion of *The Heart of an Indian* in *The Western,* 70–72.

27. Quoted in Jacobs, *Rise of American Film,* 119. Griffith's statement is a paraphrase (whether conscious or not) of the lines from Conrad's preface to *Nigger of the "Narcissus":* "My task which I am trying to achieve is, by the power of the written word, to make you hear, to make you feel—it is, before all, to make you see." See George Bluestone's discussion of this connection in *Novels into Film,* Ch. 1.

28. Many of the best silent films are now available on videotape in remastered versions. HBO, Kino, Video Yesteryear, Republic, MGM, the New York Film Annex, and Paramount have all recently released videotapes of long unseen films by Harold Lloyd, Buster Keaton, Mary Pickford, Douglas Fairbanks, Cecil B. DeMille, Harry Langdon, Lon Chaney, Rudolph Valentino, and early Chaplin, as well as compilations of "primitive" films by Edwin Porter, Auguste and Louis Lumière, George Méliès, and Cecil Hepworth, among others. One of the great boons to the silent film enthusiast is the retrieval of authentic music, as well as the writing of new music, most notably by Carl Davis. Occasionally, there are screenings of silent films at universities and museums, sometimes with live piano and, on rare occasions, orchestral accompaniment. Several web sites provide detailed, sometimes offbeat, background on silent stars and films, as well as practical information on festivals, screenings, and film and videotape availability. See *The Silents Majority* (http://www.mdle.com/ClassicFilms/indexold.htm/); *Silent Film Sources* (http://www.cinemaweb.com/silentfilm/); *Silents Are Golden* (http://www. silentsare golden.com/); and *Silent-Movies.Com* (http://www.silent-movies.com/).

Chapter 1

1. Both quoted in Robert Weisbuch, *Atlantic Double-cross,* 130. Frances Trollope's account of America in *Domestic manners of the Americans* after her 1827 visit certainly

helped to reinforce these negative stereotypes. Consider her description of dinner with a group of high-ranking military officers on board a Mississippi steamboat:

> The total want of all the usual courtesies of the table, the voracious rapidity with which the viands were seized and devoured, the strange uncouth phrases and pronunciation; the loathsome spitting, from the contamination of which it was absolutely impossible to protect our dresses; the frightful manner of feeding with their knives, till the whole blade seemed to enter into the mouth; and the still more frightful manner of cleaning the teeth afterwards with a pocket knife, soon forced us to feel that we were not surrounded by the generals, colonels, and majors of the old world (18–19).

One understands why the book caused an uproar and drove many Americans abroad to acquire "culture."

2. Quoted in R. W. B. Lewis, *The American Adam,* 15.

3. Walt Whitman, "A Backward Glance o'er Traveled Roads" (1888), in *Complete Poetry and Selected Prose and Letters,* 865.

4. Quoted in Lewis, *American Adam,* 79.

5. Emerson, "Self-Reliance" (1841), in *Essays and English Traits,* 79

6. Quoted in Lewis, *American Adam,* 103. I may be misleading in my discussion of the *Leatherstocking Tales,* which do not chart a completely linear movement back in time, but despite the deviation (*The Prairie,* written third, is actually about Bumppo's old age and death), the "feel" of the novels corresponds to Lawrence's point. See John G. Cawelti, *Adventure, Mystery, and Romance,* on the consistently darker view of civilization charted in Cooper's *Tales.*

7. James Fenimore Cooper, *The Last of the Mohicans,* 146.

8. Richard Poirier, *A World Elsewhere.*

9. James Fenimore Cooper, *Deerslayer,* 21

10. Ralph Waldo Emerson, "The American Scholar"(1837), in *Essays and English Traits,* 9; Henry David Thoreau, *Walden* (1854), in *The Portable Thoreau,* ed. Carl Bode, 363; Whitman, "Song of Myself," in *Complete Poetry,* 43.

11. Emerson, "The Poet"(1844),in *Essays and English Traits,* 179.

12. Henry James is quoted in *Ralph Waldo Emerson: A Collection of Critical Essays,* ed. Lawrence Buell, 134. Poirier, *A World Elsewhere,* 65–66, echoes James when he writes of Emerson: "His style . . . often reveals a subjection even an allegiance to the very forms and conventions which are at the same time being attacked."

13. Emerson, "American Scholar," 5, 23.

14. Thoreau, *Walden,* 563.

15. Ibid., 363.

16. Whitman, "Song of Myself," in *Complete Poetry,* 28.

17. Lewis, *American Adam,* 44.

18. Vachel Lindsay, *The Art of the Moving Picture,* 93–94.

19. Whitman, "Song of Myself," in *Complete Poetry,* 50.

20. Ibid., 74.

21. Whitman, "Democratic Vistas" (1871), in *Complete Poetry,* 663.

22. Whitman, "Poets to Come" (1860), in *Complete Poetry,* 13.

23. Whitman, "Song of Myself," in *Complete Poetry,* 84. For further discussion of Whitman's role-playing and his kinship with American performance culture, see David S. Reynolds, *Walt Whitman's America.* Reynolds quotes from Whitman's notebooks: "[A]ll things and all other beings [are] as an audience at a play-house perpetually and perpetually calling me out from behind the curtain" (161).

24. For Edison's attitude toward his invention and his place in his culture, see Neil Baldwin, *Edison.*

25. Thoreau, *Walden,* 345. In typical fashion, Thoreau would contradict this view elsewhere in *Walden* (370): "What recommends commerce to me is its enterprise and bravery"—commerce being contrasted here with "fantastic enterprises and sentimental experiments." He would probably explain this contradiction, and others throughout the book, as a case of words getting in the way of the complex reality of experience.

26. Neal Gabler, *An Empire of Their Own.* See also Benjamin B. Hampton, *History of the American Film Industry,* 125, on Edison's Motion Picture Patents Company and its monopolistic distributing arm, General Film, as they came into conflict with the emerging independent film companies. He presents the conflict as a class war, with the Edison group "never suspecting the longings and aspirations hidden beneath the mob's mental laziness" but which the "showmen" entrepreneurs, by contrast, understood and shared.

27. Quoted in Gabler, *Empire of Their Own,* 15, 24.

28. Ibid., 17.

29. See Iris Barry, *D. W. Griffith,* written as an adjunct to the first major retrospective of his films. See also see Tom Gunning, *D. W. Griffith and the Origins of American Narrative Film* and Richard Schickel, *D. W. Griffith.*

30. See Sergei Eisenstein's classic essay "Dickens, Griffith, and the Film Today" (1944), in his book *Film Form.*

31. See Walter Kerr, *The Silent Clowns,* 30, on intertitles in silent film and how the use of the definite article ("The Storm"; "The Girl") lent a mythic, generalized quality to the image on screen. Griffith was especially addicted to this style of reference, and it may be that as film grew more concerned with rendering particulars rather than generalities (or, to paraphrase Norma Desmond, as movies got smaller), his style became less acceptable.

32. Francois Truffaut, *Hitchcock,* 71.

33. Quoted in Lewis Jacobs, *The Rise of American Film,* 119.

34. Lindsay, *Art of the Moving Picture,* 94.

35. Erwin Panofsky, "Style and Medium in the Motion Picture," 22. The observation supports Judith Mayne's argument in *Private Novels, Public Films,* associating novels with the private sphere and movies with the public sphere. Also relevant is Seymour Chatman, "What Novels Can Do That Films Can't (and Vice Versa)," in *On Narrative,*

ed. W. J. T. Mitchell, which deals with film's compulsion to action and inability to describe.

36. Emerson, "Self-reliance," in *Essays and English Traits,* 72.

Chapter 2

1. Frank Capra, *The Name above the Title,* 96.

2. Quoted in David F. Burg, *Chicago's White City of 1893,* xiii. See also Stanley Applebaum, *The Chicago World's Fair of 1893.*

3. Quoted in Kenneth Silverman, *Houdini!!!,* 42.

4. Edmund Wilson, "Houdini," 125.

5. Quoted in Ruth Brandon, *The Life and Many Deaths of Harry Houdini,* 139.

6. See Gaylyn Studlar, "Barrymore, the Body, and Bliss," in *Fields of Vision,* ed. Leslie Devereaux and Roger Hillman, 166.

7. Michel Foucault, *The History of Sexuality.* See also Tim Armstrong, Introduction, *American Bodies.*

8. See Robert W. Snyder, *The Voice of the City.*

9. Quoted in James Mellon, *The Face of Lincoln,* 9.

10. Henry James, *The American,* 2; Francis Parkman, *The Oregon Trail,* 21.

11. Quoted in Mellon, *Face of Lincoln,* 9.

12. See Tim Armstrong, *Modernism, Technology and the Body,* on physical regimens of the period; also William James, *Principles of Psychology,* Ch. 4, on the ability to create oneself bodily, as well as spiritually, through the reprogramming of habits; Ed Folsom, *Walt Whitman's Native Representations,* on Whitman's "photographs of the self"; Miles Orvell, *The Real Thing,*Ch. 1, and *After the Machine,* Ch. 1, on Whitman's connection to the machine in general and to photography in particular; and Lloyd Goodrich, *Thomas Eakins,* vol. I, 126–130, on the Eakins-Muybridge connection.

13. Brandon, *Life and Many Deaths of Houdini,* takes a loosely Freudian approach to his career and interprets his drive to "expose" as a need to retaliate against or enter terrain guarded by real and imagined fathers (121). This interpretation could easily be applied to the immigrant filmmakers of the next generation.

14. Silverman, *Houdini!!!,* 111.

15. Robert Allen, *Vaudeville and Film,* 114, explains that when film was first introduced, it was initially a headline act (the penultimate place on the vaudeville program) but that it quickly gravitated to the closing act, designated for visual novelties.

16. See my "Helen Keller and the American Myth," 1–20, on the evolution from word to live body to imaged body in American culture, using Keller's case as paradigmatic of the change. Parker Tyler, "Movies and the Human Image," in *Film,* ed. Richard Dyer MacCann, makes the fascinating observation that film, by adding movement to the rendering of the body's image, "saved" the body for representation at a point when the other arts had discarded it in favor of abstraction.

17. See the comments of Marcus Loew on the relationship of vaudeville and film as it had evolved by 1927 in Charles W. Stein, ed. *American Vaudeville as Seen by Its Contemporaries,* 346. Loew answered questions at the Harvard Business School, of all places, after a talk arranged by Joseph P. Kennedy, of all people: "Q: Which carries the greater weight [the vaudeville act or the picture]? A: The picture, both as to entertainment and drawing power."

18. See Tom Gunning, "Cinema of Attraction[s]."

19. For biographical information on Keaton, see Rudi Blesh, *Keaton,* and Tom Dardis, *Keaton: The Man Who Wouldn't Lie Down;* for a discussion of the influence of Keaton's childhood on his future career and psyche, see Judith Sanders and Daniel Liberfeld, "Dreaming in Pictures: The Childhood Origin of Buster Keaton's Creativity." Keaton, in his autobiography (with Charles Samuels), *My Wonderful Life of Slapstick,* 51, discusses watching Houdini "like a hawk . . . from all parts of the theatre, from both wings of the stage, from the orchestra and both sides of the balcony and gallery." He was already thinking cinematically, and the description puts one in mind of his short film *The Playhouse,* where multiple perspectives are translated into multiple images of the self in a theater setting.

20. Blesh, *Keaton,* 93.

21. James Agee, "Comedy's Greatest Era,"(1949), in *Agee on Film,* 143.

22. See Robert Knopf, *The Theater and Cinema of Buster Keaton,* on the continued influence of vaudeville technique and conception on Keaton's films, even after his entry into feature-length comedy.

23. See Walter Kerr, *The Silent Clowns,* Part II, for delightful discussion of the differences among the three great silent comedians and their place in film comedy and film history more generally.

24. See *Buster Keaton's* Sherlock Jr., ed. Andrew Horton, for a collection of interpretations of the film. See also Daniel Moews, *Keaton* and Miles Orvell, "The Camera and the Magic of Self-transformation in Buster Keaton," in *After the Machine,* on the transformative aspects of Keaton's films.

25. See Gerald Mast, *The Comic Mind,* 131. See also Robert Goff, "Buster Keaton and the Play of Elements," in *Laughing Matters,* ed. John Durant and Jonathan Miller, for another reading of Keaton's mechanistic relationship to experience.

26. Garrett Stewart, "Keaton through the Looking Glass," 359. The conceit is the basis of Neal Gabler, *Life the Movie.*

27. See Michael F. Blake, *Lon Chaney.*

28. The classic feminist essay on the "male gaze" is Laura Mulvey, "Visual Pleasure and Narrative Cinema," in *Visual and Other Pleasures.* Wendy Lesser may go further than I do in qualifying the hard-line feminist position not only for film but also for visual representation in general. See her *His Other Half: Men Looking at Women Through Art.*

29. Molly Haskell, *From Reverence to Rape: The Treatment of Women in the Movies,* "The Twenties," discusses the difficulties that women had in silent comedy, including

the box office failure of *Exit Smiling*, but she also acknowledges the power that silent actresses had in other sorts of roles.

30. Richard Griffith and Arthur Mayer, *The Movies*, 249.

Chapter 3

1. Quoted in George N. Fenin and William K. Everson, *The Western*, 8.

2. See Barbara Novak, *American Painting in the Nineteenth Century*, on the European antecedents of American landscape painting. It should be noted that American landscape was not an unequivocal source of wonder to Europeans. The Mississippi, so awe-inspiring to Twain and Whitman, was to Charles Dickens "an enormous ditch . . . running liquid mud" (*American Notes*, 187) and to Frances Trollope, (*Domestic Manners of the Americans*, 4) "so utterly desolate, had Dante seen it, he might have drawn images of another Bolgia from its horrors."

3. See Sacvan Bercovitch, *The Puritan Origins of the American Self* and *The American Jeremiad*.

4. Ralph Waldo Emerson, "The Poet," in *Essays and English Traits* 179. Walt Whitman, "Earth's Most Important Stream" (1882), in *Complete Poetry and Selected Prose*, 765.

5. See Matthew Baigell, *Thomas Cole*. See also Bryan Jay Wolf's Lacanian reading of Cole in *Romantic Re-vision*, which discusses the artist's impulse to evade history and connect with the "real." Wolf notes that Cole's nineteenth-century biographer, Louis Legrand Noble, cast Cole "as a spiritual Benjamin Franklin" (180).

6. Novak, *American Painting*, 61.

7. The absence of accurate, realistic description in Cooper provoked the famous satire by Mark Twain, "Fenimore Cooper's Literary Offenses," in *Complete Essays of Mark Twain*.

8. Quoted in John K. Howat, *The Hudson River and its Painters*, 29.

9. Novak, *American Painting*, 66.

10. Lee Mitchell, "Bierstadt's Settings, Harte's Plots," in *Reading the West*, ed. Michael Kowalewski, 107.

11. See Novak, *American Painting*, Chs. 5 and 6, on luminism.

12. See William A. Brady, *Showman*. See also Robert Taft, *Photography and the American Scene, 1838–1889*, Ch. 10, on the popularity of the stereoscope in America.

13. Wolfgang Schivelbusch, *The Railway Journey*.

14. Angela Miller, "The Panorama, The Cinema, and the Emergence of the Spectacular."

15. Frederick Jackson Turner, "The Significance of the Frontier in American History," 463.

16. See my discussion of Freud and the *bildungsroman* in *The Daughter's Dilemma*.

17. Simon Schama, *Landscape and Memory*, 367.

18. Henry Nash Smith, *Virgin Land*, 53.

19. See Patricia Nelson Limerick's discussion of the durability of the frontier thesis in the popular imagination in "The Adventures of the Frontier in the Twentieth Century" in *The Frontier in American Culture,* ed. James R. Grossman. Limerick is one of the most vocal challengers of the Turner-based notion of the frontier in its failure to acknowledge that Native Americans lived on the so-called "free land." See Patricia Nelson Limerick, Clyde A. Milner II, and Charles E. Rankin, eds., *Trails,* for a discussion of new definitions and revised perspectives on this subject. See also Gerald D. Nash, *Creating the West,* for an overview of the Turner critique. For a more positive view of Turner, see Tiziano Bonazzi, "Frederick Jackson Turner's Frontier Thesis and the Self-consciousness of America." Bonazzi argues that "the Frontier Thesis is meant to be a gateway to a consciousness of historical continuity through change. Turner constructed it in order to show his countrymen that their basic political ideals, individualism and democracy, are not secured once and for ever, but exist only as a result of successful adaptations to ever-changing environments" (163). This argument is compatible with mine in that it manages to highlight a legacy of American self-making that, as Limerick herself acknowledges, continues to be associated with Turner's thesis in the public imagination.

20. Samuel Morse, quoted in Alan Trachtenberg, *Reading American Photographs,* 15, discusses this same photograph in a somewhat similar vein, noting that only the immobilized objects appear in the picture whereas "the objects moving are not impressed."

21. Quoted in Gunning, "An Aesthetic of Astonishment" in *Viewing Positions,* ed. Linda Williams, 120.

22. It should be noted that the footage was not really integral to the film. It was sent independently to exhibitors, who could tack it on the beginning or the end as they saw fit. That they tended to put it at the end (since so many reports refer to it as the closing shot in the film) indicates that an added sense of closure was generally felt to be needed.

23. See Seymour Stern, "*The Birth of a Nation:* The Technique and Its Influence," *The Emergence of Film Art,* ed. Lewis Jacobs, on Griffith's innovative use of another structuring motif in the film, that of "line" versus "mass," and its relationship to California topography. This anticipates Hart's use of this motif in *Tumbleweeds,* discussed later in this chapter.

24. Griffith's assistant cameraman Karl Brown, quoted in Michael Rogin, "'The Sword Became a Flashing Vision,'" in *The New American Studies,* ed. Philip Fisher, 382.

25. See William S. Hart, *My Life East and West.*

26. See Kevin Brownlow, *The War, the West, and the Wilderness,* on the mixing of fictive frontier elements with real ones during the silent period. More extreme is Jane Tompkins, *West of Everywhere,* who conceives of western landscape on film as a purely imaginative terrain used for ideologically exploitative purposes.

27. There is a general tendency among critics to see Hart as glorifying the hegemonic white, Christian American, a view not helped by the fact that one of his films is

titled *The Aryan* and refers in its intertitles to "the code of the Aryan race: 'Our women shall be guarded.'" See Diane Kaiser Koszarski, *The Complete Films of William S. Hart* and Ralph and Natasha Friar, *The Only Good Indian,* 135–38. But this view of Hart seems to me to be accurate only up to a point. Although he did embody a certain kind of Anglo-Saxon masculine type, his films helped to set in motion that shifting relationship to difference that would permit other kinds of characters to inhabit his position in future films in the genre. See John G. Cawelti, *Adventure, Mystery, and Romance,* on the evolution of the western hero.

28. Alistair Cooke, *Douglas Fairbanks,* 30. See also *The Fairbanks Album,* drawn from the Fairbanks archives by Douglas Fairbanks, Jr., with narrative by Richard Schickel (New York: New York Graphic Society, 1975), and John C. Tibbetts and James M. Welsh, *His Majesty the American.*

29. For a good discussion of Fairbanks's early films and their connection to a prevailing western mythology, see Linda Podheiser, "Pep on the Range or Douglas Fairbanks and the World War I Era Western."

30. John W. Reps, *The Making of Urban America,* 263.

31. Anne Hollander, *Moving Pictures,* 357.

32. See Devin R. McNamara, *Urban Verbs,* 106–107.

33. In fact, a screen adaptation of Twain's 1889 *A Connecticut Yankee in King Arthur's Court,* the first of several, was made in 1921, the same year as *The Mark of Zorro.*

34. Fairbanks is quoted in *Photoplay,* Feb. 1918, 40. Sherwood is quoted in Schickel, *His Picture in the Papers,* 73–74.

35. James E. West, introduction, in Douglas Fairbanks, *Youth Points the Way,* viii.

36. Turner, "Significance of the Frontier," 478.

37. Jeanine Basinger, *Silent Stars,* in her chapter on Hart and Mix also quotes this speech and praises its effect, although it seems to me she is reveling more in the charm of its quaintness than in its success at relaying meaning and emotion.

Chapter 4

1. Lillian Gish (with Ann Pinchot), *The Movies, Mr. Griffith, and Me,* 233.

2. Henry James, *The American,* 3.

3. See Alan Trachtenberg, *Reading American Photographs,* 52–60. Also see Stephen Jay Gould, *The Mismeasure of Man,* for a comprehensive overview of nineteenth-century trends in phrenology, and Charles Colbert, *A Measure of Perfection,* who argues that phrenological societies helped create an audience for photographic portraits.

4. James Mellon, *The Face of Lincoln,* 9.

5. Henry James, *Portrait of a Lady,* 35

6. See Barbara Will, "Nervous Systems, 1880–1915" in *American Bodies,* ed. Tim Armstrong.

7. Alexis de Tocqueville, *Democracy in America,* Vol. 2, 144–47.

8. Peter Gay, *The Bourgeois Experience, Vol.2: The Tender Passion,* 346–47.

9. See the photographs of female hysterics in Elaine Showalter, *The Female Malady,* 151–53.

10. Sigmund Freud and Joseph Breuer, *Studies on Hysteria,* 203–4.

11. Charlotte Perkins Gilman, *The Yellow Wallpaper.*

12. Mary Panzer, *Mathew Brady and the Image of History.*

13. Ibid., 119.

14. Tom Gunning, "Tracing the Individual Body: Photograph, Detectives, and Early Cinema," in *Cinema and the Invention of Modern Life,* ed. Leo Charney and Vanessa R. Schwartz, 23.

15. Edgar Morin, *The Stars,* 179.

16. See Van Wyck Brooks, *Helen Keller,* on the effect of Helen Keller's face.

17. Béla Balázs, "Theory of the Film," trans. Edith Bone (1953) in *Film,* ed. Daniel Talbot, 203–4; Walter Benjamin, "The Work of Art in the Age of Mechanical Reproduction," 236.

18. Gish, *Movies, Mr. Griffith, and Me,* 95–96.

19. The fan is quoted in Eileen Bowser, *The Transformation of Cinema,* 87. The reporter is quoted in Lewis Jacobs, *The Rise of American Film,* 106. See also Joyce E. Jesionowski, *Thinking in Pictures,* 2, on Griffith's belief that the screen could make us "see thoughts." See Bowser, ch. 6, for an exhaustive discussion of the development of the screen close-up. She notes that when writers first spoke of close views they were generally referring to "bust shots," even full shots (and the shot discussed in *After Many Years* might have been included here), not close-ups as we now think of them. Not until 1912 did films use facial close-ups with any consistency, and Edwin Porter maintained a static stage distance on his subjects until 1911.

20. See also Roberta E. Pearson, *Eloquent Gestures,* Ch. 3, and A. Nicholas Vardac, *Stage to Screen,* for stills comparing stage and early cinematic poses.

21. Kevin Brownlow, *The Parade's Gone By,* 97, quotes Griffith on this point: "I prefer the nervous type . . . If she is calm she has no imagination."

22. Gish, *Movies, Mr. Griffith, and Me,* 6.

23. On the subject of her directing films, Gish (*Movies, Mr. Griffith, and Me,* 223) recalls Griffith telling her, "Why shouldn't you? You know as much about making pictures as I do, and you know more about acting for them than anyone else." See also Edward Wagenknecht's paean to Gish in his "Appendix: Lillian Gish: An Interpretation," in *Movies in the Age of Innocence.*

24. Gish's performance in *True Heart Susie* has been a subject of some discussion. James Naremore, in his chapter on the film in *Acting in Cinema,* sees it as an enormously complex performance with the film "a virtual sermon on the theme of Art versus Nature" (103), whereas Charles Affron, *Star Acting,* 47–48, 47–48, finds little more than girlish sweetness in Gish's portrayal and is more taken with her performance in *Broken Blossoms.* See also William K. Everson's charming discussion of the film in *Love in the Film.*

25. Showalter, *Female Malady,* 130, summarizes the hysterical fit as follows: "At its height, the victim alternately sobbed and laughed; she might have convulsive movements of the body, heart palpitations, impaired hearing and vision, or unconsciousness." The list of symptoms certainly corresponds well to Gish's behavior in the scene discussed in *Way Down East.* In this sense, the film follows the pattern of *The Yellow Wallpaper:* the neurasthenic escalates into the hysteric, although the film ultimately recoups her to neurasthenic "normality" at the end. It is noteworthy that an article on Gish by James R. Quirk, "The Enigma of the Screen," 63, notes that "she achieves greatness of effect through a single phase of emotion—namely, hysteria."

26. David Parkinson, *History of Film,* 72–73.

27. Balázs, "Theory of Film," 214. Roland Barthes, *Mythologies,* 56.

28. See Alexander Walker, *Rudolph Valentino.*

29. Quoted in Gish, *Movies, Mr. Griffith, and Me,* 211. Griffith had also originally employed Douglas Fairbanks but viewed him as a prankster better suited to Mack Sennett's Keystone films.

30. See M. M. Marberry, "The Overloved One."

31. Quoted in Naremore, *Acting in Cinema,* 18. See also Edward Dwight Easy, *On Method Acting.*

Chapter 5

1. Twenty-two-year-old college senior, quoted in Robert Sklar, Ed. *The Plastic Age,* 45.

2. Virginia Woolf, "Mr. Bennett and Mrs. Brown" (1924), *Collected Essays,* 320.

3. See Eileen Bowser, *The Transformation of Cinema,* 112–113.

4. Moses Maimonides, *The Guide of the Perplexed,* Vol. 1, 22. For further discussion of these issues, see W. J. T. Mitchell, *Iconology,* 32–36.

5. See Elizabeth K. Helsinger, *Ruskin and the Art of the Beholder,* 169, for a discussion of Locke and his influence on representation.

6. Quoted in Mitchell, *Iconology,* 23.

7. William Wordsworth, *Prelude* (1850), Book XIV, *Selected Poems and Prefaces,* 358.

8. For the classic study of the contrast between epic and novel in terms of the loss of spiritual essence or transcendent value, see Georg Lukacs, *The Theory of the Novel.*

9. Quoted in Joyce E. Jesionowski, *Thinking in Pictures,* 3.

10. On the meaning and history of celebrity, see Leo Braudy, *The Frenzy of Renown;* Richard Schickel, *Common Fame* and *His Picture in the Papers;* and Neal Gabler, *Life the Movie.*

11. The difference between the old-style celebrity and the movie star could be understood in terms of that loss of aura that Walter Benjamin connected to the advent of mechanical reproduction.

12. Quoted in Richard deCordova, *Picture Personalities,* 57.

13. Zukor's Famous Players in Famous Plays series not only helped to gain more respectability for movies with a middle-class public but also helped make it acceptable for actors to appear in movies since theater stars like Sarah Bernhardt and Geraldine Farrar had now done so.

14. Pearl White, *Just Me.*

15. See W. J. T. Mitchell, *On Narrative;* Lionel Trilling's intriguing essay on the death instinct as it relates to narrative, "The Fate of Pleasure," in *Beyond Culture,* and Seymour Chatman, *Story and Discourse.*

16. Iris Barry, *D. W. Griffith,* 14, cites Joseph Wood Krutch's testimony of his boyhood in Knoxville, where he singled out Griffith's films as superior.

17. See deCordova, *Picture Personalities,* 34, on the emergence of a discourse on film acting.

18. Many commentators like to note Gilbert's conspicuous but lackluster debut as an extra in Hart's *Hell's Hinges* in 1916.

19. Edward Wagenknecht, *Movies in the Age of Innocence,* 24.

20. The incident is a staple in histories of early cinema (see Bowser, *Transformation of Cinema,* 112). It reflects what the "father" of public relations (and nephew of Sigmund Freud), Edward Bernays, would describe a few years later in his book *Crystallizing Public Opinion* as the "art of making news."

21. See Martin Levin, Ed., *Hollywood and the Great Fan Magazines* for an amusing compendium of fan magazine stories from the late silent and early talkie period.

22. Quoted in Richard Koszarski, *An Evening's Entertainment,* 276.

23. See Mary Pickford's *Sunshine and Shadow.* Both Gish's and Pickford's autobiographies manage to impart something of the quality of their authors' screen personas. In Pickford's case, I was disarmed by her devoting pages toward the end of the book to an unintended anti-Semitic remark she once made to a Jewish friend that she now wished to apologize for. See also Eileen Whitefield, *Pickford;* Wagenknecht's chapter on Pickford in *Movies in the Age of Innocence;* and Kevin Brownlow's essay to accompany the marvelous collection of photographs in *Mary Pickford Rediscovered.*

24. Alistair Cooke, *Douglas Fairbanks,* on Pickford, 21. Richard Griffith and Arthur Mayer, *The Movies,* 57. Benjamin B. Hampton, *History of the American Film Industry,* 147, recounts that Mary's mother overheard the remark about "wrapping the program around Mary's neck." Whitefield, *Pickford,* 143, recounts the incident of the contract and the baby.

25. Quoted in Lary May, *Screening out the Past,* 125–26. See also Wagenknecht, *Movies in the Age of Innocence,* 156–57, on Pickford's remark that "I became, in a sense, my own baby."

26. See Booton Herndon, *Mary Pickford and Douglas Fairbanks,* 44–46, on Fairbanks' lies.

27. Douglas Fairbanks, *Laugh and Live.*

28. Michael Rogin's argument in *Black Face, White Noise* about the assimilative

function of blackface performance for Jews can be applied to Fairbanks here (and the fact that he was part Jewish and wanted to hide it reinforces the connection). I will deal with functional differences between Jolson's blackface and Fairbanks's suntan in chapter 6.

29. See deCordova, *Picture Personalities,* and May, *Screening Out the Past,* for chapters on the star scandals and the creation of the Hays Office; see Kenneth Anger, *Hollywood Babylon,* for a more prurient version of the events.

30. Frances Denton,"The Lonely Princess," 46.

31. Billy Bates, "The Pickford-Fairbanks Wooing," 70.

32. See Paul Trent, *The Image Makers.*

33. See Richard Dyer, *Heavenly Bodies.* For related ideas, see Andrew Britton, *Katharine Hepburn,* and Christine Gledhill, "Signs of Melodrama," *Stardom,* in which both address the role that genre plays in shaping the star image. These views seem to me to be versions of what Siegfried Kracauer in *Theory of Film,* 95, meant when he said that "the film actor must seem to be his character in such a way that all his expressions, gestures, and poses point beyond themselves to the diffuse contexts out of which they arise. They must breath a certain casualness marking them as fragments of an inexhaustible texture."

34. William K. Everson, *American Silent Film,* Ch. 12.

35. Quoted in Koszarski, *Evening's Entertainment,* 307.

36. Ibid., 311. It is said that Mayer sabotaged Gilbert's career in talkies because of that punch, somehow arranging his projection of a higher voice on screen than he would normally have. But Gilbert didn't need any help in disappointing the public, given the unrealizable expectations that his silent image had created.

37. See Miriam Hansen, "Pleasure, Ambivalence, Identification: Valentino and Female Spectatorship," and Gaylyn Studlar, "The Perils of Pleasure? Fan Magazine Discourse as Woman's Commodified Culture in the 1920s," in *Silent Film,* ed. Richard Abel, for a discussion of the complex appeal of Valentino to women. Both argue that Valentino was "more than a consumerist spectacle orchestrated from above" (Hansen, "Pleasure, Ambivalence," 7).

38. See Mary Ann Doane, "Film and Masquerade."

39. Studlar, "Perils of Pleasure?" in Abel, *Silent Film;* Pickford is quoted in Diane MacIntyre,"The Little Girl Who Couldn't Grow Up: The Phenomenon of Typecasting." http:www.mdle.com/ClassicFilms/FeaturedStar/maryx.htm> (Jan. 20, 2000).

40. Quoted in Bernard P. Brennan, *William James,* 63; James's emphasis.

41. William James, *Principles of Psychology,*745.

42. Balázs, "Theory of Film," in *Film,* ed. Daniel Talbot, 208.

43. Daniel J. Boorstin, *The Image,* 57.

44. William Leach, *Land of Desire,* xiii.

45. Steven J. Ross, *Working-Class Hollywood,* 195.

46. James R. Quirk, "The Public Just Won't Let Mary Pickford Grow Up," 36. Cooke, *Douglas Fairbanks,* 31.

47. Alexander Walker, *Joan Crawford.* For a discussion of the relationship among Crawford, her roles, and her female fans, see Charlotte Cornelia Herzog and Jane Marie Gaines, "Puffed Sleeves Before Tea" in Gledhill, *Stardom.*

48. See Lionel Trilling, "Mansfield Park," *The Opposing Self.*

49. Carl York, "Studio News and Gossip," 42; advertisement, March 1926; "How to Spoil the Effect of Beautiful Clothes," 64.

50. See Herzog and Gaines, "Puffed Sleeves Before Tea," 83, on fan magazine advice to women to adapt star outfits to their own needs, and Jackie Stacey, "Feminine Fascinations: Forms of Identification in Star-Audience Relations" in Gledhill, *Stardom,* 157, on the ways in which women identified with stars and acted on that identification. For a discussion of the relationship of fashion to self-expression in culture that dovetails with my argument about fan consumerism, see Anne Hollander, *Sex and Suits,* and assorted essays in her *Feeding the Eye.*

51. See Sumiko Higashi, *Cecil B. DeMille and American Culture,* on the commodity culture and DeMille, and Mary Ann Doane, *The Desire to Desire,* on film's relationship to female consumption. Whereas I see movie-generated consumerism as linked to narrative, Doane, sees the opposite, arguing that "the desire to possess displaces comprehension as the dominant mechanism of reading" (31).

Chapter 6

1. Erwin Panofsky, "Style and Medium in the Motion Picture," in *Film,* ed. Daniel Talbot, 20–21; the film critic is quoted in Kevin Brownlow, *The Parade's Gone By,* 666.

2. Another variable that affected silent films, at least during their earlier years, was projection speed. Walter Kerr, *The Silent Clowns,* 36, quotes a 1911 projectionist's advice to colleagues: "The operator 'renders' a film, if he is a real operator, exactly as a musician renders a piece of music, in that, within limits, the action of the scene being portrayed depends entirely on his judgment . . . I have often changed speed half a dozen times on one film of 1000 feet."

3. Andrew Sarris, "The Cultural Guilt of Musical Movies: *The Jazz Singer,* Fifty Years After." *The Jazz Singer,* though retrospectively presented as an immediate hit, was actually slower to gain notice, and it was really Jolson's next film, the 1928 *The Singing Fool,* that made a fortune at the box office and precipitated the wholesale shift to sound. See Donald Crafton, *The Talkies,* Ch. 20, and Larry Swindell, "The Day the Silents Stopped."

4. Walter Benjamin, "The Work of Art in the Age of Mechanical Reproduction," 237. In my systemic approach to the arrival of speech in film I may call to mind André Bazin's "myth of total cinema," which saw film as moving asymptotically toward "an integral realism, a recreation of the world in its own image" (*What Is Cinema?,* 2).

5. Christian Metz, *Film Language,* 50.

6. David Bordwell, "The Introduction of Sound," in David Bordwell, Janet

Staiger, and Kristin Thompson, eds., *The Classical Hollywood Cinema,* 306. Taking the other extreme, Scott Eyman, *The Speed of Sound,* 22, calls talkies "a mutation, a different art form entirely" from silent movies.

7. Quoted in Brownlow, *Parade's Gone By,* 667.

8. Eyman, *Speed of Sound,* 379–80, describes Fairbanks's reaction when, halfway through filming, the set of *The Iron Mask* was retrofitted for sound. On the issue of cause and effect for technological and conceptual change, see John Dewey, *Art as Experience,* 141: "Significant advances in technique occur . . . in connection with efforts to solve problems that are not technical but that grow out of the need for new modes of experience."

9. The partial sound format of *The Jazz Singer* was also a masterful public relations maneuver on behalf of sound, for by alternating between sound and silence, Warners was able to "negatively emphasize silence" (Eyman, *Speed of Sound,* 15) and thus make a silent film appear more stodgy and outmoded than an all-talkie.

10. Quoted in Swindell, "Day the Silents Stopped," 27. It should be noted that Jolson had tried to make an all-silent movie with D. W. Griffith as his unlikely director in the mid-1920s, but he supposedly left the project when he saw the rushes of the love scenes. His willingness to return to film was presumably because of the money promised and the opportunity to record the combination of his body and voice for posterity. See Harry M. Geduld, *The Birth of the Talkies,* 167.

11. On Sam Warner, see Neal Gabler, *An Empire of Their Own,* 123–43.

12. See Michael Rogin, *Black Face, White Noise,* for an exhaustive discussion of the relationship between blackface and Jewish assimilation.

13. The Vitaphone sound-on-disk system, which required the camera to be enclosed in a soundproof booth so that its whirring would not be recorded, was eventually replaced by the more user-friendly sound-on-film method, which Fox had adopted earlier and had used for newsreels and outdoor footage when Warner's was still confined to a sound stage. For discussion of the technological considerations involved with the transition to sound, see Douglas Gomery, "The Coming of Sound: Technological Change in the American Film Industry," in *The American Film Industry,* ed. Tino Balio.

14. See Rick Altman, *The American Film Musical,* for a discussion of Berkeley's place in the genre.

15. See Ann Douglas, *Terrible Honesty.*

16. See Charlene Register, "Stepin Fetchit: The Man, The Image, and the African American Press."

17. See Aldous Huxley, "Silence Is Golden," a diatribe against sound film and *The Jazz Singer* in particular, in his essay collection, *Do What You Will.*

18. Crafton, *Talkies,* 422.

19. Ibid.

20. Panofsky, "Style and Medium," 21.

21. Vachel Lindsay, *The Art of the Moving Picture,* 94.

Epilogue

1. Michael Levine, *The Princess and the Package,* 226, 310.

2. See M. M. Marbury, "The Overloved One," 85–87.

3. Commentators quoted in Levine, *Princess and Package,* 308, 309. It is interesting to consider in the context of the American myth the monarchical stipulation that the royal bride be a virgin. On the one hand, virginity conforms to the idea of innocence, which is basic to the myth; on the other, it runs counter to the idea that one can begin again—that innocence need not be lost and can be revisited, as an ever-expanding frontier. The virgin bride is also a one-of-a-kind artifact and, in a world of mechanical reproduction through cinema and other technologies (re Walter Benjamin, "The Work of Art in the Age of Mechanical Reproduction"), would represent an archaic value.

4. See A. N. Wilson, *The Rise and Fall of the House of Windsor,* 36.

5. Ibid., 43.

6. It is amusing to speculate on how Adolph Zukor or Louis B. Mayer would have "managed" Diana and whether her fate would have been happier under their care. We might also think of Diana as a metaphor for the rise of the independent producer and the fall of the studio system. In this case, the monarchy stands not in opposition to Hollywood but as the counterpart to the once all-controlling Hollywood studio that has now lost that omnipotent control.

BIBLIOGRAPHY

Abel, Richard, ed. *Silent Film.* New Brunswick, N.J.: Rutgers University Press, 1996.

Affron, Charles. *Star Acting: Gish, Garbo, and Davis.* New York: Dutton, 1977.

Agee, James. *Agee on Film.* Boston: Beacon Press, 1966.

Allen, Robert. *Vaudeville and Film: 1895 – 1915: A Study in Media Interaction.* New York: Arno Press, 1980.

Altman, Rick. *The American Film Musical.* Bloomington: Indiana University Press, 1987.

Anger, Kenneth. *Hollywood Babylon.* New York: Dell, 1975.

Applebaum, Stanley. *The Chicago World's Fair of 1893: A Photographic Record.* New York: Dover, 1980.

Armstrong, Tim, ed. *American Bodies: Cultural Histories of the Physique.* New York University Press, 1996.

———. *Modernism, Technology and the Body.* New York: Cambridge University Press, 1998.

Baigell, Matthew. *Thomas Cole.* New York: Watson-Guptill Publications, 1985.

Baldwin, Neil. *Edison: Inventing the Century.* New York: Hyperion, 1995.

Balio, Tino, ed. *The American Film Industry.* Madison: University of Wisconsin Press, 1985.

Barry, Iris. *D. W. Griffith: American Film Master.* New York: Museum of Modern Art, 1940.

Barthes, Roland. *Mythologies.* Trans. Annette Lavers. New York: Hill and Wang, 1975.

Basinger, Jeanine. *Silent Stars.* New York: Knopf, 1999.

Bates, Billy. "The Pickford-Fairbanks Wooing." *Photoplay,* June 1920: 70.

Bazin, André. *What Is Cinema?* Trans. Hugh Gray. Berkeley: University of California Press, 1961.

Benjamin, Walter. "The Work of Art in the Age of Mechanical Reproduction" (1936). In *Illuminations: Essays and Reflections.* Ed. Hannah Arendt. Trans. Harry Zohn. New York: Schocken Books, 1968.

Bercovitch, Sacvan. *The American Jeremiad.* Madison: University of Wisconsin Press, 1978.

———. *The Puritan Origins of the American Self.* New Haven: Yale University Press, 1975.

Berger, John. *Ways of Seeing.* New York: Penguin, 1972.

Bernays, Edward. *Crystallizing Public Opinion*. 1923. Reprint, New York: Liveright, 1961.

Blake, Michael F. *Lon Chaney: The Man Behind the Thousand Faces*. Vestal, NY: Vestal Press, 1993.

Blesh, Rudi. *Keaton*. New York: Collier, 1966.

Bluestone, George. *Novels into Film: The Metamorphosis of Fiction into Cinema*. Berkeley: University of California Press, 1957.

Blum, Daniel. *A Pictorial History of the Silent Screen*. New York: Grosset and Dunlap, 1953.

Bode, Carl, ed. *The Portable Thoreau*. New York: Viking, 1964.

Bonazzi, Tiziano. "Frederick Jackson Turner's Frontier Thesis and the Self-Consciousness of America." *Journal of American Studies* 27, 2 (1993): 149–71.

Boorstin, Daniel J. *The Image: A Guide to Pseudo-Events in America*. New York: Atheneum, 1975.

Bordwell, David, Janet Staiger, and Kristin Thompson, eds. *The Classical Hollywood Cinema: Film Style and Mode of Production to 1960*. New York: Columbia University Press, 1985.

Bowser, Eileen. *The Transformation of Cinema, 1907–1915*. Berkeley: University of California Press, 1994.

Brady, William A. *Showman*. New York: Dutton, 1937.

Brandon, Ruth. *The Life and Many Deaths of Harry Houdini*. New York: Kodansha International, 1995.

Braudy, Leo. *The Frenzy of Renown: Fame and its History*. New York: Oxford University Press, 1986.

Brennan, Bernard P. *William James*. New York: Twayne Publishers, 1968.

Britton, Andrew. *Katharine Hepburn: The Thirties and After*. Newcastle upon Tyne, England: Tyneside Cinema, 1984.

Brooks, Van Wyck. *Helen Keller: A Sketch for a Portrait*. London: J. M. Dent, 1956.

Brownlow, Kevin. *Mary Pickford Rediscovered*. New York: Harry N. Abrams, 1999.

——. *The Parade's Gone By . . .* New York: Ballantine Books, 1968.

——. *The War, the West, and the Wilderness*. New York: Knopf, 1979.

Buell, Lawrence, ed. *Ralph Waldo Emerson: A Collection of Critical Essays*. Englewood Cliffs, N.J.: Prentice Hall, 1993.

Burg, David F. *Chicago's White City of 1893*. Lexington: University Press of Kentucky, 1976.

Capra, Frank. *The Name Above the Title*. New York: Macmillan, 1971.

Card, James. *Seductive Cinema: the Art of Silent Film*. New York: Knopf, 1994.

Cavell, Stanley. *The World Viewed: Reflections on the Ontology of Film*. New York: Viking, 1971.

Cawelti, John G. *Adventure, Mystery, and Romance: Formula Stories as Art and Popular Culture*. Chicago: University of Chicago Press, 1976.

Chapman,Charles D. "Providing Yourself with the Proper Period," *Photoplay,* March 1926: 64–65.

Charney, Leo, and Vanessa R. Schwartz, eds. *Cinema and the Invention of Modern Life.* Berkeley: University of California Press, 1995.

Chatman, Seymour. *Story and Discourse: Narrative Structure in Fiction and Idea.* Ithaca, NY: Cornell University Press, 1978.

Cohen, Paula Marantz. *The Daughter's Dilemma: Family Process and the Nineteenth-Century Domestic Novel.* Ann Arbor: University of Michigan Press, 1991.

——. "Helen Keller and the American Myth." *The Yale Review,* 85, 1(January 1997):1–20.

Colbert, Charles. *A Measure of Perfection: Phrenology and the Fine Arts in America.* Chapel Hill: University of North Carolina Press, 1998.

Conrad, Joseph. *The Nigger of the "Narcissus."* 1898. Reprint, Garden City, NY: Double-day, 1947.

Cooke, Alistair. *Douglas Fairbanks: The Making of a Screen Character.* New York: The Museum of Modern Art, 1940.

Cooper, James Fenimore. *Deerslayer.* 1841. Reprint, New York: P.F. Collier, 1892.

——. *The Last of the Mohicans.* 1826. Reprint, New York: Signet, 1962.

Crafton, Donald. *The Talkies: American Cinema's Transition to Sound, 1926–1931.* Berkeley: University of California Press, 1997.

Crary, Jonathan. *Suspensions of Perception: Attention, Spectacle, and Modern Culture.* Cambridge, MA: MIT Press, 1999.

Dardis, Tom. *Keaton: The Man Who Wouldn't Lie Down.* New York: Scribner's, 1979.

deCordova, Richard. *Picture Personalities: The Emergence of the Star System in America.* Chicago: University of Illinois Press, 1990.

Denton, Frances. "The Lonely Princess." *Photoplay,* June 1920: 46+.

Devereaux, Leslie and Roger Hillman, eds. *Fields of Vision: Essays in Film Studies, Visual Anthropology, and Photography.* Berkeley: University of Calif. Press, 1995.

Dewey, John. *Art as Experience.* 1934. Reprint, New York: Perigee Books, 1980.

Dickens, Charles. *American Notes.* 1842. Reprint, NY:Collier, N.D.

Doane, Mary Ann. *The Desire to Desire: The Woman's Film of the 1940's.* Bloomington: Indiana University Press, 1987.

——. "Film and Masquerade: Theorizing a Female Space." *Screen* 23, 3–4 (September–October, 1982): 74–87.

Douglas, Ann. *Terrible Honesty: Mongrel Manhattan in the 1920s.* New York: Farrar, Straus and Giroux, 1995.

Durant, John, and Jonathan Miller, eds. *Laughing Matters: A Serious Look at Humour.* New York: Longman, 1988.

Dyer, Richard. *Stars.* London: British Film Institute, 1979.

——. *Heavenly Bodies: Film Stars and Society.* New York: Macmillan, 1987.

Easy, Edward Dwight. *On Method Acting.* New York: Ivy Books, 1994.

Eisenstein, Sergei. *Film Form.* Trans. Jay Leyda. New York: Harvest, 1977.

Emerson, Ralph Waldo. *Essays and English Traits.* New York: P. F. Collier and Son, 1909.

Everson, William K. *American Silent Film.* New York: Oxford University Press, 1978.

——. *Love in the Film: Screen Romance from the Silent Days to the Present.* Secaucus, NJ: Citadel Press, 1979.

Ewen, Stuart and Elizabeth. *Channels of Desire: Mass Images and the Shaping of American Consciousness.* New York: McGraw-Hill, 1982.

Eyman, Scott. *The Speed of Sound: Hollywood and the Talkie Revolution, 1926–1930.* Baltimore, MD: Johns Hopkins University Press, 1997.

Fairbanks, Douglas. *Laugh and Live.* 1917. New York: Amereon Ltd., 1989.

——. *Youth Points the Way.* New York: D. Appleton and Co., 1924.

Fenin, George N., and William K. Everson. *The Western: From Silents to the Seventies.* New York: Penguin, 1973.

Fisher, Philip, ed. *The New American Studies: Essays from Representations.* Berkeley: University of Calif. Press, 1991.

——. *Still the New World: American Literature in a Culture of Creative Destruction.* Cambridge, MA: Harvard University Press, 1999.

Folsom, Ed. *Walt Whitman's Native Representations.* Cambridge: Cambridge University Press, 1994.

Foucault, Michel. *The History of Sexuality,* Vol. I: *An Introduction* . Trans. Robert Hurley New York: Vintage Books, 1980.

Franklin, Joe. *Classics of the Silent Screen.* New York: Citadel Press, 1959.

Freud, Sigmund, and Joseph Breuer, *Studies on Hysteria.* Trans. A. A. Brill. London: Penguin, 1980.

Friar, Ralph and Natasha. *The Only Good Indian: The Hollywood Gospel.* New York: Drama Book Specialists, 1972.

Gabler, Neal. *An Empire of Their Own: How the Jews Invented Hollywood.* New York: Anchor Books, 1989.

——. *Life the Movie: How Entertainment Conquered Reality.* New York: Knopf, 1998.

Galbraith, John Kenneth. *The Affluent Society.* Boston: Houghton Mifflin, 1958.

Gay, Peter. *The Bourgeois Experience,* vol. 2: *The Tender Passion.* New York: Oxford University Press, 1986.

Geduld, Harry M. *The Birth of the Talkies: From Edison to Jolson.* Bloomington: Indiana University Press, 1975.

Gilman, Charlotte Perkins. *The Yellow Wallpaper.* 1892. Reprint, New York: The Feminist Press, 1973.

Girgus, Sam B. *The Law of the Heart: Individualism and the Modern Self in American Literature.* Austin: University of Texas Press, 1979.

Gish, Lillian (with Ann Pinchot). *The Movies, Mr. Griffith, and Me.* New York: Prentice Hall, 1969.

Gledhill, Christine, ed. *Stardom: Industry of Desire.* New York: Routledge, 1991.

Goodrich, Lloyd. *Thomas Eakins,* 2 vols. Cambridge, MA: Harvard University Press,
    1982.

Gould, Stephen Jay. *The Mismeasure of Man.* New York: Norton, 1981.

Griffith, Richard, and Arthur Mayer. *The Movies.* New York: Bonanza Books, 1957.

Grossman, James R., ed. *The Frontier in American Culture.* Berkeley: University of Cali-
    fornia Press, 1994.

Gunning, Tom. "Cinema of Attraction[s]." *Wide Angle,* 8, 3–4(1986): 68–70.

———. *D. W. Griffith and the Origins of American Narrative Film: The Early Years at Bio-
    graph.* Urbana: University of Illinois Press, 1991.

Hampton, Benjamin B. *History of the American Film Industry from its Beginnings to 1931.*
    1931. Reprint, New York: Dover Books, 1970.

Hansen, Miriam. *Babel and Babylon: Specatorship in American Silent Film.* Cambridge,
    MA: Harvard University Press, 1991.

———. "Pleasure, Ambivalence, Identification: Valentino and Female Spectatorship."
    Cinema Journal 25 (summer 1986): 6–32.

Harris, Neil. *Humbug: The Art of P. T. Barnum .* Boston: Little, Brown and Co., 1973.

Hart, William S. *My Life East and West.* New York: Benjamin Blom, 1929.

Haskell, Molly. *From Reverence to Rape: The Treatment of Women in the Movies,* 2nd edi-
    tion. Chicago: University of Chicago Press, 1987.

Helsinger, Elizabeth K. *Ruskin and the Art of the Beholder.* Cambridge, MA: Harvard
    University Press, 1982.

Herndon, Booton. *Mary Pickford and Douglas Fairbanks.* New York: Norton, 1977.

Higashi, Sumiko. *Cecil B. DeMille and American Culture: The Silent Era.* Berkeley: Uni-
    versity of California Press, 1994.

Hollander, Anne. *Feeding the Eye.* New York: Farrar, Straus and Giroux, 1999.

———. *Moving Pictures.* New York: Knopf, 1989.

———. *Sex and Suits.* New York: Knopf, 1994.

Horton, Andrew, ed. *Buster Keaton's* Sherlock Jr. Cambridge: Cambridge University
    Press, 1997.

"How to Spoil the Effect of Beautiful Clothes." *Photoplay.* January 1926: 64+.

Howat, John K. *The Hudson River and its Painters.* New York: Viking, 1972.

Huxley, Aldous. *Do What You Will.* New York: Harper and Row, 1929.

Jacobs, Lewis, ed. *The Emergence of Film Art.* New York: Hopkinson and Blake, 1969.

———. *The Rise of American Film.* New York: Teacher's College Press, 1939.

James, Henry. *The American.* 1877. Reprint, New York: Bantam, 1971.

———. *Portrait of a Lady.* 1881. Reprint, New York: Penguin, 1983.

James, William. *Principles of Psychology.* 1890. Reprint, Chicago: Encyclopedia Britan-
    nica, 1952.

Jesionowski, Joyce E. *Thinking in Pictures: Dramatic Structure in D. W. Griffith's Biograph
    Films.* Berkeley: University of California Press, 1987.

Keaton, Buster (with Charles Samuels). *My Wonderful Life of Slapstick.* New York: Dou-
    bleday, 1960.

Kerr, Walter. *The Silent Clowns*. New York: Random House, 1979.

King, Richard H., and Helen Taylor, eds. *Dixie Debates: Perspectives on Southern Cultures*. New York: New York University Press, 1996.

Knopf, Robert. *The Theater and Cinema of Buster Keaton. Princeton, NJ:* Princeton University Press, 1999.

Koszarski, Richard. *An Evening's Entertainment: The Age of the Silent Feature Picture, 1915–1928*. Berkeley: University of California Press, 1990.

Koszarski, Diane Kaiser. *The Complete Films of William S. Hart: A Pictorial Record*. New York: Dover, 1980.

Kowalewski, Michael, ed. *Reading the West*. New York: Cambridge University Press, 1996.

Kracauer, Siegfried. *Theory of Film*. New York: Oxford University Press, 1960.

Leach, William. *Land of Desire: Merchants, Power, and the Rise of a New American Culture*. New York: Vintage, 1993.

Lennig, Arthur. *Stroheim*. Lexington: University Press of Kentucky, 2000.

Lesser, Wendy. *His Other Half: Men Looking at Women Through Art*. Cambridge, MA: Harvard University Press, 1991.

Levin, Martin. ed. *Hollywood and the Great Fan Magazines*. New York: Arbor House, 1970.

Levine, Michael. *The Princess and the Package*. Los Angeles: Renaissance Books, 1998.

Lewis, R. W. B. *The American Adam: Innocence, Tragedy, and Tradition in the Nineteenth Century*. Chicago: University of Chicago Press, 1955.

Lifton, Robert Jay. *The Protean Self: Human Resilience in an Age of Fragmentation*. Chicago: University of Chicago Press, 1993.

Limerick, Patricia Nelson, Clyde A. Milner II, and Charles E. Rankin, eds. *Trails: Toward a New Western History*. Lawrence: University of Kansas Press, 1991.

Lindsay, Vachel. *The Art of the Moving Picture.* 1915. Reprint, New York: Liveright, 1970.

Lukacs, Georg. *The Theory of the Novel*. Trans. Anna Bostock. Cambridge: MIT Press, 1971.

Lynn, Kenneth Schuyler. *Charlie Chaplin and His Times*. New York: Simon and Schuster, 1997.

MacCann, Richard Dyer, ed. *Film: A Montage of Theories*. New York: Dutton, 1966.

MacIntyre, Diane. "The Little Girl Who Couldn't Grow Up: The Phenomenon of Typecasting," *The Silents Majority*. 1996–97. <http:www.mdle.com/ClassicFilms/ FeaturedStar/maryx.htm> (Jan. 20, 2000).

Maddox, Lucy, ed. *Locating American Studies*. Baltimore, MD: Johns Hopkins University Press, 1999.

Maimonides, Moses. *The Guide of the Perplexed*. 2 vols. Trans. Shlomo Pines. Chicago: University of Chicago Press, 1963.

Marberry, M. M. "The Overloved One." *American Heritage: Special Issue–The 20's* XVI, 5 (August 1965): 84–87.

Marx, Leo. *The Machine in the Garden: Technology and the Pastoral Ideal in America.* New York: Oxford University Press, 1964.

Mast, Gerald. *The Comic Mind: Comedy and the Movies.* New York: Bobbs-Merrill Co., 1973.

May, Lary. *Screening out the Past: The Birth of Mass Culture and the Motion Picture Industry.* Chicago: University of Chicago Press, 1983.

Mayne, Judith. *Private Novels, Public Films.* Athens: University of Georgia Press, 1988.

McNamara, Devin R. *Urban Verbs: Arts and Discourses of American Cities.* Stanford: Stanford University Press, 1966.

Mellon, James. *The Face of Lincoln.* New York: Viking, 1979.

Melnick, Jeffrey. *A Right to Sing the Blues: African-Americans, Jews, and American Popular Song.* Cambridge, MA: Harvard University Press, 1999.

Melville, Herman. *The Confidence-Man: His Masquerade* 1857. Reprint, New York: Grove Press, 1949.

Mencken, H. L. "The Future of English." 1935. Reprint, *Harper's,* September 1999: 86–90.

Metz, Christian. *Film Language:A Semiotics of the Cinema.* Trans. Michael Taylor. Chicago: University of Chicago Press, 1974.

Miller, Angela. "The Panorama, The Cinema, and the Emergence of the Spectacular," *Wide Angle,* 18, 2:38–39

Miller, David, ed. *American Iconology: New Approaches to Nineteenth-Century Art and Literature.* New Haven: Yale University Press, 1993.

Mitchell, W. J. T. *Iconology: Image, Text, Ideology.* Chicago: University of Chicago Press, 1986.

——, ed. *On Narrative.* Chicago: University of Chicago Press, 1981.

Moews, Daniel. *Keaton: The Silent Features Close-up.* Berkeley: University of California Press, 1977.

Morin, Edgar. *The Stars.* Trans. Richard Howard. New York: Grove Press, 1960.

Mountbatten: Eighty Years in Pictures. New York: Viking, 1979.

Mulvey, Laura. *Visual and Other Pleasures.* Bloomington: Indiana University Press, 1989.

Munsterberg, Hugo. *The Photoplay: A Psychological Study.* New York: D. Appleton and Co., 1916.

Musser, Charles. *The Emergence of Cinema: The American Screen to 1907.* Berkeley: University of California Press, 1990.

Naremore, James. *Acting in Cinema.* Berkeley: University of Calif. Press, 1988.

Nash, Gerald D. *Creating the West: Historical Interpretations 1890–1990.* Albuquerque: University of New Mexico Press, 1991.

Novak, Barbara. *American Painting in the Nineteenth Century.* New York: Praeger, 1969.

Orvell, Miles. *After the Machine: Visual Arts and the Erasing of Cultural Boundaries.* Jackson: University Press of Mississippi, 1995.

——. *The Real Thing:Imitation and Authenticity in American Culture, 1880–1940.* Chapel Hill: University of North Carolina Press, 1989.

Panzer, Mary. *Mathew Brady and the Image of History.* Washington, DC: Smithsonian Institution Press, 1997.

Parkinson, David. *History of Film.* New York: Thames and Hudson, 1995.

Parkman, Francis. *The Oregon Trail.* 1849. Reprint, New York: Signet, 1964.

Pearson, Roberta E. *Eloquent Gestures: The Transformation of Performance Style in the Griffith Biograph Films.* Berkeley: University of Calif. Press, 1992.

Pickford, Mary. *Sunshine and Shadow.* New York: Doubleday, 1955.

Podheiser, Linda. "Pep on the Range or Douglas Fairbanks and the World War I Era Western." *The Journal of Popular Film and Television,* Fall 1983: 122–130.

Poirier, Richard. *A World Elsewhere: The Place of Style in American Literature.* New York: Oxford University Press, 1966.

Pratt, George C. *Spellbound in Darkness: A History of Silent Film.* New York Graphic Society, 1973.

Pudovkin, V. I. *On Film Technique.* Trans. Ivor Montagu. London: Vision Press, 1950.

Quirk, James R. "The Enigma of the Screen." *Photoplay,* March 1926: 63+.

——. "The Public Just Won't Let Mary Pickford Grow Up." *Photoplay,* September 1925: 36+.

Ramsaye, Terry. *A Million and One Nights.* 1926. Reprint, New York: Simon and Schuster, 1964.

Register, Charlene. "Stepin Fetchit: The Man, The Image, and the African American Press." *Film History* 6, 4 (Winter 1994): 502–21.

Reps, John W. *The Making of Urban America.* Princeton, NJ: Princeton University Press, 1965.

Reynolds, David S. *Walt Whitman's America: A Cultural Biography.* New York: Vintage Books, 1996.

Rogin, Michael. *Black Face, White Noise: Jewish Immigrants in the Hollywood Melting Pot.* Berkeley: University of California Press, 1996.

Ross, Steven J. *Working-Class Hollywood.* Princeton, NJ: Princeton University Press, 1998

Rotha, Paul, and Richard Griffith. *The Film Till Now: A Survey of World Cinema.* London: Spring Books, 1960.

Sanders, Judith, and Daniel Liberfeld. "Dreaming in Pictures: The Childhood Origin of Buster Keaton's Creativity." *Film Quarterly,* 47, 4 (Summer 1994): 14–28.

Sarris, Andrew. "The Cultural Guilt of Musical Movies: *The Jazz Singer,* Fifty Years After," *Film Comment,* 13 (September–October 1977): 39–41.

Schama, Simon. *Landscape and Memory.* New York: HarperCollins, 1995.

Schatz, Thomas. *Hollywood Genres.* New York: Random House, 1981.

Schickel, Richard. *Common Fame: the Culture of Celebrity.* New York: Pavilion, 1985.

——. *D. W. Griffith: An American Life.* New York: Simon and Schuster, 1985.

——, ed. *The Fairbanks Album.* Boston: New York Graphic Society, 1975.

———. *His Picture in the Papers: A Speculation on Celebrity in America Based on the Life of Douglas Fairbanks, Sr.* New York: Charterhouse, 1973.

Schivelbusch, Wolfgang. *The Railway Journey: Trains and Travel in the Nineteenth Century.* Trans. Anselm Hollo. New York: Urizen, 1977.

Seldes, Gilbert. *The Movies Come from America.* 1937. Reprint, New York: Arno Press, 1978.

Shi, David E. *Facing Facts.* New York: Oxford University Press, 1995.

Showalter, Elaine. *The Female Malady.* New York: Pantheon, 1985.

Silverman, Kenneth. *Houdini!!!* New York: Harper Collins, 1996.

Singer, Irving. *Reality Transformed: Film as Meaning and Technique.* Cambridge: MIT Press, 1998.

Sklar, Robert. *City Boys: Cagney, Bogart, Garfield.* Princeton, NJ: Princeton University Press, 1992.

———, ed. *The Plastic Age, 1917–1933.* New York: George Braziller, 1970.

Smith, Henry Nash. *Virgin Land: The American West as Symbol and Myth* Cambridge, MA: Harvard University Press, 1950.

Snyder, Robert W. *The Voice of the City: Vaudeville and Popular Culture in New York.* New York: Oxford University Press, 1989.

Sontag, Susan. *On Photography.* New York: Anchor Books, 1973.

———. *Styles of Radical Will.* New York: Dell, 1969.

Staiger, Janet. *Interpreting Films: Studies in the Historical Reception of American Cinema.* Princeton, NJ: Princeton University Press, 1992.

Stein, Charles W., ed. *American Vaudeville As Seen By Its Contemporaries.* New York: Knopf, 1984.

Stephens, Mitchell. *The Rise of the Image and the Fall of the Word.* New York: Oxford University Press, 1998.

Stewart, Garrett. "Keaton through the Looking Glass." *Georgia Review* 33, 2 (Summer 1979): 348–67.

Swindell, Larry. "The Day the Silents Stopped." *American Film* 3 (Oct. 1977): 24–31.

Taft, Robert. *Photography and the American Scene, 1838–1889.* New York: Macmillan, 1938.

Talbot, Daniel, ed. *Film: An Anthology.* Berkeley: University of Calif. Press, 1967.

Thoreau, Henry David. *The Portable Thoreau.* Ed. Carl Bode. New York: Viking, 1964.

Tibbetts, John C., and James M. Welsh, *His Majesty the American: The Films of Douglas Fairbanks, Sr.* New York: A. S. Barnes, 1977.

Tocqueville, Alexis de. *Democracy in America,* 2 vols. 1835 and 1840. Reprint, New York: Vintage Books, 1945.

Tompkins, Jane. *West of Everywhere.* New York: Oxford University Press, 1992.

Trachtenberg, Alan. *Reading American Photographs.* New York: Hill and Wang, 1989.

Trent, Paul. *The Image Makers: Sixty Years of Hollywood Glamour.* New York: Bonanza Books, 1982.

Trilling, Lionel. *Beyond Culture: Essays in Literature and Learning.* New York: Viking, 1965.

——. *The Opposing Self.* New York: Viking, 1955.

Trollope, Frances. *Domestic Manners of the Americans.* 1832. Reprint, New York: Vintage, 1960.

Truffaut, Francois. *Hitchcock.* Revised edition. New York: Touchstone, 1985.

Turner, Frederick Jackson. "The Significance of the Frontier in American History." 1893. Reprint, *The Annals of America,* Vol. 11. Chicago: Encyclopedia Britannica, 1968.

Twain, Mark. *Complete Essays of Mark Twain.* Ed. Charles Neider. New York: Doubleday, 1985.

"Uncle Sam's Adopted Children," *Photoplay,* January 1926: 68+.

Vardac, A. Nicholas. *Stage to Screen: Theatrical Method from Garrick to Griffith.* Cambridge, MA: Harvard University Press, 1949.

Wagenknecht, Edward. *The Movies in the Age of Innocence.* Norman: University of Oklahoma Press, 1962.

Walker, Alexander. *Joan Crawford: The Ultimate Star.* New York: Harper Collins, 1983.

——. *Rudolph Valentino.* New York: Stein and Day, 1976.

Watt, Ian. *The Rise of the Novel.* 1957. Berkeley: University of California Press, 1971.

Weisbuch, Robert. *Atlantic Double-cross: American Literature and European Influence in the Age of Emerson.* Chicago: University of Chicago Press, 1986.

White, Pearl. *Just Me.* New York: Doran, 1919.

Whitefield, Eileen. *Pickford.* Lexington: University Press of Kentucky, 1997.

Whitman, Walt. *Complete Poetry and Selected Prose and Letters.* London: Nonesuch Press, 1938.

Williams, Linda, ed. *Viewing Positions: Ways of Seeing Film.* New Brunswick: Rutgers University Press, 1994.

Wilson, A. N. *The Rise and Fall of the House of Windsor.* New York: Norton, 1993.

Wilson, Edmund. "Houdini," *The New Republic,* June 24 1925: 125+.

Wolf, Bryan Jay. *Romantic Re-Vision: Culture and Consciousness in Nineteenth-Century American Painting and Literature.* Chicago: University of Chicago Press, 1982.

Wollen, Peter. *Signs and Meaning in the Cinema.* Bloomington: Indiana University Press, 1972.

Wood, Michael. *America in the Movies.* New York: Basic Books, 1975.

Woolf, Virginia. *Collected Essays,* vol. I. New York: Harcourt, Brace and World, 1967.

Wordsworth, William. *Selected Poems and Prefaces.* Ed. Jack Stillinger. Boston: Houghton Mifflin,1965.

York, Carl. "Studio News and Gossip," *Photoplay,* January 1926: 42+

INDEX

Page numbers in italics refer to illustrations and photographs.